W9-ADP-198

The
Short = War
Illusion

TWENTIETH CENTURY SERIES

LYMAN H. LEGTERS

Series Editor

German National Socialism, 1919-1945
Martin Broszat

We Survived: Fourteen Histories of the Hidden and Hunted of Nazi Germany
Eric H. Boehm

International Relations Research: Problems of Evaluation and Advancement
E. Raymond Platig

Native Fascism in the Successor States, 1918-1945
Peter F. Sugar, Editor

The Bolshevik Seizure of Power
S.P. Melgunov
S.G. Pushkarev, Editor

The Czechoslovak Reform Movement, 1968:
Proceedings of a Conference Held at Reading University 12-17th July 1971
V.V. Kusin, Editor

The
Short = War
Illusion

GERMAN POLICY,
STRATEGY & DOMESTIC AFFAIRS
AUGUST-DECEMBER 1914

L.L. FARRAR, JR.

Foreword by JAMES JOLL

Santa Barbara, California   *Oxford, England*

Library of Congress Catalog Card Number 72-95267
ISBN Clothbound Edition 0-87436-118-4
Paperbound Edition 0-87436-119-2

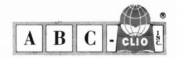

American Bibliographical Center—Clio Press, Inc.
2040 Alameda Padre Serra
Santa Barbara, California

European Bibliographical Center—Clio Press
30 Cornmarket Street
Oxford OX1 3EY, England

Designed by Barbara Monahan
Composed by Camera-Ready Composition
Printed and bound by Publishers Press
in the United States of America

TO

MY MOTHER
who taught me the pleasure of taking something seriously,

MY FATHER
who taught me the importance of taking myself lightly, and

MY WIFE
who helps me remember the difference

CONTENTS

FOREWORD

The origins and the course of World War I continue to fascinate readers and writers of history. In spite of all the critical events of the past sixty years, the outbreak of the First World War still seems of exceptional importance and marks the moment after which things were never to be the same again, the starting point for the upheavals and sufferings, the revolutions and wars which we have since experienced. It was the end, or so it now seems, both of the age of liberalism and of the unquestioned domination of Europe over the rest of the world. Moreover, the opening of the government archives in Germany, in Britain and, most recently, in France, as well as the ever-growing volume of material from other sources, has obliged historians to look again in the light of the new evidence at the old arguments about responsibility for the war and the continuity of foreign policy between one generation and another; and this in turn has led to fresh controversies and renewed discussions.

Lancelot Farrar's book is, it seems to me, one of the most interesting and original of those which have appeared since the reassessment of war aims in the First World War began in the early 1960s. By his careful and perceptive analysis of the sources, and especially of the material in the German archives, he has shown how the nature of the war, and with it the nature of its historical consequences, had changed within six months of its beginning. The strategy and the diplomacy of the war had everywhere been based on the assumption that the war would be a short one. The French soldiers scribbled *A Berlin* on the railroad coaches taking them to the front; the British assured one another that "It will all be over by Christmas"; the Germans expected a "bright and jolly" (*frisch-fröhlich*) war. Within a few months, however, these hopes were buried in the mud of the Western Front, and a new, total war had to be planned.

The result was not only that the war permanently affected the social and economic organization of all the belligerent countries, but it also changed the nature of international relations. Like almost all the other aspects of government, diplomacy was never to be the same again. "War," as Professor

Farrar remarks, "alters the practice of diplomacy." In the short run, as this book demonstrates, this led to the Germans trying, almost successfully, to split their enemies by persuading one or other of them to make a separate peace. In the long run, it was the experience of wartime diplomacy and the subsequent exposure of the secret commitments into which the belligerents entered in order to win neutral support or to keep their allies in the war which confirmed the worst suspicions about the "old diplomacy" and increased the demand for a new style in international relations, based on "Open covenants openly arrived at."

The acceptance of the necessity of a long war paradoxically made the attainment of peace all the harder; for, to quote Professor Farrar again, "Stalemate made compromise undesirable but logical and made continuation desirable but illogical." As the toll of sacrifices mounted and the price of victory became ever greater, so the rewards had to be greater still if the sufferings inflicted on the people of Europe were to be justified. As long as either side felt that they had a chance of winning, they rejected any compromise peace. To return to the situation as of July 1914 seemed a trifling outcome for so much expense of money, materials and blood. A long war could only be worth fighting if it brought massive gains or permanent changes in the world balance of power.

A short war could be fought on the principle expressed by the British slogan "Business as Usual." A long war presupposed increasing government intervention and control and fundamental changes in the relations between government and society. At the same time, the end of the "short-war illusion" forced leaders of the belligerent countries to think about the conditions on which they might be prepared to make a victorious peace. In September 1914, when victory seemed to be within their reach, the Germans had already formulated extensive plans for annexation in west and east; and, as Fritz Fischer has shown, this provided a program which they were reluctant to abandon. On the other hand, although as the war went on the French and British hoped for new possibilities of imperialist expansion—especially in the lands under Ottoman rule—they were primarily concerned to restore the European balance of power by the liberation of Belgium from German control and the return to France of Alsace-Lorraine and, above all, by establishing a situation in which another German attempt to upset the balance would be impossible. It was the rival views of the international system as a whole that made the two sides irreconcilable. In the eyes of the British, as Lancelot Farrar points out, the system must be adjusted so as to contain German power. "But the Germans sought a system which would reflect rather than balance power. Permanent peace in their view required an adjustment of the system to allow their power to develop."

It is this kind of analysis which gives *The Short-War Illusion* its importance as a study which helps us to understand the crisis of the winter of 1914-1915 and to show that this was at least as significant as that of July 1914 which led to the outbreak of the war. Too often diplomatic historians are content with facts and no theory. Too often political scientists are content to construct their models without much regard for the facts which inconveniently refuse to fit them. Professor Farrar uses his skill as a diplomatic historian to unravel the complexities of the making and execution of German policy and he has made a substantial contribution to the debate started by Fritz Fischer. However, he is not content with the establishment of a diplomatic or military record; he places that record in a conceptual framework. By combining political and strategic analysis with some of the theoretical insights of political science, his book has the merits but not the defects of both approaches. This is a book that tells us about the European crisis of 1914; but it does not only do that. In examining the international system in the first phase of the First World War, it tells us much about the international system in general. It will be widely read by students of twentieth century history and of international relations, and both historians and political scientists will derive much profit from it.

JAMES JOLL

ACKNOWLEDGEMENTS

One of the great pleasures in finishing a book is the opportunity to acknowledge the contributions of other persons. My interest in diplomatic history was aroused by the teaching and scholarly examples of three former teachers and now friends—Gordon A. Craig, James Joll and A.J.P. Taylor. Lyman H. Legters, the editor of the Twentieth Century Series in which this book appears, gave encouragement and support without which the book would not have been published. Lloyd W. Garrison, the editor of Clio Books, invested gargantuan time and effort far beyond the call of duty. Barbara Monahan, production editor of Clio Books, was an author's ideal of efficiency. My girls, Livi and Shepi, were wise beyond their years about the foibles of a writing father and provided the diversion of childish fantasies just when they were most needed. Above all I want to thank my wife, Marjorie—gentle overseer, resident therapist, wise counselor, colleague and friend.

INTRODUCTION

Every author runs the risk of exaggerating the importance of his subject. The
danger exists even when the subject is generally regarded as important. It is,
however, difficult to overemphasize the significance of World War I. In reviewing
Albertini's *Origins of the War of 1914,* Max Beloff observed: "The more one
looks at the contemporary scene the more it appears that it was 1914 and not
1939 that decisively unleashed the forces of evil." The basic assumption of the
present study is that the outbreak of war in 1914 marked the beginning of a
revolutionary era which lasted until 1945 and compares to previous revolutionary periods such as 1789-1815. In fact the events of 1914-1945 were more
revolutionary and indeed unique because they caused the end of European
history in the traditional sense of Europe's being the power center of the world.
Since Germany played an important if not critical role in this development,
comprehension of European history during its final stage requires an understanding of German behavior during World War I.

One testimony as to the importance of German policy before and during
the World War is the debate on the subject. It has been prolonged, lasting during
much of the interwar period and reviving in the 1960s. The debate has been
intense and aroused heated emotions, particularly in Germany but also
elsewhere. It has been extensive; even since 1960 it has precipitated hundreds of
books, reviews, conferences, radio broadcasts and articles. Several excellent
larger studies and many thorough monographs on German policy during the
World War have appeared in the last decade. It is therefore valid to doubt the
justifiability of another study on the subject. This doubt, in fact, suggests the
primary justification. The mass of new material and recent scholarship is great,
and the debate is complex, dispersed and extensive. The present study
complicates the problem further by adding new material from the German
Foreign Office archives. But if this book makes a contribution, it is primarily as
a synthesis and interpretation of recent scholarship.

The main concern of this study is German power. Although complexity
and diversity make generalization difficult, the debate has generally focused on

the question of whether German policy was arrogant or anxious. This study questions the utility of this dichotomy and suggests instead that German policy may have been an ominous mix of both. The more general concern is therefore with the effects of power on policymakers.

The organization of the book implies certain assumptions. It assumes that German policy is understood best if it is integrated with, rather than isolated from, other factors. All studies must be limited in scope and subject because of practical considerations. The magnitude of new material on German policy reinforces this necessity. But practical limitations should not distort the subject. Isolation of German policy from the policies of the other belligerents or neutrals makes German policy appear unique and precludes evaluation of its realism. Separation of German policy from German strategy and domestic politics both oversimplifies policymaking and fails to explain the oscillations of policy. The present study consequently puts German policy into the context of German strategy and politics, as well as the policies, strategies and politics of the other belligerents and neutrals.

Such a broad and integrated approach imposes its own limitations. In particular it necessitates a short period. The present study therefore concentrates on the first five months of the war. Like all historical phenomena, the events of this period are related to previous and subsequent developments. Since the war developed gradually, stages can be distinguished only very roughly and are artificial devices to suit intellectual convenience. To the extent that periods can be perceived, however, the first five months of the war constitute such a stage. It began in August 1914 with the outbreak of war and the prevalence of certain assumptions, above all, that the war would be short. It ended when this short-war assumption proved to be an illusion in December 1914.

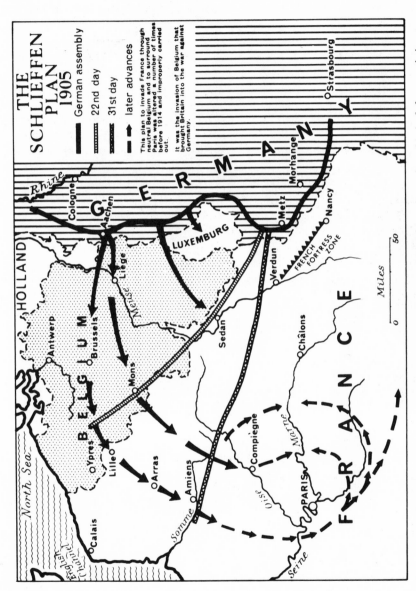

Acknowledgement is due to The Macmillan Company and Weidenfeld and Nicolson Limited for permission to reproduce the map taken from the Recent History Atlas by Martin Gilbert © 1966.

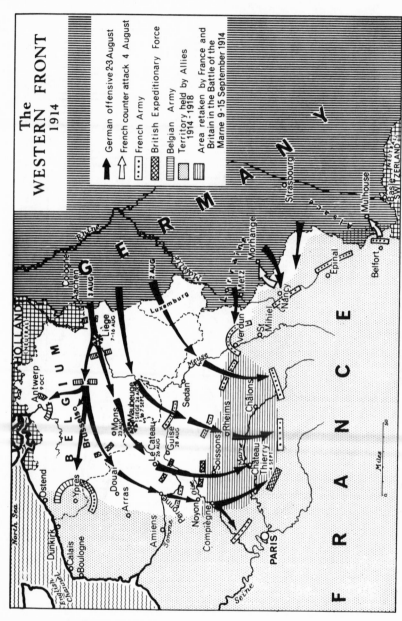

The WESTERN FRONT 1914

German offensive 23 August
French counter attack 4 August
French Army
British Expeditionary Force
Belgian Army
Territory held by Allies 1914-1918
Area retaken by France and Britain in the Battle of the Marne 9-15 September 1914

HOLLAND (NEUTRAL)

North Sea

English Channel

Dunkirk
Calais
Boulogne
Ostend
Antwerp 9 OCT
Ypres
Douai
Arras
Amiens
Somme
Noyon
Compiègne
Seine

BELGIUM
Brussels
Mons 23 AUG
Le Cateau 26 AUG
Guise 29 AUG
Soissons
Château Thierry 4 Sept
PARIS

Liège 7-16 AUG
1 AUG
Aachen
Cologne

GERMANY

Luxemburg

Maubeuge SIEGE 24 AUG to 9 SEPT
Sedan
Rheims
Châlons

Meuse

2 AUG

Verdun
St Mihiel
Metz
Morhange
Nancy
Strasbourg

Epinal
Belfort
Mulhouse

SWITZERLAND (NEUTRAL)
Basle

F R A N C E

Miles
0   50

Acknowledgement is due to The Macmillan Company and Weidenfeld and Nicolson Limited for permission to reproduce the map taken from the Recent History Atlas by Martin Gilbert © 1966.

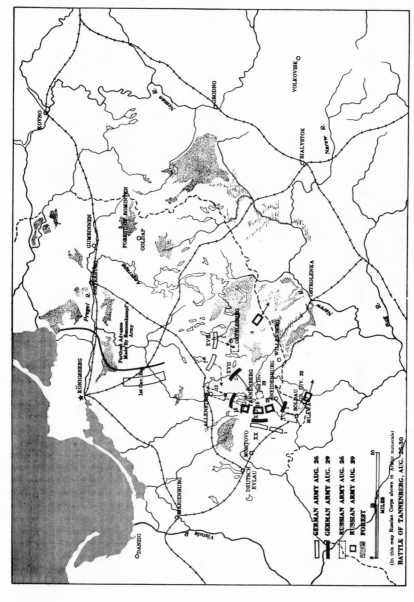

Acknowledgement is due to The Macmillan Company and Russel & Volkening, Inc. for permission to reproduce the map taken from The Guns of August by Barbara W. Tuchman ©1962.

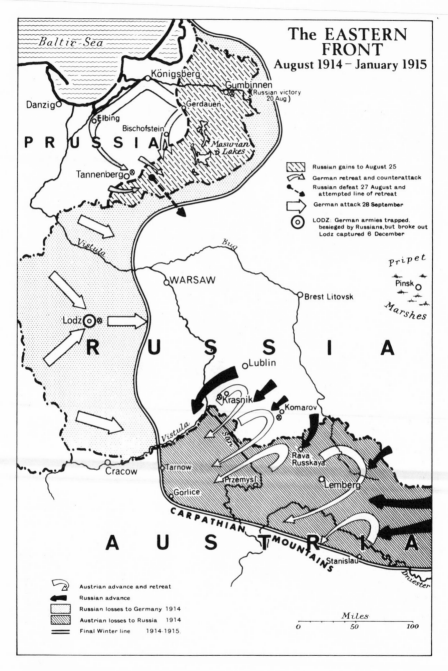

The **EASTERN FRONT**
August 1914 – January 1915

Baltic Sea

Königsberg

Danzig

Elbing

Gumbinnen
(Russian victory
20 Aug)

Gerdauen

Bischofstein

P R U S S I A

Masurian Lakes

Tannenberg

	Russian gains to August 25
	German retreat and counterattack
	Russian defeat 27 August and attempted line of retreat
	German attack 28 September
	LODZ: German armies trapped, besieged by Russians, but broke out Lodz captured 6 December

Vistula

Bug

Pripet

Pinsk

WARSAW

Brest Litovsk

Marshes

Lodz

R U S S I A

Lublin

Krasnik

Komarov

Vistula

San

Rava Russkaya

Tarnow

Cracow

Przemysl

Lemberg

Gorlice

CARPATHIAN MOUNTAINS

A U S T R I A

Stanislau

Dniester

Austrian advance and retreat
Russian advance
Russian losses to Germany 1914
Austrian losses to Russia 1914
Final Winter line 1914-1915.

Miles
0   50   100

Acknowledgement is due to The Macmillan Company and Weidenfeld and Nicolson Limited for permission to reproduce the map taken from the Recent History Atlas *by Martin Gilbert* ©*1966.*

Part I

The Assumption Tested

(August-October 1914)

PURSUIT OF VICTORY:
THE MILITARY ASPECTS

THE SHORT WAR: POLICY BY OTHER MEANS

An understanding of German wartime strategy, diplomacy and politics involves the question of historical continuity. The problem has figured prominently in the debate over Germany's role during the First World War. The advocates of continuity see German wartime policy as a logical extension of German prewar policy, whereas the advocates of discontinuity perceive wartime and prewar policies as essentially different. The debate hinges on an interpretation of the July crisis. The advocates of continuity argue that Germany was primarily responsible and even provoked the crisis in order to fight a preventive war, whereas the advocates of discontinuity insist that responsibility for the crisis must be shared or even placed elsewhere. These two perspectives have fundamentally different implications. If continuity is accepted, German wartime policy is conceived as a response to conditions which prevailed both before and during the war. If discontinuity is accepted, German wartime policy is understood as a reaction to new conditions created by the war. The problem of continuity must therefore be confronted at the outset.[1]

The present study accepts continuity, although not in the sense argued by the advocates of primary German responsibility for the July crisis. The continuity question cannot be resolved unless the term is rigidly defined to mean a persistence of essential elements such as the determination of the great powers to maintain their status by whatever means seemed necessary. German policy, like the policies of the other European powers, was a tense mixture of anxiety and arrogance, i.e., a desire to defend and expand its power. This tension was more severe in Germany's case because it had the greatest power and therefore provoked the most intense response. The persistence of these elements after August 1914 is evidence of the continuity of German policy. It was, however, due less to conscious German decisions than to circumstances. Since the basic circumstances remained the same, the policies in response to them remained the same. In this sense, circumstances determined policy.

The behavior of the great powers during the early months of the war can therefore be understood in terms of their prewar policies. These policies collided during the July crisis when each sought diplomatic victory, and, under the circumstances, a diplomatic victory for one power would have required a diplomatic defeat for another. Since none of the powers were willing to accept diplomatic defeat, all chose war as a less undesirable alternative. There were, however, other more positive reasons for electing war as far as Berlin, Vienna, Paris, St. Petersburg and Belgrade were concerned (these views were probably not shared in London and certainly were not in Brussels). War seemed to be a means of achieving the objectives which eluded diplomacy. By choosing war Germany sought to shore up its alliance with Austria-Hungary and to shatter the Anglo-Franco-Russian alliance. Similarly, war was a means by which Austria-Hungary might preserve itself and increase its influence in the Balkans. Russia was anxious to preserve its alliance with France and to dominate the Balkans. France desired to preserve itself and the alliance with Russia and to resuscitate its great power status. Only Britain wanted to maintain the *status quo* which served British interests. All the continental powers probably also entertained more ambitious objectives which would have fundamentally altered the state system. But none of the powers specifically sought war to destroy the system, and each envisaged what it perceived as reconstruction rather than revolution. Thus, the prewar ends remained basically the same, but the means were changed from diplomacy to war. War seemed merely policy by other means.[2]

The approaching war was perceived in this way because of the prevailing view that it would be short. Even more significant than the prevalence of the short-war view was the fact that those who expected a long war did little to prepare for it. Their inaction was due to the widespread assumption that the state of Europe's political and economic development made such preparations either unnecessary or impossible.[3]

The assumption of a short war dominated German strategy. It had not always been so. Bismarck's Chief of General Staff Helmuth von Moltke predicted that the war would last seven or even thirty years. At the other end of the political spectrum, Friedrich Engels shared this view, though he estimated more accurately—three or four years. The turning point in German strategic thinking occurred with Moltke's second successor, Alfred von Schlieffen, who assumed that a lengthy conflict was impossible "in an age in which the existence of nations is based on the uninterrupted progress of trade and commerce. . . . A strategy of exhaustion is impossible when the maintenance of millions necessitates the expenditure of billions." Schlieffen's successor, Moltke's nephew Helmuth von Moltke, was characteristically ambivalent; sometimes he predicted a long, sometimes a short, war. Regardless of his varied predictions, his strategy remained constant—he planned a short war. The short-war assumption was apparently shared by most of the German officer corps and was implied in prewar discussions about the possibility of a preventive war. Germany's initial military successes during the first weeks of the war seemed to confirm the assumption. Though shaken by the Marne setback in September, that assumption was revived during October only to be shattered by the end of 1914.[4]

The same assumption underlay German diplomacy. Chancellor Theobald von Bethmann Hollweg reportedly predicted that the war would be a "brief storm." The Kaiser and court seem to have shared this view. The government's discussion of war aims was based on the expectation that France would be defeated quickly and that England would resign itself to French defeat. Despite fluctuation, this assumption remained the basis of Germany diplomacy until the end of 1914.[5]

To the extent that they expressed themselves, German financiers and industrialists probably shared the short-war assumption because of the government's statements. Although Schlieffen justified his short-war assumption in economic and political terms, he virtually ignored these considerations in his planning for war, as did his successor, the younger Moltke. Some effort was made on the eve of war to foresee the economic implication of a conflict, but little was accomplished, due to bureaucratic inertia and because it was assumed that a short war would make preparations unnecessary. Consistent with this assumption, factories and farms were subordinated to the military front—industrial and agricultural workers were drafted as the war began. A few industrialists and financiers doubted that the war would be short, in particular, that England would accept a French defeat. But most seem to have expected the conflict to end quickly, indeed, perhaps too quickly, and even agitated against "premature peace."[6]

German politicians, leaders of the Bundesstaaten, and the masses apparently shared these views. Those conservatives who felt that war would reinforce the domestic *status quo* assumed that the conflict would be short and successful. This opinion was echoed by at least one Socialist member of the Reichstag. Other members of the Reichstag considered a long war to be economically infeasible. The unanimous acceptance of the domestic political truce declared in August was justified by the anticipation that it would be temporary; politics were to resume when the Reichstag reconvened in December following a German victory. This view was encouraged by the Kaiser's assurance that victory would be won "before the leaves fall." The assumed brevity of the war caused the government and leftist politicians to discuss postwar problems in September and October. The demands from leaders of several Bundesstaaten for war aims were prompted by an expectation of imminent victory. Since the government assumed that the masses expected a short war, it concealed German military setbacks, and Bethmann considered not attending the Reichstag in December.[7]

Austro-Hungarian leaders evidently shared the assumption. Franz Conrad von Hötzendorf, the Austro-Hungarian Chief of General Staff, repeatedly demanded a preventive war. The hopes of Leopold von Berchtold, the Austro-Hungarian Foreign Minister, and others for a rapid punitive expedition against Serbia were based on the short-war assumption. Hungarian Minister President Stephan Tisza was ambivalent; he expected an Austro-Hungarian attack on Serbia to be successful but feared that it might precipitate a protracted European conflict.[8]

British leaders generally seem to have assumed that the war would be short. Anglo-French strategic discussions during the prewar decade focused on the question of how quickly and where British troops should be sent to aid the French, since the critical battles would presumably be fought early. When war broke out, those who had dominated these discussions persuaded the cabinet to send British troops quickly. But this decision was opposed by Lord Kitchener, Secretary of State for War, who did not participate in the prewar discussions and expected the war to last several years. Foreign Secretary Edward Grey's attitude was unclear; his disinclination to send troops to the continent indicated that he expected a short war, but his oft-quoted remark about the lights going out implied a destructive and thus long war. Members of the British cabinet were shocked by Kitchener's prediction of a long conflict but nonetheless accepted it. The British financial community shared writer Norman Angell's prediction that war would destroy the European financial structure and thus could not last long.[9]

French leaders likewise expected a short war. The French General Staff assumed it and French strategy implied it. Chief of the General Staff Joseph Joffre predicted that the coming war would be long, but his emphasis on speed and optimism at the beginning of the war suggested the opposite; most importantly, he made no preparation for a long conflict. Despite the French setbacks during August 1914, some French generals—notably Ferdinand Foch—predicted (in September) that the war was "virtually ended." The French government and politicians apparently shared this expectation.[10]

The same assumption was reflected in the Russian strategy. The Turkish, Italian and Bulgarian governments expected a rapid German victory. The Japanese government grabbed German colonies in Asia while Germany was engaged in Europe, in part because they probably shared the short-war assumption. American observers were ambivalent; some expected a rapid German victory, while others foresaw a protracted struggle ending in German defeat.[11]

The short-war assumption was related to policy objectives which were initially projected as reformist rather than revolutionary. A short, successful war

was necessary to achieve these goals, whereas a long war—even if successful—
might become revolutionary and preclude them. Consequently, the assumption
of a short war was a precondition of the decision to pursue prewar objectives by
war rather than diplomacy. In this sense, the desire was father to the belief. The
belief that the war would be short permeated strategy, diplomacy and domestic
politics during the first months of the war. It proved to be the war's greatest
illusion.

ENCIRCLEMENT VERSUS BREAKTHROUGH:
THE MILITARY PLANS

All military plans are forward looking since they prescribe future action;
conversely, actions based on plans are retrospective. During the early months of
the war military strategies were based on prewar assumptions and aspirations.

The German strategic blueprint, the Schlieffen plan, was based on the
assumption that Germany and Austria-Hungary would go to war against Russia,
France and probably Great Britain. The German objective was victory, not mere
survival. Germany could win only if the war was short, which was possible only
if the enemy forces were rapidly encircled and annihilated. The annihilation of
enemy forces depended upon the superiority of German forces and room to
maneuver. The relative speeds of mobilization and space factors rendered French
forces more susceptible to encirclement than the Russian army. Schlieffen thus
decided to concentrate German forces on his northern flank facing France and
to reduce German forces both on the French southern front and on the eastern
front facing Russia. The consequent risks seemed congruent with the assumption
that victory depended upon a short war, i.e., short-term security on all fronts
might lessen the chance for rapid success and thus risk long-term failure. The
operation was to develop in three stages. The German armies would be mobilized
rapidly and move westward through Belgium until they were spread out along
the Franco-Belgian border. They would then move generally southward through
the northern French plains west of the main French armies. Finally, they would
wheel eastward to encircle and annihilate the French army.[12]

Although the Germans could determine the disposition of their own
forces, victory depended upon several factors beyond their control. The
Schlieffen plan was developed as a solution to the problem of a two-front war,
but its success required what, in practice, would be a one-front war. Germany
could win only if Russian power remained ineffective until Germany defeated
France. The outcome thus depended on whether Russia decided to remain
inactive. German success was also dependent on the French dispositions. The
French army could be encircled quickly only if it concentrated and advanced
rapidly at the German center, but not if it was divided, withdrawn, or slow in
advancing.[13] Consequently, the outcome depended on French decisions. Finally,

German success required French surrender immediately after military defeat. Although hypothetically possible, surrender was unlikely in view of French behavior in 1870-71, when they had not capitulated immediately after military defeat, but only after they had been unable to find allies and to confront domestic turmoil. The Germans assumed that a French decision to surrender would be precipitated by military events but it would probably be more dependent on diplomatic and domestic considerations. In particular, French surrender after military defeat in 1914 would probably have required French diplomatic isolation. France would have been isolated only in the event that Russia and Great Britain renounced their alliances during the July crisis. If the ᵔlliances had collapsed, France would probably have accepted diplomatic defeat rather than fight alone against Germany. In that case, the Schlieffen plan would not have been implemented. Thus, the Schlieffen plan might have succeeded only in circumstances which would have made it unnecessary (i.e., a one-front war against France). But the Schlieffen plan was necessary when France elected to fight with the support of Russia and Great Britain in 1914. That support, however, made a French surrender unlikely even after military defeat. Consequently, the Schlieffen plan was implemented under conditions which made its success unlikely. It was therefore caught in a dilemma—it might have succeeded under conditions which would render it unnecessary, but was implemented when it was unlikely to succeed.

French decisions were probably determined primarily on the basis of political, rather than military, considerations, but military events were nonetheless important. German military success depended on French strategy. The revival of French self-confidence on the eve of war encouraged the development of a strategy which paradoxically increased the probability of a French defeat. The French Plan XVII, like the Schlieffen plan, was based on the assumption that victory necessitated an offensive. French strategists accordingly proposed to exploit the diversion of the main German force in Belgium in order to break through the German center. French and German strategies thus reinforced each other; they differed, however, in formulation. The Schlieffen plan stipulated an ultimate objective (i.e., annihilation of the French army), whereas Plan XVII did not. Plan XVII presumed that a French breakthrough and increasing Russian pressure on the eastern front would cause the Germans to renounce their offensive, withdraw in confusion, and surrender at the prospect of a long war. Like the Schlieffen plan, Plan XVII was based on the assumption that military events would determine the political decision to surrender. Subsequent events contradicted this assumption. Even when quick victory eluded the Germans in 1914, they did not opt for a compromise peace. Germany might have sued for peace if it had been much weaker or if its alliance with Austria-Hungary had collapsed during the July crisis. In either event, Germany would probably have accepted diplomatic defeat rather than fight alone against France, Russia and

Great Britain. If Germany had not chosen war, France would not have implemented Plan XVII. Consequently, Plan XVII might have succeeded only under conditions which would have made it unnecessary. But Plan XVII was necessary because the German alliance did not collapse, Germany was not weak, and Germany elected to fight. The considerations which persuaded the Germans to fight, however, made it unlikely that they would surrender. Plan XVII was implemented under circumstances which virtually precluded success. It was caught in the same conceptual dilemma as the Schlieffen plan.[14]

Plan XVII was probably even less likely to succeed militarily than the Schlieffen plan. The French breakthrough was possible only if the German center was depleted. The German attack through Belgium would weaken the German center, but Plan XVII also predicated massive German withdrawals to the eastern front which would occur only if the Russians attacked. Yet, Russia would attack Germany only if France promised an offensive against Germany. Since the French armies were closer to the Germans and mobilized faster than the Russians, the French attack was likely to be over before Russian pressure could force German withdrawals to the east. Consequently, German withdrawals to the east would facilitate a French breakthrough only if they were made before war broke out. The Germans would have redeployed their forces in this way only if they had expected an immediate Russian attack, i.e., a genuinely two-front war. In such an eventuality, they would probably not have implemented the Schlieffen plan which assumed a slow Russian attack, i.e., effectively a one-front war. The Germans were therefore unlikely to divert large forces simultaneously to attack through Belgium and defend the eastern front. Both actions were essential, however, if the French were to break through the German center. Plan XVII was consequently unlikely to produce military success.

The proposed French strategy may, however, have avoided French political failure. By committing their forces to an immediate attack, the French received a Russian declaration of war against Germany and assurances of an eventual offensive on the eastern front. The French would therefore not be diplomatically isolated and would not need to surrender even if defeated on the battlefield. But an immediate French surrender following military defeat was a precondition for German success. Plan XVII's most important results were probably least expected. Designed to produce military victory, it might prevent military defeat. It assumed a short war, yet virtually assured a long one. Disastrous military strategy thus proved to be a desirable political policy.

Like all alliances, the Franco-Russian alliance was selfishly and contra-dictorily interpreted by its adherents. Whatever the French might gain, the Russians would lose; and whatever the Russians gained would result in a comparable French loss. If the alliance caused Germany to concentrate against France, Russia could concentrate against Austria-Hungary. If instead the alliance caused Germany to divide its forces, France might win a breakthrough. France and Russia accordingly made a calculated bargain. The Russian calculation better served German interests, since it allowed Germany to concentrate on France rather than fight a genuine two-front war. Conversely, the German interpretation of the Austro-German alliance served Russian interests better, since it allowed Russia to concentrate on Austria-Hungary rather than fight a genuine two-front war. The immediate interests of both Russia and Germany coincided because both sought to convert two-front wars into one-front wars by using their allies as diversions.

Austro-Hungarian and French interests likewise coincided since their positions were analogous in many ways. The decline of both as great powers had been accelerated by defeat at the hands of Germany, and the prospect of one-front wars further threatened their great power status. Since they could improve that status with a victory over a genuine great power, each urged its ally to concentrate against its primary protagonist. France wanted Russia to concentrate against Germany, while Austria-Hungary asked Germany to concentrate against Russia. Each minimized the other as a threat to its ally—France dismissed the Austro-Hungarian threat to Russia; Austria-Hungary depreciated the French threat to Germany. Their allies refused, however, to comply, and so each was compelled to meet its opponent virtually alone. Both nonetheless committed themselves to risky offensives in order to insure the minimal assistance proffered by their allies. These offensives risked immediate military defeat and were therefore poor strategically, but they were good policy since they insured future aid from their allies. In summary, France and Austria-Hungary sought political gains by taking military gambles.

In the last analysis, France and Austria-Hungary probably benefited more than their allies from their respective alliances. Russian and German strategies were caught in the same kind of vicious cycle in that success in both instances depended upon the immediate surrender of their main enemies after military defeat. The defeat of Austria-Hungary would have required a Russian concentration against it, just as a German concentration was needed against France to insure French defeat. Russian concentration against Austria-Hungary required that France divert Germany. A German concentration against France needed an Austro-Hungarian diversion of Russia. But French diversion of Germany was not likely without Russian assurances of future aid to France, just as Austria-Hungary required a German promise of future aid before it would divert Russia. This prospect of future aid from their allies virtually assured, however, that France and Austria-Hungary would not surrender immediately. Consequently, the German commitment to Austria-Hungary almost certainly precluded a Russian victory, whereas the Russian commitment to France significantly diminished the probability of a German victory. In each case, the preconditions for German and Russian military victory legislated against their political success.

The risks of military failure taken by Austria-Hungary and France, on the other hand, may have prevented their political failure.

Logically, the situation almost precluded a short war. A short war would have ensued if the defeated powers surrendered immediately after defeat which they might have done if their alliances had collapsed leaving them politically isolated. But if the alliance systems had collapsed, there would probably have been no war. The war occurred because the alliance system continued. Since the alliance system insured that military defeat would not result in political isolation, the defeated nations would not be inclined to surrender immediately. The war was therefore likely to be long.

VICTORY PROVES ELUSIVE:
THE MILITARY EVENTS (4 AUGUST-14 SEPTEMBER)

Events subsequently demonstrated that there was no escape from this dilemma for any of the participants. Since the short-war assumption implied that it was necessary to win the initiative, the operative military question during the first weeks of the war was whether the Franco-Russian alliance would drive into central Europe or whether the Austro-German alliance would break out. The struggle for the initiative resulted in a mobilization mania involving political and military aspects. Political obstacles to mobilization did not materialize despite prewar governmental anxieties, and the technical military aspects of mobilization proceeded relatively smoothly. The governments were consequently most successful in areas where they were least confident. They were, however, least correct where they were most confident, i.e., in their assumption that mobilization would have the desired effect on subsequent military events. The powers mobilized and concentrated their forces at different rates. The French attacked the Germans first, the Russians attacked the Germans first, and the Austro-Hungarians attacked the Russians first. These attempts to seize the initiative were expected, prepared for, and produced no long-run advantages. On the contrary, these attacks were terribly expensive, reinforced enemy strategies, and allowed the enemy in each case to win the initiative during subsequent operations. The military advantage of rapid mobilization thus proved as illusory as the short-war assumption on which it was based.

The French were first to win and then lose the initiative. They sought to break through the German center and thereby isolate the German forces advancing through Belgium. The calm with which the French commander Joffre regarded the German advance is explained neither by icy nerves nor stupidity (as later criticism implied), but by the conviction that the German strategy served his purpose by weakening the German center. Although the initial French attacks were repulsed with heavy losses, Joffre ordered his major attack in the expectation that the German center had been depleted. In fact, the German center was superior because it had been reinforced in anticipation of the French attack. Joffre eventually recognized that his offensive had failed but might have persevered nonetheless if he had perceived some prospect of success, had expected aid from the Russians, and had security on his flanks. Since these requirements were lacking, he chose to discontinue the attack, withdraw to preserve his forces, and reinforce his west wing to meet the German advance through Belgium. This decision was typical during the early weeks of the war; the Belgian and British decisions were similar in August, as were Russian, Austro-Hungarian, and German decisions in September. The French decision was probably the most crucial, however, since a continued French attack against the German center and German superiority on the west wing were essential to the success of the Schlieffen plan. Joffre's withdrawal and redeployment prevented both eventualities. By sacrificing Plan XVII Joffre thus scuttled the Schlieffen plan.[15]

German strategy now became the operative element in the unfolding situation. The Germans overcame initial Belgian resistance, advanced rapidly westward through Belgium, and spread out along the Franco-Belgian border in preparation for a sweep southwestward through the northern French plains in pursuit of the retreating French and British forces. The pursuit operations began with great optimism among German leaders, but they soon realized that the French were not yet defeated and were withdrawing in order. Despite their rapid advance and success in several encounters, the Germans failed to turn the French flank as Joffre continued to withdraw.

The speed of the Germans' advance presented them with the need for a critical decision. As his right wing approached Paris, Moltke had the choice of passing either west or east of the city. If he swung west, he would gain an advantage by encircling Paris but risk a French breakthrough which would isolate the German army west of Paris. If he chose to pass east of Paris, he would consolidate his forces and concentrate them on the main French army but expose his west flank to the Paris garrison. Moltke elected to move east of Paris and counter the danger from Paris by turning his flank against it. He has frequently been criticized for this decision, but it is unlikely that it made a significant difference to the outcome of the campaign. Had the French and German armies on the west flank met west instead of east of Paris, they would merely have fought in different terrain and, in fact, might have been less, rather than more, critical to the outcome at the Marne. As it turned out, Moltke's decision to pass east of Paris may have offered an unexpected advantage to the Germans. By inducing the French to discontinue their withdrawal and to counterattack, this decision gave the Germans their one hypothetical opportunity to encircle the Anglo-French forces. The Germans thereby improved their chances of military success by risking military failure.

The battle of the Marne (September 5-9) was important because it ended the German pursuit, marked the farthest point of German advance, and saved

Paris. The critical question in evaluating the Marne, however, is whether the battle reversed, or merely revealed, the course of events. Traditionally the Marne has been perceived as a miraculous reversal, which implies that a German victory was likely and that Anglo-French forces turned back superior German forces; otherwise it would be illogical to describe the outcome as a miracle. This view is accepted by many German as well as Anglo-French historians. German historians sought to make the Marne battle "come out right" by altering various details and decisions. Their favorite scapegoats were Moltke and his emissary Lieutenant Colonel Hentsch who actually ordered the withdrawal of the German west wing. This criticism is emotionally understandable but largely irrelevant. Although the commanders on the German west wing resisted Hentsch's instruction to withdraw, few of them claimed that they could immediately resume the rapid advance which encircling the Anglo-French required. Their troops were simply too weak and exhausted. The German success during August had been deceptive. The German right wing could advance rapidly only as long as the French concentrated their forces elsewhere. But when the French redeployed enough forces to give them superiority over the German west wing, the German advance ground to a halt. In view of these factors, the Marne must be considered less a miracle than a logical result of the similar strength of the opposing armies and the strategies they employed.[16]

The weakness of the German west wing has frequently been attributed to mistaken decisions made by the German command. It is claimed that Moltke deprived his west wing of the forces necessary to surround the French by deploying them to strengthen his south wing. Clearly if the Germans had been vastly stronger at the Marne, they might have threatened the Anglo-French with encirclement. Several considerations, however, argue against such an eventuality. Technical difficulties (particularly limited logistic capabilities) reduced the possibility of strengthening the German west wing early in the campaign. Had troops been shifted from the German south to west wing during the pursuit stage, it is likely that the French would have more than canceled any German advantage by shifting more troops more rapidly. In that case the Marne would have involved more troops but the outcome would probably have been much the same.

It is also claimed that Moltke's deployment of troops elsewhere critically affected the Marne battle. His shipment of several corps to the eastern front was certainly a mistake, since it reduced the strength of his west wing and these troops, in any case, arrived on the eastern front too late to be effective. It is, however, doubtful that those forces were sufficient to alter the outcome of the Marne even if they had been sent to the west wing. Some German forces on the western front were involved in siege operations (most importantly against the Belgian army in its sanctuary of Antwerp). Those German troops would undoubtedly have been useful at the Marne—but so would the Belgian forces which they tied down. The Germans eventually expelled the Belgians from

Antwerp in early October, gaining both troops and artillery for their main operations but thereby drove these Belgian forces into the Anglo-French lines where they played an important role in the October operations. The net gain to the Germans turned out to be slight.

In summary, the criticism of Moltke's decisions is double-edged. Although they probably reduced German forces at the Marne (if it is assumed that they would have been sent there at the critical moment), enemy forces might also have been larger. In the final analysis, such changes in the relative strength of forces at the Marne would probably not have fundamentally altered the course of events in the sense of allowing either side to encircle and annihilate the other.[17]

Meanwhile events in the east made a rapid German victory even less likely. The Russians mobilized more rapidly than the Germans had expected and attacked before the Marne began (on September 5). The German victory of Tannenberg (August 25-30) in fact was a demonstration of the preconditions for success of the Schlieffen plan. The Russian army at Tannenberg attacked the German middle, neglected its own flanks, and thereby allowed the Germans to encircle and annihilate it. When during the subsequent operations of early September in East Prussia the Russians refused to attack the German middle and withdrew to protect their flanks, the Germans were unable to encircle them. The Germans won a resounding victory at Tannenberg because the Russians in fact made a decision unlike any other during the early months of the war. Tannenberg constituted an immediate military advantage for the Germans because it made the deployment of large forces to the east unnecessary and allowed them to pursue their objective of defeating France first. But Tannenberg also implied a political disadvantage for the Germans since it proved that Russia was committed to war. France consequently could count on Russia's future, if not immediate, help and was unlikely to surrender even if it was defeated in the field. Tannenberg was consequently a short-term military success for Germany but it signaled the possibility of long-term political failure.

VICTORY ESCAPES AGAIN:
THE MILITARY EVENTS (15 SEPTEMBER-3 NOVEMBER)

The events of August and early September marked the first attempt by both sides to win a quick victory. It was not yet clear that a short war was impractical under existing conditions. The major fact of the initial stage of military operations was the failure of either side to win a decisive success. Although the armies engaged had been too weak to keep the initiative, all had been strong enough to avoid annihilation. Each side counted on victory and feared defeat but had, in fact, achieved a draw. Following the frenetic events of the first month, each side paused to consolidate its forces. This hiatus was required by the catastrophic casualties and confusion of the initial campaigns. The antagonists' roles had dramatically reversed. The initiative on the western front had been taken first by the French, then by the Germans, finally by the Anglo-French. The initiative on the eastern front had been first taken in the north by the Russians and then the Germans, and first in the south by the Austro-Hungarians and then the Russians. By the middle of September a rough strategic balance had been established.[18]

These events had contradictory implications. The Germans had won the most striking successes, but their inability to achieve victory was more serious for them than for their enemies. Since the Germans had assumed that they could win only if they won quickly and could win quickly only if they won decisively, the failure to win a decision constituted a failure in terms of their own strategy and argued for regaining the initiative as soon as possible. Conversely, since the Anglo-French prospects were better in a long war, the lack of a decision was less ominous for them and perhaps even argued for remaining on the defensive. The French desire to liberate territory occupied by the German invasion, however, argued for a resumption of their offensive. Consequently, the French strategists, governed by desire more than logic, would be on the offensive as much as the Germans during the first year of the war. Similar contradictions occurred on the eastern front. It would have been logical for the Germans to assume the defensive after repelling the Russians, but the Russian threat to Austria-Hungary argued for resuming the offensive. Conversely, the Russian failure against Germany and their success against Austria-Hungary were logical arguments for concentrating against Austria-Hungary, whereas the need to encourage a new Anglo-French offensive required a renewal of the attack against Germany. In the situation at hand, Austria-Hungary, like France, would probably have been well-advised to assume the defensive; they were similarly obsessed with their lost territories and elected the offensive.

The decision on German strategy was primarily the responsibility of Erich von Falkenhayn, who succeeded the sick Moltke in mid-September. Since Moltke implemented Schlieffen's strategy, Falkenhayn had to make the first fundamental strategic modifications. Falkenhayn's actions were complicated because of his awkward personality, his previous exclusion from the decision-making process, and the concealment of his succession in order to avoid the appearance of defeat. These disadvantages were offset both by the support given Falkenhayn by the Kaiser and his military cabinet and by Falkenhayn's experience with the problems of mobilization as Prussian minister of war. Falkenhayn's strategy oscillated between postponing and pursuing the initiative. He rejected an offensive on the eastern front before the Anglo-French were defeated but was unclear as to how victory could be achieved on the western front where he pursued an ambiguous policy. Although he argued that an offensive was impossible for several weeks—until new recruits were trained, losses replaced, railroad and communication problems solved, and munitions deficiencies repaired—he nonetheless hoped for immediate success on his west wing. Falkenhayn's undeniable indecisiveness has been severely criticized. It is, however, debatable whether different decisions and greater decisiveness would have substantially altered the subsequent course of events. Even if the mobility of the German west wing had been reestablished by a rapid, tactical withdrawal (as Falkenhayn's critics advocated), it is dubious that the Germans were strong enough to achieve victory. The reasons for German failure at the Marne still applied.[19]

In any case, the French strategy militated against German success. French dispositions were roughly analogous to German movements. After recognizing that the Germans had reestablished their front, the French and British slowed their own advance and fortified the occupied territory. Like Falkenhayn, Joffre mixed caution with confidence. He too recognized that the shortage of men and munitions reduced chances for a rapid victory, but the desire to liberate French territory and the advantage of superior mobility encouraged Joffre to seek the initiative against the German west wing. Despite Falkenhayn's efforts to tie him down with attacks elsewhere, Joffre shifted forces to the west of the German west wing.

The struggle for the initiative was resumed at the end of September when each army groped for the other's west flank. The roles were ambiguous since both sides sought to encircle and to avoid encirclement at the same time. Falkenhayn attacked in the hope that the whole front could be set in motion again, while Joffre sought a success but lacked the men and munitions to achieve it. Falkenhayn rejected the alternative of regaining mobility by ordering a tactical withdrawal because it would appear as another defeat. Instead he sought unsuccessfully to break through the French west wing. He thus tried general attack, breakthrough and encirclement without success. Both sides suffered so severely from exhaustion of men and munitions that operations threatened to desist altogether. The front had been extended westward but no fundamental strategic change had occurred.

Although victory eluded them, the Germans avoided defeat and had limited tactical success. They maintained the cohesion of their forces and their control over conquered territory by repelling Anglo-French attacks against their front and by removing the threat of Anglo-Belgian attacks on their rear. The Germans attacked the Belgian army in its Antwerp sanctuary at the end of September and took the city in early October. The capture of Antwerp was a contradictory success. It secured the German rear and freed artillery and men for the campaign in France. But it also forced the Belgian army out of its sanctuary and back into the Anglo-French lines where it could become an important factor during October. The net effect was therefore a further concentration of military forces on the west wing of both sides.

The Germans made a final attempt to win quickly in late October. The fall of Antwerp and the availability of newly trained reserve corps remedied the troop shortage. The Germans sought first to outflank the enemy along the coast and then to break through farther inland. Although they severely tested Anglo-French-Belgian resistance, these attacks failed by the beginning of November. The Germans again won the initiative but not victory. Falkenhayn had chosen to gamble on a rapid success instead of preparing for a long war, a choice justified only if the chances for success were favorable. When he made the original decision to attack in early October, there was a possibility of success because troops on the German west wing were about twice as numerous as their opponents. But Anglo-French-Belgian transferrals toward the coast diminished German superiority and thus Falkenhayn's chance for success. In fact, the salient characteristic of these operations was precisely the similarity of the moves made by both sides at the same time in the same terrain with forces of roughly the same size. A stalemate was the logical result. These operations during October had important implications. By committing his newly formed corps, Falkenhayn exhausted his fresh reserves and destroyed the potential leaders of the German army's future expansion. Men and munitions were exhausted on both sides and the offensive spirit had expired.

Roughly analogous events had taken place in the east. There both sides paused to regroup and continued to spar for the initiative during the latter half of September. The Russian and Austro-Hungarian forces, the pursuers and the pursued, were equally exhausted, and the German army lacked sufficient power to continue its advance. Like their counterparts in the west, the commanders in the east now had to decide on future operations. German options were limited by Falkenhayn's decision not to shift significant forces east until victory had been won in the west. Nonetheless the desire to eject the Russians from East Prussia and the requests for help from Conrad, the Austro-Hungarian Chief of General Staff, argued for operations against the Russians in Poland. An acrimonious dispute between the allies developed on what these operations should be. Hindenburg and Ludendorff advocated an offensive into Poland from the north which Conrad had requested since early August, but Conrad now asked instead for German reinforcements in the south. In the face of Conrad's threat not to resume operations, Falkenhayn decided in his favor and it was finally agreed that a combined offensive should be launched in the south. After six weeks of war, the principle, though not the actual practice, of Austro-German military coordination had finally been established. But contemporaneous Russian decisions virtually precluded an Austro-German success. Previous Russian losses and the possibility of a German attack from the north persuaded Grand Duke Nicholas, the Russian supreme commander, to await reinforcements before resuming his offensive against the Austro-Hungarians.

Both sides sought a decisive victory in October. The Germans and Austro-Hungarians tried first. Conrad had high hopes as their combined offensive began, but Hindenburg and Ludendorff sought only local success in order to gain time until German reinforcements arrived from the west. The Austro-German objective was a double encirclement of Russian forces in southern Poland by the Germans from the west and the Austro-Hungarians from the south, but it became impossible when the Russians withdrew on the German front. The roles of attacker and the attacked were reversed when the Russians tried to turn the German northern flank. The issue then became a question of whether the Russians could encircle the Germans in the north before the Austro-Hungarians could defeat the Russians in the south. The Russians eventually forced both their opponents to withdraw at the end of October, but pursued cautiously and halted at the beginning of November.[20]

As in the west, no decisive outcome occurred in the east. The northern campaign was indecisive because Russian numerical superiority was nullified by superior German mobility. Operations in the south were likewise indecisive because the Austro-Hungarian numerical superiority was offset by inconducive terrain and Austro-Hungarian offensive weakness. The prospect for a decisive outcome would have been better if the situation had been reversed, i.e., if the Russians had attacked the Austro-Hungarians or if the Germans had attacked the Russians. The Germans nonetheless achieved their immediate purpose of avoiding a diversion from the west. The Austro-Hungarians gained little in October but had at least lost little. Like the Germans in the west, the Russians won the initiative but not victory.

The events of August and September were confirmed in October. The inability of the powers to gain victory suggests that their failure was due less to particular incidents and personalities than to the general circumstances. The comparable strengths and counterbalancing strategies of the opposing armies probably precluded a decisive outcome. Without such an eventuality, a short war was unlikely. The faith proved to be an illusion.

ARROGANCE & ANXIETY:
GERMAN FOREIGN POLICY

POLICY & STRATEGY: A DECEPTIVE DICHOTOMY

War alters the practice of diplomacy. If war and diplomacy are defined as mutually exclusive, diplomacy desists when war is declared. But if diplomacy is defined broadly as the pursuit of state interests by all means except actual military operations, diplomacy often performs an important function in wartime. The second definition is applied here. Like peacetime diplomacy, war diplomacy can be divided for analysis into the two general areas of ends and means. In establishing ends, war diplomacy projects the conditions under which war stops and peace resumes; in this sense, war diplomacy defines the moment when its function ends. These objectives are formulated as war aims which can be separated into confidential and public aims. Confidential aims reflect the goals actually sought by governments, whereas public aims, though not unrelated to confidential aims, serve primarily domestic political purposes and are therefore less reliable indicators of governmental aspirations.

In addition to establishing aims, war diplomacy performs an important function as a means of war in conjunction with military operations. This aspect is important in bilateral conflicts and critical in coalition wars. War diplomacy seeks on the one hand to strengthen the friendly alliance by consolidation and adhesion of new members, on the other to weaken the enemy alliance by defection and revolution. All the participants in World War I sought all these objectives in varying forms and situations. Although convenient as analytical categories, means and ends were, however, not always clearly distinguished by the governments involved. Contradictions frequently existed between the two, and means sometimes determined ends. The relationship between means and ends also fluctuated as a result of changes in the general situation. As long as military means seemed sufficient to win a short war, the establishment of ends was the primary function of war diplomacy. But when military means proved insufficient by the end of 1914, war diplomacy was called upon to assist in the pursuit of victory, and the distinction became even less clear between means and ends.

War alters policymaking. Among other things, war requires a redefinition of the relationship between military and civilian authority. The civil-military conflict in Germany (and elsewhere) has traditionally been regarded as significant. Historians frequently sympathize with the civilians whom they perceive as being less aggressive than the soldiers. These civil-military frictions which certainly existed before, during and after the war were clear from its beginning. Bethmann and Moltke disagreed over the timing of mobilization and proclamations to the German and Polish peoples. Moltke not only suggested diplomatic moves to assist strategy but he, Admiral Alfred von Tirpitz, Admiral Hugo von Pohl and General Wilhelm Groener also severely criticized the civilians. These frictions were due in part to differences in personality and training. They were reinforced by the persistence of the peacetime habit of isolating civilian and military functions. Further complications were caused by adjustments in authority necessitated by war; soldiers rather than statesmen suddenly had the authority for making the most critical decisions. Different perceptions of the relationship between strategy and policy naturally resulted. The soldiers generally subordinated political considerations to military operations which they expected to resolve German problems. Furthermore, their criticism of Bethmann's lack of clarity was partly justified. The considerable disagreements which ensued should therefore not be minimized.[1]

These frictions tend, however, to obscure the basic agreement on fundamental assumptions and long-range goals. Soldiers and statesmen alike accepted the necessity of war, assumed it would be short and victorious, and hoped it would preserve the Austro-German alliance while shattering the Franco-Russian alliance. An emphasis of their differences is also misleading since it implies that the long-range policy aspirations of German leaders affected the course of events during the early months of the war. In fact these aspirations were in large measure determined by previously established military plans and events beyond the control of either soldiers or statesmen. Despite certain superficial conflicts, strategy and policy complemented one another and therefore the assumption of a sharp dichotomy is deceptive.[2]

BEGINNINGS OF POLICY (4-24 AUGUST)

German war policy was a synthesis of possible and desirable goals. Objectives reflected the military situation: when military prospects were favorable, aspirations expanded; when military prospects were unfavorable, aspirations contracted. Since the expectation for a short and successful war seems to have been fairly general among German leaders, they were initially confident. Their confidence gave way to concern because of the dangers on the eastern front, but it was revived just as abruptly when Germany finally won the initiative in the west. In short, policymakers vacillated as military prospects varied, and the prewar oscillation between anxiety and arrogance persisted. Likewise, they evolved policy as some desiderata proved impossible and other possibilities became desirable. A residue of objectives nonetheless remained through all vicissitudes and the general form, if not the precise content, of German policy was established at the beginning of the war.[3]

German policy toward France reflects some of these paradoxes. Although the immediate object of German military operations was a French defeat, France was infrequently mentioned and inconsistently perceived by German leaders. In their Reichstag speeches at the beginning of August, the Kaiser emphasized but Bethmann minimized the Franco-German conflict. In confidential discussions during August among German leaders, Bethmann expressed hope for an alliance with France through British mediation and advocated limiting the occupation of France so that Germany could aid Austria-Hungary. The Kaiser seems to have been won over to this view, but Tirpitz felt French and Belgian territory should be retained as a pawn in subsequent bargaining with Britain. Others, such as the banker Arthur von Gwinner, advocated a German demand for indemnity and colonies from France. Amity and enmity seemed to operate simultaneously in the evolution of German policy.[4]

German policymakers gave Russia much attention in contrast to that accorded France. In part, German leaders sought to compensate for their momentary military inadequacy in the east with political means. Russia also was perceived to be the greatest threat by some German leaders (including Bethmann and Jagow). The Kaiser minimized the Russian danger in his Reichstag speech at the beginning of August, while Bethmann maximized it. German leaders, unwilling to make significant transfers from the western front, used the political recourse of encouraging revolt among the border peoples under Russian rule. Despite their public affirmations of "monarchical solidarity," the conservatives who formulated German policy had remarkably few inhibitions about using revolution as a tool. Poland, the barometer of Russo-German relations since the 18th century, was appropriately chosen as the first target for revolution. Through proclamations and by encouraging dissidents, the German government sought unsuccessfully to establish an outsized, German-dominated Polish state to disrupt the Russian war effort and act as a buffer against Russia. Berlin likewise began to encourage rebellion among the Finns, Russian Jews and Caucasus minorities. Vienna, understandably reticent about promoting nationalist revolts because of its own vulnerability, was nonetheless the first to foster social revolution in Russia by expediting the return of exiled revolutionaries to Russia. The Germans applied the same idea in encouraging Ukrainian socialists. National and social revolution was consequently intended to serve both as a means of winning the war and as an end in extending German influence in eastern Europe.[5]

German policy toward Britain was a contest between conciliation and compulsion. Bethmann, Jagow and the former German ambassador in London Karl von Lichnowsky advocated conciliation. Bethmann's efforts to keep Britain neutral during the July crisis continued to the eve of war; when they failed, he sought to postpone military and especially naval contact as long as possible. He, Jagow and perhaps even Moltke hoped that Anglo-German relations could be reestablished rapidly after a brief conflict in which Britain was not deeply involved. The German government encouraged a rapid settlement by claiming publicly that it had sought peaceful Anglo-German relations during the July crisis, and Lichnowsky hoped commercial considerations would make the British seek peace. But the advocates of compulsion disagreed. Tirpitz regarded Bethmann's policy as fallacious and sought to reverse its priorities: he considered Britain, not Russia, to be the main enemy. Admiral Pohl turned Lichnowsky's argument around and urged lengthening rather than shortening the war in order to hurt Britain economically. The banker Gwinner argued, however, that a protracted war would not hurt, but help, Britain's economy. Whether sooner or later, means had to be found to make Britain conclude a peace favorable to Germany. As in the case of Russia, revolution seemed the panacea since military means were unavailable. The Kaiser and Moltke accordingly advocated and the Foreign Office began to encourage insurrection in India, Egypt and South Africa.[6]

German relations with Britain implicated Belgium, which complicated the conciliatory approach toward Britain. Some German leaders felt that active British intervention could be discouraged only by a rapid defeat of France. But a French defeat would require a violation of Belgian neutrality which would insure British belligerence. Bethmann and Jagow tried to escape this vicious circle by seeking Belgian permission to German passage, which would not only expedite French defeat but also perhaps encourage British neutrality. When the Belgians refused and conciliation proved less practical, compulsion seemed more promising. Tirpitz urged using Belgium as a threat to Britain, while the Kaiser and the King of Bavaria advocated annexation of Belgium. Although he may have considered offering Belgian territory as compensation to France for demands Germany might make, Bethmann opposed outright German annexation of Belgian territory. German policy toward Britain thus reflected the ambiguities of prewar Anglo-German relations, a lack of significant military contact between them, and Germany's uncertain military prospects.[7]

PLANNING FOR VICTORY (24 AUGUST-14 SEPTEMBER)

The vicissitudes of German military fortunes during late August and early September were reflected in the mercurial moods of German leaders. The news that Germany had won the initiative in the west caused a sense of euphoria and an expectation of imminent victory. Moltke believed that the Germans had already won, and his head of operations, Gerhard Tappen, asserted that the war would be over in six weeks. Tirpitz, who was initially skeptical, began to hope that the war would end quickly, that the power of the French army had been broken, and that the British were near defeat. Groener was in an ebullient mood. Admiral Georg Alexander Müller wrote that the German forces were jubilant over their successes on the western front and that a "great catastrophe" would befall the Anglo-French forces when the Germans encircled them. After the initial uncertainty, operations seemed to be developing according to plan.[8]

This general optimism was not enjoyed long. It soon became clear that a pursuit was necessary because Anglo-French withdrawals had preserved their forces. During this period, German anticipation of success gave way to caution and despondency to the point that optimists were criticized. Tirpitz recognized that the Anglo-French fought tenaciously, that their withdrawal precluded an immediate encirclement, and that the ultimate outcome was difficult to predict. Groener's ebullience gave way to the sober realization that the encirclement and annihilation envisaged by Schlieffen had not yet occurred, and he predicted that more battles would be necessary. Müller realized that the British forces were unlikely to be encircled. Moltke observed that the Germans had won successes but had not annihilated or captured the enemy forces because the French were conducting a planned and orderly retreat. The Kaiser was aware that the situation was serious despite initial successes. Despondency and pessimism grew. Müller lost his optimism, and Moltke, Bethmann and Jagow became more serious, almost depressed. The concern at all levels was compounded by the uncertainty of events on the eastern front and the possibility of Anglo-Russian naval operations in the Baltic. The news of Tannenberg raised spirits at German headquarters and the Kaiser became overly optimistic again, but Müller and Moltke criticized the Kaiser for being unrealistic. The continuing German advance nonetheless encouraged Moltke and Bethmann to be cautiously hopeful. The psychology which permeated the German pursuit was therefore an amalgam of fears and hopes.[9]

The Anglo-French counterattack at the Marne augmented feelings of anxiety and anticipation. Moltke became increasingly depressed. Kuhl, chief of staff of the army on the extreme west wing, was concerned by the French army's ability to maintain coherence. Tirpitz realized that the war had not yet been won, predicted that the hardest fighting was still to come, and doubted the possibility of German success. Groener likewise recognized that the critical victory remained to be won. The criticism which is a characteristic reaction to frustration and failure began to be expressed: Groener and Falkenhayn thought Moltke had lost control of operations. But optimism was more characteristic. The Kaiser became expectant, commanders on the German right wing hoped for imminent victory, Admiral Pohl was confident, and Tirpitz mixed hope with his doubts. Many of Moltke's advisers (including Tappen, Domnes, Groener, Stein and Plessen) recognized that the French counterattack offered the Germans their best opportunity to encircle and annihilate the French.[10]

The confrontation at the Marne ended, however, in German withdrawal, not victory, and their mood plummeted. Moltke became so severely depressed that he was replaced by Falkenhayn. Tirpitz wrote that everyone was anxious and doubtful as to whether the situation could be saved. Groener concurred, Bethmann and Jagow became increasingly pessimistic and complaining, the Kaiser reverted to depression, and Lyncker became seriously worried for the first time. Others were less dejected but still concerned. Hentsch felt that the withdrawals were not as serious from the military as from the political point of view. Plessen believed that the withdrawals were necessary but only minor and temporary. The mood of German leaders thus evolved from optimism to confidence to depression as German military fortunes varied from success to pursuit to withdrawal.[11]

German leaders were under the influence of these changing moods as they developed policy. The imminence of victory in late August implied the necessity of planning for peace. The resulting policy toward France was a contradictory mixture of carrot and stick. In answer to Jagow's request for his views, Colonial Secretary Wilhelm Solf argued that the French (as well as Belgian and Portuguese) colonies could be taken following a French defeat. Bethmann asked Imperial Secretary of the Interior Clemens von Delbrück and the banker Karl Helfferich to evaluate French ore deposits in Briey-Longwy and the extent of German investments in them. Bethmann's interest in these deposits was probably reinforced by requests for their annexation from industrialists Karl Röchling, Emil Kirdorff, Fritz Thyssen and the Catholic Centrist politician Matthias Erzberger. Bethmann also asked Delbrück and Helfferich to estimate how much indemnity France (and Belgium) could pay. The Kaiser suggested that the non-German population of Alsace-Lorraine by expelled and dispossessed to create a military front by settling the area with former German non-commissioned officers. Tirpitz took an opposing tack by urging the offer of moderate conditions in order to win France as an ally. The banker Gwinner argued for economic domination instead of outright annexation, as did the economist Walther Rathenau, Undersecretary of Foreign Affairs Arthur Zimmermann, and Bethmann's private secretary, Kurt Riezler. German leaders consequently began to consider desiderata by the end of August but had not yet worked out a systematic program.[12]

When the possibility of a French defeat increased at the beginning of September, timing became as important as the terms of peace. If the war was to be short, nonmilitary factors would have to be excluded as much as possible. German leaders therefore became increasingly anxious to pacify the French civilian population and to discourage a popular or revolutionary struggle as had occurred in 1870-1. Using the threat of reprisal for resistance and the promise of restraint for compliance, Moltke sought to discourage guerrilla activities and thus "a national rising." When it seemed that the French would defend Paris, the Germans dropped on the city both bombs and bombastic proclamations recommending surrender. Bethmann urged that the occupying German forces handle French private property carefully, apparently to encourage the French middle and upper classes to seek a settlement.[13]

The most specific German effort to encourage peace with France was a proclamation to be delivered to the French people. It was prepared by three of Bethmann's intimates—his private secretary, Riezler; his cousin, Gerhard von Mutius; and Wilhelm von Radowitz, a counselor in the Foreign Office. The proclamation began with an assertion of German victory, but it expressed no rancor and even praised the bravery of French troops. It claimed that Germany did not want the war which was forced upon it by the intransigence of the Entente. Similar to the previous statements, the proclamation promised that response would be rewarded and resistance punished. It guaranteed private property, assured that occupation costs would be minimized and urged a return to normal peacetime activities. It threatened, however, that occupation would last until the French government and allies allowed peace to be concluded. It therefore implied an effort to split France from its allies and the French people from their government which had proclaimed its determination to continue the war despite military setbacks. In essence the proclamation offered the French people peace in exchange for a renunciation of their country's great power status. The proclamation was postponed when Joffre's order to counterattack was intercepted. Bethmann was indeed already worried that the war might be protracted because France was not disposed to peace and Moltke predicted a vast war between peoples. German leaders thus hoped for a new Treaty of Frankfurt by winning another Sedan but feared another Commune.[14]

Paradoxically, these extensive preparations for peace with France were made at a time when peace had become less likely. The Anglo-French counterattacks at the Marne and the Entente's declaration that they would not make a separate peace caused Bethmann to conclude that "the war has not been decided and it appears instead that England has succeeded in holding its allies for a resistance *à outrance.*" He nonetheless felt that it was necessary to prepare "for the eventuality of sudden negotiations which should not be protracted." The resulting memorandum stipulated that "the general goal of the war was the security of the German Empire to the west and east for the foreseeable future." To achieve this objective, "France must be so weakened that it cannot revive again as a great power. Russia must be pushed back as far as possible from the German border and its dominion over the non-Russian vassal peoples broken." A "cohesive *Mittelafrika* colonial empire" should also be sought. Since it postponed the Russian and colonial questions, omitted Britain and concentrated on western and central Europe, the memorandum was probably designed as preparation for a separate peace with France and Belgium. Germany would allow its generals to decide the specifics of territorial demands, seek the ore basins of

Briey, and force the French government to assume responsibility for transferring the iron works to German ownership. The memorandum also proposed a commercial treaty to make France economically dependent on Germany and to exclude British commerce. It urged an indemnity sufficiently high to preclude French rearmament for the next eighteen to twenty years. France would effectively become a German satellite.

The Bethmann memorandum also proposed that Belgium be even more harshly handled. "Although it would retain the appearance of a state, Belgium must sink to the level of a vassal state, grant Germany the right of occupying any important military posts, place its coast at the military disposal of Germany and become an economic province of Germany." Since such an arrangement would offer Germany all the advantages without the problems of annexation, the suggested territorial demands were relatively limited. Even such severity did not satisfy the Kaiser and several generals who demanded that Belgian and French territory be annexed without inhabitants, designated as "military colonies," and resettled by German soldiers. Bethmann thought the suggestion involved practical difficulties, but regarded it as appealing. Bethmann recommended that Holland be handled more deviously though with the same objective, that it be made apparently independent, but in fact dependent on Germany. By these means the independence of Germany's other western neighbors was to be destroyed.

Peace with France and Belgium was only part of a larger scheme for German domination over Europe. A "middle European economic union" was to be established through customs agreements with France, Belgium, Holland, Denmark, Austria-Hungary, Poland and possibly Italy, Sweden and Norway. The proposed union was to have no constitutional head and would apparently preserve equality among its members. In fact it was to be dominated by Germany and establish German economic preponderance over Europe.[15]

Bethmann's memorandum was a synthesis of prevailing German ideas. All its major points—a quick separate peace with France; *Mitteleuropa* and *Mittelafrika*; concern for Belgian and French forts which had resisted the German advance; French ore basins; economic domination of France and Belgium; and a war indemnity—had been proposed before the memorandum was prepared. The memorandum in turn caused further discussion and Bethmann continued to canvass his colleagues for suggestions. Rathenau argued for a moderate peace with France on the model of 1866 in order to bring it into "a *Mitteleuropa* unified under German leadership and protected politically and economically against England and America on the one side and Russia on the other." Minister of Interior Delbrück opposed the annexation of Belgium and Holland and the customs union with Austria-Hungary which he regarded as impractical and restrictive for Germany. The conservative Delbrück was skeptical of the *Mitteleuropa* idea because of practical and political difficulties, but he nonetheless recognized the great advantages of a German-dominated economic entity "from the Pyrenees to the Memel, from the Black Sea to the North Sea, from the Mediterranean to the Baltic," which would allow Germany to compete with the United States for world economic domination. He therefore concluded that "we should thank God that the war gives us the impulse and opportunity to renounce an economic system which is in the process of passing beyond the acme of its success." Bethmann granted some of Delbrück's objections but ordered him to pursue the *Mitteleuropa* scheme. Unlike Delbrück, Tirpitz and Falkenhayn rejected as premature the whole premise of discussing peace with France since they regarded a continuation of the war necessary to preserve Germany's world power status. Such exclusive reliance on military means was, however, castigated by some of Bethmann's advisers who had contributed to the memorandum—e.g., Riezler, Rathenau and Gwinner—since they felt it would preclude achieving their objective of German domination over Europe. Consequently, if Germany had been able to dictate peace in September 1914, German leaders would have agreed on the general objective but not on the form of German domination over Europe.[16]

Peace with France was the immediate German objective, but neither was it an end in itself nor was France perceived as the primary enemy. Having seemed to be a possible neutral in July and a reluctant belligerent in early August, Britain became Germany's main opponent in late August and September. Some German officials, particularly the Kaiser and Tirpitz, perceived Britain in this role before the war and continued to do so. The conversion to this view of those—like Bethmann, Jagow and the shipping magnate Albert Ballin—who had previously regarded Britain in more favorable terms was important, but the reason for this change can only be inferred. Increased British military and naval participation in the war during late August was probably the main impulse. The British blockade, propaganda and diplomatic activity—particularly the public rejection of a separate peace—probably contributed. The possibility that Britain would induce its ally Japan to enter the conflict touched racial sensitivities.[17]

Therefore, in the eyes of many German leaders, including Müller, Falkenhayn, Ballin, Solf, Rathenau, Tirpitz and Gwinner, Britain now became Germany's central problem. Both the carrot and stick were suggested as a means of achieving peace with Britain. Defeat of the British army in France was obviously the most desirable means, but a naval confrontation was also a hypothetical option. Bethmann opposed any intensification of naval operations by arguing that England would make peace only if Germany still had its fleet as a potential threat. Tirpitz advocated greater naval activity and concluded that Bethmann and the Foreign Office wanted to make naval concessions to win peace with Britain. Bethmann won over all his colleagues except Tirpitz (i.e., Müller, Pohl, Ingenohl, Falkenhayn) and persuaded the Kaiser not to augment radically naval operations. Other means were meanwhile sought. Economic warfare in response to the British blockade was suggested by Rathenau, Gwinner, and Helfferich. Bethmann answered British propaganda with denials and countercharges of his own, while he, the Kaiser and Rathenau encouraged efforts to revolutionize the British empire. The problem of forcing Britain to conclude peace nonetheless remained.[18]

Bethmann's memorandum and the resulting discussion sought to resolve this problem. Rathenau argued that Germany had to make Britain capitulate since Britain would seek to protract the war which allowed Britain to dominate world trade. Since he believed Britain was militarily invulnerable, Rathenau advocated economic warfare, intensified naval activity from the Channel ports, air attacks and colonial insurgence after Germany had arranged peace with Belgium and France. Bethmann and others at German headquarters apparently agreed and some of Rathenau's ideas were incorporated into Bethmann's memorandum. The changed attitude of German leaders toward Britain altered their perception of Belgium. While some of them continued to see Belgium as a pawn in eventual peace negotiations with Britain, their mounting antipathy toward Britain caused most German leaders to see Belgium as an object for annexation and a base of future operations against Britain. The most striking feature of the discussions was the realization that projected German war aims could affect Britain only indirectly—in Belgium and France, in its empire, and in international trade—but not directly. Indeed this was the basic dilemma of German policy toward Britain: Britain was the most obstinate but least vulnerable opponent.[19]

German policy toward Russia received less attention for the moment, but German aims at Russian expense remained extensive. Bethmann postponed discussion of Russia yet asserted that "Russia must be pushed back as far as possible from the German border and its domination over the non-Russian vassal peoples broken," i.e., replaced by Germany. Bethmann and Zimmermann realized that the fulfillment of these objectives required continuation of the war against Russia after France was defeated. Rathenau's attitude toward Russia was contradictory: he advocated financial cooperation with Russia to exclude Anglo-American competition but viewed the projected *Mitteleuropa* as a means of competing with both the Russians and Anglo-Americans. Despite the postponement of extensive planning in regard to Russia, the annexation of a border strip of Russian-Polish territory was discussed. Still unable to concentrate large military forces in the east, the Germans and the Austro-Hungarians continued to encourage revolution in Russia. German policy and strategy thus concentrated on the west. [20]

PLANNING DESPITE UNCERTAINTY
(15 SEPTEMBER-3 NOVEMBER)

Germany's military prospects during the autumn were reflected in the attitudes of German leaders. As the situation changed, their moods varied between pessimism, skepticism, cynicism, stoicism and occasionally optimism. Pessimism prevailed immediately after the Marne. When the situation stabilized, German leaders realized that the war would be longer, more difficult and less certain than they had anticipated. The sparring for the initiative in late September and early October instilled moderate hope which soon vied with fear, frustration and doubt. The fall of Antwerp and German advances in Poland at the beginning of October caused optimism varying from excessive to moderate. The second attempt to win a decision over the Anglo-French-Belgian forces in Flanders during late October and early November was accompanied by new hopes, worries and disappointments. German withdrawal from Poland at the end of October caused both serious concern and confidence. As Tirpitz and Groener observed, "fears very much increase and decrease" at German headquarters and the German people would have to accustom themselves to a "fluctuating fate in the war."[21]

German military failures resulted in recriminations, fears of the future, and self-pity among German leaders. German strategy was castigated, and the German people and army were subjected to criticism for their excessive optimism. Moltke and his advisers, Falkenhayn, the Kaiser, as well as Bethmann and his civilian colleagues all received a share of blame from several quarters for their prewar and wartime policies. Paradoxically, few critics specifically blamed Germany's enemies for the situation. German leaders increasingly recognized the likelihood of a long war and the obstacles to victory created by static warfare. They perceived the future pessimistically and the feeling that Germany had been persecuted and abandoned grew in all quarters.[22]

The uncertain military prospects caused German leaders to plan less intensively for peace than they had in September, but considerable aspirations nonetheless persisted in the minds of many. Bethmann and Jagow realized the implications of the Marne, and Bethmann became unresponsive in discussions on war aims. Since they did not enlighten any of their subordinates (except Zimmermann) on the military situation, planning initiated during the first half of September continued and suggestions poured in. Bethmann had Delbrück pursue the *Mitteleuropa* scheme but no decision was reached. When the possibility of military victory seemed to recur in the second half of October, Bethmann's enthusiasm for planning revived. In short, planning reflected events on the battlefield.[23]

In contrast with the first half of September, discussions of peace with France diminished. Unexpected French tenacity impressed many German leaders and caused Bethmann to doubt rumors of French domestic paralysis. Demands at French expense nonetheless remained considerable, and the conditions outlined in Bethmann's memorandum remained the starting point for discussions of a peace with France. Although he granted that "it seems too early for such considerations and their achievement is not yet sure," Bethmann ordered an investigation of the annexation of the Briey mines. He decided in late October that the campaign in Flanders warranted more active preparations for peace. As he told Delbrück, "we must reckon with the possibility that one of our opponents [i.e., either Belgium or France] may suddenly collapse even though there is still no sign of it. This possibility must not surprise us." They should therefore continue to collect "detailed materials on what is worth striving for in case of peace negotiations." He asked Delbrück and Zimmermann to determine a scale of indemnities sufficient to weaken France and Belgium as economic competitors and suggested that an annexation of the Briey ore basin was desirable, since France would then become dependent on Germany for ore and thus be unable to compete with Germany. Delbrück concurred, but argued that France be compensated with Belgian territory. Prussian Minister of Interior Loebell urged that France be destroyed as a great power by losing its ore deposits, eastern fortresses and African colonies. Friedrich Naumann, who published the best known argument for *Mitteleuropa* a year later, expressed comparable views. Only Rathenau urged moderation toward France as a means of reconciling it with a *Mitteleuropa* designed to continue the war against Britain and Russia. These aims at French expense deterred neither Jagow nor Bethmann from trying to encourage Anglo-French antipathies or seeking contacts with French politicians who might be inclined toward peace.[24]

German interest in dominating Belgium intensified in October when Antwerp fell, most of the country was occupied, and the defeat of the Belgian army became a possibility. Bethmann reiterated the guidelines established in his memorandum when he asked Delbrück and Zimmermann to suggest a war indemnity large enough to cripple Belgium as an economic competitor and to seek a political arrangement "which does not encumber us with the administration [of Belgium] but allows economic penetration and insures us of military control over the coasts, fortresses and transport facilities in the eventuality of future wars." Delbrück urged taking the Belgian coast and giving France a large slice of Belgium as compensation for Briey. Naumann suggested that Belgium be divided between France, Luxemburg and Holland. The German government justified German domination of Belgium by publishing captured Belgian documents which it claimed were proof that Belgium had renounced neutrality by a secret prewar alliance with Britain. The theme of using Belgium as a lever on Britain recurred only in a suggestion from Loebell.[25]

Discussions of Britain were characterized more by exasperation than aspirations at British expense. The bitterness of German leaders toward Britain was expressed publicly and privately, and it was intensified by the first prolonged Anglo-German military contact in Flanders and British blockade measures. They were left with the problem of translating their antipathy into action. In response to Falkenhayn's suggestion that all available means be used, Tirpitz revived the issue of intensified activity by the High Seas Fleet, but the

Kaiser again refused on the advice of Bethmann, Pohl and Müller. U-boat operations were, however, increased and produced striking successes: while seeking to disrupt transportation of British troops to the continent, a boat was sent into the Channel and sank three British cruisers. Ingenohl advocated using U-boats in a systematic campaign against British trade in retaliation for British minelaying in the Channel. But that proposal was not acted upon while a rapid victory over France seemed possible.[26]

The concentration of German leaders on the western front continued to divert their attention from Russia, which they regarded as an unfortunate distraction. They were more interested for the moment in parrying the Russian threat than in projecting their eastern aims. They therefore encouraged a social and national revolution in Russia to paralyze the Russian war effort and to prepare for subsequent German expansion eastward. Meanwhile the alternative of a separate peace with Russia was suggested for the first time. Loebell and the Bavarian envoy to Berlin, Hugo von Lerchenfeld, argued that a separate peace should be sought with Russia if Germany could not defeat all its opponents. Russia could then be used as a tool in Germany's struggle with Britain and Japan for international economic superiority. This suggestion was revealing. It indicated that some German leaders were beginning to realize that German power was insufficient to fulfill all their aspirations and that compromises might become necessary. Lerchenfeld and Delbrück felt it was doubtful that "all Europe would lie at our feet" or that even "decisions like 1870 could be expected." They also realized that policy depended on power: "policy is being made at the moment on the battlefields [and] only when the decision has occurred there will the great questions of the future be raised [including] the future reconstruction of the map of Europe." In short, "as long as the size of our victories is uncertain, no decision can be made on the size of our peace conditions." While strategy was in adversity, policy should remain in abeyance.[27]

ALLIANCE OF INCONVENIENCE:
AUSTRO-GERMAN RELATIONS

In addition to postulating objectives and weakening the enemy alliance, German policy was confronted with the problem of consolidating its own alliance. German leaders were dependent on their Austro-Hungarian allies to divert Russia, but they communicated remarkably little with Vienna. German civilian leaders, like their military colleagues, were fascinated at the prospect of victory in the west and regarded the eastern front as an unfortunate distraction.

Evidence of these attitudes toward Austria-Hungary was initially scant and contradictory but it became increasingly clear in September and October. Some Austro-German disagreements emerged immediately after war broke out. When the prospects of Austro-German success against Russia looked favorable in

August, disputes arose over the spoils, particularly Poland. Austro-Hungarian Foreign Minister Berchtold sought German agreement for Austro-Hungarian annexation of Russian Poland. Moltke, Bethmann and Jagow recognized that the proposed annexation would preclude the establishment of Polish and Ukrainian buffer states under German control, but they did not immediately reject the proposal in order to forestall disagreements with their ally. The question became academic at the end of August when the Austro-Hungarian forces were expelled from Russian Poland. Subsequent Austro-German disputes arose from strategic problems. The Germans accused the Austro-Hungarians of incompetence since they felt reverses on the eastern front jeopardized the German campaign in the west. The Austro-Hungarians countered that they had been betrayed and sacrificed to selfish German aims. Military operations thus produced more mutual denunciation than cooperation.[28]

The Austro-Hungarian complaints had serious implications—the ultimate danger was that they might leave the war. German leaders accordingly sought to parry them. Falkenhayn's decision in favor of Conrad during the disputes over strategy in September was, in his own words, "politically desirable." When Berchtold hinted in early September that Vienna might conclude a separate peace (ostensibly to extract more military aid from Germany). Bethmann sought to reassure the Austro-Hungarian Ambassador Gottfried Hohenlohe-Schillingsfürst that Germany would join Austria-Hungary against Russia after France was defeated. Hohenlohe felt that the Germans had lost none of "the old confidence" although the Marne had dampened German enthusiasm. He reported that the Germans were determined "to defeat France and England as severely as possible" and "Russia as completely if not more so." Hungarian Minister President Stephan Tisza was more critical—he accused the Germans of dragging Austria-Hungary into the war. The tension between the two allies was intensified by the possibility of a Rumanian entry into the war. Germany pressed Vienna for concessions to buy off Rumania but the Austro-Hungarians indignantly refused. As in many other questions, the two allies pulled in opposite directions. The Germans made strategic concessions to Austria-Hungary in Poland in order to encourage Austro-Hungarian diplomatic concessions to Rumania, whereas the Austro-Hungarians sought strategic concessions to make diplomatic concessions unnecessary. Hohenlohe recognized this fundamental divergence and warned his government that Austria-Hungary would have to protect its interests because Germany's main enemies were France and Britain, whereas Austria-Hungary's was Russia.[29]

German political aspirations probably threatened Austro-Hungarian interests even more than Hohenlohe suspected. The discussions among German leaders on future economic relations revealed their attitude toward Austria-Hungary. Delbrück opposed the unlimited customs union proposed by Rathenau, because it would restrict German economic development and could be imposed on Austria-Hungary only by force. Bethmann, however, accepted the idea that force might have to be used against Austria-Hungary when he argued that "unification of central Europe [into a *Mitteleuropa* under German control] will not be achieved on the basis of an agreement on joint interests but only through a peace dictated by us under pressure of political superiority. This consideration will likewise be decisive for the Austrian side of the problem since we shall probably be able to use whatever political superiority we have against Austria-Hungary." Austria-Hungary was not only an ally, and thus a German means of war, but also a German war aim.[30]

These disagreements could not be resolved but only concealed or postponed. Yet such a tactic was threatened by the prolongation of the war. On the one hand, the allies became more dependent on each other as the war continued; on the other, a longer war necessitated choices between German and Austro-Hungarian interests which would intensify their disputes. The alliance thus became more important, but less harmonious, as the war continued.

CONTINUITY, CONSENSUS, CONSISTENCY, CONDUCT, CONDEMNATION: INTERPRETING GERMAN POLICY

The meaning and significance of German policy discussions during the first three months of the war are the subject of a continuing debate. This is appropriate since those discussions were the source of many problems in evaluating German policymaking during the whole war. It is therefore essential to isolate and confront these issues if an analysis of German policy is to be coherent.[31]

The debate raised the question of continuity, i.e., whether German policy was consistent from the autumn of 1914 through the summer of 1918. Professor Fritz Fischer, who brought Bethmann's memorandum to light, asserted that it was "the first war aims program" which "continued to exist during [the war's] duration as a firmly defined conception." Professor Hans Herzfeld questioned Fischer's interpretation and argued that German policy was characterized by "permanent [i.e., recurring] crises" and a "continuity of errors" rather than "continuity." Fischer adamantly maintained that "the continuity of German war aims policy from autumn, 1914, to mid-summer, 1918," remained, although he granted that there were insignificant deviations and that "responsible German leaders retained their war aims when and where the war circumstances seemed to allow it." Professor Gerhard Ritter's contradictory interpretation both granted and denied that Bethmann's memorandum remained the outline of Bethmann's war aims. Fischer castigated what he regarded as Ritter's effort to "disqualify" Bethmann's aims as a "temporary concession" to popular demands or a "passing and forgivable weakness." Professor Egmont Zechlin doubted Fischer's argument of continuity and asserted that Bethmann dropped important elements of his memorandum by November 1914. Fischer nonetheless believed that the memorandum "remained despite all crises a true reflection of the aspirations of the geopolitical central power of Europe."[32]

The debate will remain unresolved and indeed unrevealing until it has been determined which elements of German policy were essential and the degree of permanence required to make that policy continuous. If the essential element in the discussions was a demand for German domination over Europe, then continuity existed in German policy because that aspiration persisted throughout the war. If, however, all elements of Bethmann's program are regarded as essential elements of German policy, that policy was not continuous because some elements disappeared and reappeared or received different emphasis. Both interpretations are important. The persistent German desire to dominate Europe was the central fact of the war, but German wartime policy cannot be understood unless the oscillations and adjustments in German war aims are explained. Thus, the question of continuity depends on the level of interpretation. There was continuity on the level of general policy but not on the level of specific detail or degree.

The debate involved the issue of consensus, i.e., whether agreement on war aims existed among German leaders and between German leaders and people. Fischer asserted that there was a "general unity of the war aims movement, military and political leadership." Herzfeld doubted this contention, and Ritter implied that Bethmann sought essentially different aims from the Kaiser and military. Zechlin claimed that Fischer did not distinguish between moderate and extreme annexations which Zechlin felt reflect the difference between wisdom and foolishness.[33]

The meaning of consensus is also critical—the essential elements and the degree of similarity need definition. If the essential element is defined as a demand for German domination over Europe, then a consensus existed among German leaders. If all elements are defined as being essential, then a consensus did not exist since there were disagreements over questions of form, degree, method, and timing. Both points of view are important. General agreement among German leaders on the desirability of increasing German power was the starting point for all discussions throughout the war. The difference between German leaders was therefore not between moderation and immoderation (as some have suggested), but between degrees of immoderation. But these differences were not insignificant because they were matters of degree—most disputes revolve around questions of detail. German policy debates become explicable only if it is recognized that these differences mattered to German leaders. Thus, the problem of consensus reduces to a question of appearances and implications. Although their differences appeared significant to German leaders, the implications of all their views were similar.

The debate raised the issue of consistency, i.e., whether German policy was consistently arrogant or anxious. Herzfeld argued that German leaders were not the supremely confident men Fischer supposed but were characterized instead by "oscillation between mania and depression," by self-doubts and self-delusion. To Fischer these doubts and delusions were insignificant because they were uncharacteristic of most German leaders and they did not preclude extensive aims. Ritter argued at first that German aspirations were offensive but later reversed himself and contended that Bethmann's war aims program was "defensive in character," a response to British economic war, an effort to free Germany from "continental 'encirclement,' " a result of "military-political anxieties and economic wishes," and necessary to maintain both German morale and Bethmann's own position. Zechlin contended that German leaders feared they could not win the war and that Bethmann's program was a response to British economic warfare rather than a blueprint for German domination over Europe. Fischer rejected Zechlin's interpretation and insisted that the memorandum reflected German confidence in victory.[34]

Both interpretations have been argued on different levels. Herzfeld, Ritter and Zechlin have contended that German leaders were simultaneously confident of victory and concerned about defeat. There is much evidence to indicate they were ambivalent. To contend that German leaders were consistently confident or concerned, it is necessary to reject the conflicting evidence as irrelevant or suspect. Furthermore, the assumption of German consistency implies that the impulses for a policy are identical with the implications of policy. Thus, if a policy is aggressive, the policymakers must be aggressive; conversely, if the policymakers are anxious, their policy cannot be aggressive. But this assumption is tenuous and misleading. It does not explain how an aggressive German policy could be advocated by statesmen who alternated between arrogance and anxiety. The ambivalence of German leaders made German aspirations no less aggressive; in fact it made German policy more dangerous by precluding a more realistic evaluation of German prospects. Only total confidence or a total lack of confidence might have produced a consistent policy. German policy therefore reflected a mixture of arrogance and anxiety on the part of its leaders which seemed to erase the distinction between the offensive and defensive. Self-preservation seemed to demand domination.

The debate provides some insights into how policy is conducted. Fischer claimed that Bethmann's program affected, even determined, later policy. Zechlin, Herzfeld and Ritter contended instead that the memorandum was a product of immediate circumstances and that it was dropped when those circumstances changed. Both views may be misleading. It is doubtful that statesmen bind themselves by, or even refer to, previous policy statements. Continuity in policy is due more to recurring circumstances and aspirations than to prior commitments. Thus, the memorandum was temporal in the sense of being unbinding. But it was not temporal in the sense implied by Zechlin, Ritter and Herzfeld—i.e., unique and unlike subsequent policy. On the contrary, the memorandum remained typical of German policy through the summer of 1918. It therefore represented, but did not determine, German policy.[35]

The debate involved the problem of ends and means. Fischer perceived Bethmann's memorandum as primarily a statement of long-range goals and only incidentally of short-range objectives. Zechlin reversed the proposition and saw it less as an outline for the future than conditions for an impending peace with France and means to continue the war with England. This distinction is probably unrealistic and misleading. Both aspects were important and inextricable. The memorandum indicated not only that German leaders sought European domination but also how they hoped to make Britain accept it. The discussions of August-October 1914 suggest that ends and means grow simultaneously and interdependently. A German-dominated *Mitteleuropa* necessitated a successful war with Britain as much as a successful war with Britain necessitated a German-dominated *Mitteleuropa*.[36]

The study of these discussions also illuminates the relationship between policy and strategy. Bethmann and his advisers made plans to dictate peace to France while the German army was being forced to withdraw at the Marne. This anomaly resulted because Bethmann was poorly informed on the immediate military situation, and policy would continue to lag behind military events throughout the war, particularly when situations changed rapidly. The shock of failure during September was reflected in the tentative tone of subsequent policy discussions in which German statesmen realized that the shape of peace depended on the size of victory. Above all, they realized that policy and strategy were interdependent. The September discussions provide a particular insight into the nature of policymaking during crises. Zechlin cited the prevailing freneticism in German headquarters to prove that the policies of September 1914 were impermanent. But his conclusion is not the only one which can be drawn. Historically, such crises have caused chaotic policymaking and inconsistent policy. The behavior of German policymakers emphasizes the significance, rather than unimportance, of decisions made in September 1914.[37]

The debate has been conducted in an atmosphere of moral condemnation. When Fischer and others accused, most German historians excused. Herzfeld, Ritter and most German historians accepted the assertion that Germany's extreme war aims were reprehensible, but they differed on the identity of the sinners and the extent of the sins. This moralistic tone, however, obscures more than it clarifies. German policy was a natural reflection of the circumstances in which it developed. Observers on both sides expected a German victory and the French regarded the Marne as a miracle. In a state system based on power, the expectation of great military success is logically expressed in extreme aims. The moral tone of the historical debate therefore introduces a consideration which was largely irrelevant to the statesmen of 1914. Some German apologists defend Germany by accusing the Entente powers of having ambitious aims. This assertion is valid but the implication is deceptive. Whereas the achievement of even the most extreme Entente aims would have divided Europe between three great powers and thereby reinforced the balance of power, German aims implied a concentration of power and the consequent destruction of the balance of power. The impulses behind the policies of all the powers were therefore comparable, but the implications were contradictory.[38]

These considerations are important for an understanding of German policy. German policy depended ultimately, however, on German power. When German power could not prevail, German policy could not prescribe.

PROCRASTINATION &
PACIFICATION:
GERMAN DOMESTIC AFFAIRS

PATRIOTISM PRECLUDES POLITICS: THE *BURGFRIEDEN*

A nation's war potential is a function of its power, policies and politics. Success depends on winning popular support, limiting domestic opposition, retaining control over policy, maintaining morale, and mobilizing material resources.

All governments sought to arouse popular support for the war. The short-war assumption increased the need since rapid mobilization required mass cooperation. When war seemed inevitable in late July, the German government sought to place the blame on Russia in order to win popular support. These efforts met with success when the Reichstag voted unanimously for war credits. Although Socialist support insured against overt opposition, it did not guarantee enthusiasm. Opponents of war within the Socialist Reichstag delegation had not been persuaded but merely delayed their protest until a more propitious moment rather than shatter party unity. Consequently, in their speeches the Kaiser and Bethmann sought to arouse public enthusiasm by reiterating German innocence, enemy guilt, and national unity. These assertions were widely accepted within Germany, and the popular enthusiasm for a hard line during the July crisis became fervid when war was declared. The government's assertions were echoed by the press and politicians including moderate Socialists. In fact, acceptance of the official claims was so widespread that it suggests government propaganda may have been superfluous or even a concession to, rather than the cause of, popular enthusiasm. Public support for the war did not determine or even significantly influence policy, but it did indicate that the government and the people perceived the war in basically similar terms. Furthermore, popular enthusiasm buttressed the short-war assumption, and the short-war assumption reinforced enthusiasm because it united the country and promised maximum rewards at minimum cost. Popular feeling and policy therefore complemented each other.[1]

National unity precluded partisan politics. Most Germans assumed that domestic conflicts would defer, and possibly preclude, victory. Since it implied differences, party politics was unpatriotic, and a political moratorium was necessary. The German moratorium on politics (the *Burgfrieden* or "civil peace") was declared when the Reichstag renounced its powers and recessed until December, when the war was expected to be over. The end of politics was implied when the Kaiser proclaimed with characteristic flamboyance that he no longer recognized parties but only Germans. The Reichstag's abdication has been severely criticized by liberal historians. This criticism is understandable from the liberal point of view but is unhistorical. The Reichstag had failed to assert itself in peacetime when it was easier, and it was unlikely to do so in wartime when even the more established British and French parliaments acceded to the dictates of their government and military. Even if the Reichstag had retained its powers, its policy would probably not have been different or wiser than the government's since they shared many of the same assumptions. The Reichstag's abdication is more important as a feature of the moment than as a failure. Sharing both the popular fears and enthusiasm for war, most politicians regarded their decision as a contribution to the war effort and not a capitulation. They may even have accepted Bethmann's view that party politics was selfish, and thus immoral, in wartime. Although the government did not declare war as an escape from political problems, the political truce nonetheless seemed one of the positive by-products. Consequently, war seemed not only to require a moratorium on party politics but a moratorium on politics also required war.[2]

However necessary it seemed, such a moratorium on politics had serious implications. Politics can be narrowly defined as the nonviolent accommodation of domestic differences. The renunciation of politics in this sense implies the absence, postponement or denial of differences. Since serious prewar differences persisted, problems could only be postponed or denied. The *Burgfrieden* could be interpreted in either sense. It might work if the war proved short and successful but not if the war was long or unsuccessful. The *Burgfrieden* was therefore a gamble which seemed to augment the chances of victory at the risk of greater political problems in case of defeat. It also altered the options. By renouncing the middle road of accommodating domestic disagreement through the nonviolent political process, the *Burgfrieden* left only the extreme options of international war and civil truce on the one hand or international truce and civil war on the other. The *Burgfrieden* consequently implied an internal revolution just as the Schlieffen plan implied an international revolution.

COOPERATION WITHOUT CONCESSIONS:
POLITICAL PROBLEMS PERSIST

A political moratorium was easier to proclaim than to maintain. Partisan differences had been sublimated but not solved, and the *Burgfrieden* was threatened by dissent over both domestic and diplomatic problems. The government's problem was, therefore, to establish cooperation between traditionally competitive elements while avoiding pressures for political concessions.

Cooperation proved less difficult though by no means easy. Prewar antipathies between left and right intensified on the eve of war, but patriotism temporarily obscured bitterness. The "Imperial League against Social Democracy" suspended its activities because the Socialists had voted for war credits. This event correctly recognized the critical contribution of the moderate Socialists to the war effort. Several moderate Socialists served on government missions to neutral countries, and the first member of the Reichstag killed in battle was a former leader of the SPD, Ludwig Frank. Traditional conflicts were, however, an obstacle to genuine cooperation. Mutual suspicion between Socialists and Conservatives almost precluded proclamation of the *Burgfrieden,* and Conservative acquiescence was grudging. Conservative Prussian bureaucrats criticized cooperation with the Socialists and Prussian Minister of Interior Loebell opposed removal of restrictions on the Socialist paper, *Vorwärts.* The army was dominated by conservatives who used martial law to justify legal injustice and to maintain rigid censorship. Bethmann sought to overcome conservative opposition by arguing that their cooperation with the Socialists was a prerequisite for success in war. Falkenhayn sought to mollify the Socialists by removing restrictions on *Vorwärts.* Cooperation, though imperfect, was sufficient to allow the government to conduct war.[3]

The possibility of demands for domestic political concessions was a more serious problem since the Social Democrats proposed domestic political reform as their reward for cooperation. The moderate Socialist Eduard David warned Imperial Minister of Interior Delbrück that "a chasm will be created between the people [and the government] which will not be bridged for decades" if the Socialist soldier was not rewarded with reforms for his support of the war. Delbrück relayed this argument to Bethmann and concluded that "something would have to change in the area of domestic politics" if the Socialists were to be reconciled to the existing political system. Another moderate Socialist, Max Cohen-Reuss, told Delbrück's subordinate Arnold von Wahnschaffe that the moderates wanted to render their vote of war credits "a turning point for the party by making peace with the Monarchy and Army" in return for suffrage reform. In effect, the moderate Socialists wanted concessions in exchange for cooperation.[4]

The government was in a dilemma since it would be damned whether it refused or acceded to the Socialist demands. A refusal created the danger that moderate leaders of the SPD would be displaced by their more radical colleagues. This radicalization of the SPD seemed entirely possible. Immediately after Falkenhayn removed restrictions, the radical editors of *Vorwärts* began to discuss war aims and were censored by the government. Radical Socialist Karl Liebknecht and several local Socialist organizations agitated for a party statement on war aims which was subsequently rejected by the moderate-dominated party executive. Moderate Socialists were thus caught between the government's appeal for cooperation and the radicals' demand for change. The moderates sought to increase their power by achieving both. They supported the *Burgfrieden* out of patriotic conviction and the political calculation that it would augment their authority by allowing them to act as spokesmen for all workers. They meanwhile sought to squelch opposition within their party by playing up the danger of government reprisal. Since they could not permanently repress dissent, they bought peace with the government at the expense of peace within their party. Cohen assured Wahnschaffe that his moderate colleagues (including Albert Südekum, David, and Philipp Scheidemann) wanted a reconciliation with the government enough to risk a split in the party. Whereas opposition to the government had held the party together in peacetime, cooperation between the moderates and the government would eventually split the party in wartime. A tenuous truce therefore prevailed among Socialists as in the country at large.[5]

There was a danger of conservative reaction if the government granted the Socialists' demand for change. Delbrück warned Bethmann that alterations in the domestic political structure would be resisted by conservatives. Loebell was a good case in point: he opposed government concessions to the Socialists by arguing that "nationalistic circles," industry and agriculture would be alienated. His opposition was confirmed by Wahnschaffe, who reported that opponents of reform were actively propagandizing heavy industrialists and extreme conservatives against "overly extreme concessions to democratic wishes after the conclusion of peace." Politicians on the right, like those on the left, perceived a connection between change and cooperation; but conservatives, unlike the Socialists, would cooperate only if the existing system was unchanged.[6]

Confronted with this dilemma, the government employed the tactics of procrastination and pacification. Since the attitudes of right and left toward change were irreconcilable, the issue had to be avoided and the connection severed between cooperation and concessions. Furthermore, the government had to foster cooperation between the competing interests without sacrificing control of policy. Considering the complexity of these issues, it is not surprising that the government's policy was devious and contradictory.

The government's interrelated wartime domestic and diplomatic policies began to evolve simultaneously in September under the influence of the expected military victory. Delbrück was the first to articulate the problem. The question of "how our domestic politics will be oriented after the war" had already "aroused emotions generally without being spoken of in public." He had been sounded out by all parties except the Conservatives, who opposed all change. He recognized the close connection between domestic and diplomatic policies, particularly with regard to war aims. The *Mitteleuropa* envisaged by Bethmann would cause a fundamental departure in German economic and political organization. Although Delbrück granted the advantages of the economic changes that would result, he argued that they would be resisted by the right and that the support of the center and left would be essential if the needed changes were to be achieved. He therefore urged that a definite policy be developed: the government should decide upon and proclaim reforms rather than await demands if such concessions were to have "political effect," i.e., preserve the conservative system. The government should also prepare the public with propaganda. Since these reforms would cause domestic conflicts, they should be delayed until after the war and "we must try to get as far as we can with this delaying policy." Postponement of the necessary political preparation argued for delaying the *Mitteleuropa* scheme until after the war. In short Delbrück urged a pragmatically conservative policy.[7]

Bethmann also linked domestic and diplomatic policies. The *Mitteleuropa* he espoused implied the need for political and economic reforms. Postwar domestic political problems, he felt, could "certainly not be resolved by a return to principles" rooted in the past. He granted that domestic changes would be resisted by conservative elements, which should therefore not be consulted. He also accepted Delbrück's argument that the domestic changes implied by *Mitteleuropa* required concessions to the Socialists which would cause a "new orientation of our whole domestic policy." Bethmann's perception of postwar politics was, however, hardly a radical reconstruction. In exchange for superficial concessions, the Socialists would be required to renounce fundamental changes. They would have to recognize that "the German Empire and the Prussian state in particular can never be severed from the firm ground on which it has grown—namely, that respect for the state and system which the Social Democrats have heretofore branded as militarism. . . . A re-orientation of our domestic policy" would therefore be possible only when "the German left is in a position to accept this system."[8]

Bethmann's policy involved a fundamental contradiction. On the one hand, he postulated a *Mitteleuropa,* which would have revolutionary implications for the German political and economic system; it would consequently require the support of the center and left to overcome resistance from the right. On the other hand, he was unwilling to pay for this support with real concessions, and he demanded acceptance of the existing system which would in any case be altered by *Mitteleuropa.* Bethmann's refusal to grant revolutionary concessions to achieve revolutionary changes was a characteristic feature of policymaking which differentiated German leaders in the two world wars. This contradiction may be explained by Bethmann's expectation of military victory which would allow him to override domestic as well as foreign resistance. His vision of the postwar domestic situation was essentially a perpetuation of the *Burgfrieden* into peacetime. Partisan politics in the sense of a process of resolving domestic differences would be unnecessary because Germany's increased power would allow it to satisfy all parties and thus resolve all political problems.

The views of Delbrück and Bethmann were moderate by comparison with other German leaders. Loebell represented the rigid conservative position in resisting all concessions because they would alienate the right. Tirpitz typified the rabid nationalist view which would emerge increasingly during the war and culminate in his founding of the Fatherland Party. He and Admiral Paul von Hintze agreed that the "lack of leadership of the ruling classes" would force them to forfeit their position whether the war eventuated in victory or defeat. Concessions to the Socialists—i.e., their inclusion in the government and a reform of Prussian suffrage—were needed to harness the "gigantic [national] upheaval" for war. Tirpitz concluded in typically dramatic fashion that "it is all up now with the rule of caste and class. Victory or defeat, we shall get democracy." Unlike Bethmann, Tirpitz implied that he would make radical concessions to unify the nation for a total war which would achieve radical international changes. Although they were less outspoken or radical than Tirpitz, Rathenau, the historian Friedrich Meinecke and the Bavarian Catholic Minister President Georg Hertling also foresaw postwar political changes. German leaders gradually began to sense the interdependence of domestic and diplomatic questions.[9]

In its public statements, the government sought to obscure the political issues it could not resolve. Unable to confront political and social differences, German leaders pretended that they would be cured by the war. Bethmann asserted to the Democrat Conrad Haussmann that the war had created German "unity" and thus "a nation," diminished class distinctions, and would cause a "new time" after the war when "barriers must fall." The theme of national unity, and by implication absence of political disunity, was repeated incessantly by German leaders. They also made vague promises of postwar political changes. Delbrück dropped Bethmann's phrase "new orientation" publicly at the end of October but postponed changes until after the war "since they would cause conflicts between the parties." The government meanwhile parried Socialist demands for wartime concessions in exchange for continued cooperation. Probably on orders from Bethmann, Delbrück's subordinate Wahnschaffe warned the moderate Socialist Cohen that "if the Social Democrats expect concessions, they must first change fundamentally and reconcile themselves with our monarchical system . . . in which the Army plays such a decisive role and must continue to play in the future." According to Wahnschaffe, Cohen and his associates (including Südekum, David and Scheidemann) accepted this condition. For the moment, the government's tactics seemed successful.[10]

POWER REPLACES POLITICS:
POPULAR WAR AIMS

The *Burgfrieden* was jeopardized not only by domestic, but also diplomatic, questions, in particular, the problem of war aims. In fact German leaders increasingly perceived an inversely proportional relationship between war aims and reforms. A victory and achievement of war aims would obviate demands for reform, while defeat and failure to achieve war aims would result in reform, if not revolution.

This politicization of the war aims issue almost precluded the *Burgfrieden* before it had been proclaimed. When Hugo Haase, the Socialist spokesman, hinted that peace conditions would be attached to his party's vote for war credits, the Conservative leader, Kuno von Westarp, threatened to make a counterstatement. The annexationist Pan-Germans were among the first to recognize and articulate a relationship between war aims and prewar political conflicts. In the first wartime meeting of Pan-German leaders, Chairman Heinrich Class asserted that the alternative to achieving war aims was domestic reform. Consequently, he and other Pan-German leaders demanded extensive annexations. Westarp made a similar argument while the publisher Rippler warned the historian Hans Delbrück (cousin of Clemens Delbrück, Imperial Minister of Interior) that the German people would revolt against the peace without annexations advocated by the official Socialist paper *Vorwärts.*[11]

The war aims question implicated the constitutional as well as the political structure of Germany. Some of the Bundesstaaten—particularly Bavaria—feared that Prussia would take an inordinate share of the booty and thus dominate the empire even more than it already did. Although consciously related by many, war aims did not exclusively reflect domestic politics. For many Germans, war aims merely expressed the hysterical patriotism released by war. In still other cases, war aims represented a cooler calculation of special interests. Public war aims were thus motivated by a mixture of politics, particularism, patriotism and special interests.

Politicians from extreme Conservatives to moderate Socialists advocated expansionist war aims. The Conservatives supported the extreme aims of the Pan-Germans in general outline. The National Liberals—particularly their most outspoken leader, Gustav Stresemann—shared the anglophobia of most Germans and urged pushing Russia eastward. The Catholic Center Party—especially the ubiquitous Matthias Erzberger—advocated German domination of Europe and opposed a premature peace. The other middle parties were less outspoken but shared the prevailing bitterness toward England. There was dissension among the

Socialists. Moderate Socialists favored limited annexations, whereas radical Socialists increasingly opposed annexations after September. Insufficient influence over party organization and the muzzling of radical groups (particularly the editors of *Vorwärts*), however, reduced the effectiveness of radical dissent.[12]

Statements of war aims from the Bundesstaaten and special interest groups were less frequent but no less extreme. King Ludwig of Bavaria and King William of Württemberg advocated division of Alsace-Lorraine and Belgium among various Bundesstaaten. Their prime ministers were more subtle and expressed regret that these demands had been stated so early. The Bavarian prime minister, Georg von Hertling, nonetheless hoped that the war would produce territorial changes favorable to Germany. The special interest groups advocated aims which would serve their adherents. The industrialists were the most outspoken. August Thyssen, Emil Kirdorf and Karl Röchling sought unsuccessfully to extract from the government a promise that the French mines in Briey-Longwy would be annexed. The "War Committee of German Industry" urged Bethmann to prolong the war rather than to conclude a peace which would require renouncing the territory that Germany already occupied. Other groups advocated annexation of French and Belgian territory but none of their demands matched those of the outspoken and ambitious Pan-Germans.[13]

The aspirations of the intelligentsia were equally ambitious and more articulate. The vast majority of German intellectuals, particularly academics, advocated expansion. Several urged the German domination of Europe and a few suggested Napoleon's empire as the appropriate model. Many demanded that Germany compete for "world power" and "world policy" particularly with Britain. The annexation or domination of Belgium was a frequently enunciated goal. The war was idealized by Max Weber and militarism was defended by Ernst Troeltsch. Like the policymakers, academics mixed anxiety with their aggressiveness. Friedrich Meinecke asserted that "we now want to win for ourselves room to breathe and security for a century." Hans Delbrück observed that, after initial concern for self-defense, public opinion had "reversed itself into a desire that we should be secure forever and that could happen only if we conquered."

The responses to the infrequently voiced pleas for moderation were as revealing as the extremism expressed by most commentators. The only academic who consistently urged restraint was Hans Delbrück. He agreed that Germany should follow Napoleon's example by seeking to shatter British "hegemony at sea," but he asserted that it would be a mistake to repeat Napoleon's attempt to dominate the continent. He believed that security could be achieved only if maximum military power were exercised with political moderation. He therefore concluded: "World political equality and colonial expansion—yes; striving for continental hegemony—no!" Delbrück argued that colonial expansion (primarily in Africa) should be achieved by using Belgium as a lever on Britain and by seeking reconciliation with Britain's allies, France and Russia. Delbrück's views were published in October, and he was subsequently anathematized as a defeatist by the Pan-Germans, criticized by his academic colleagues, warned by the censor, and disavowed by Bethmann. Restraint was out of season.[14]

Public pressures for extensive war aims were a problem for the government, despite the general unanimity on German goals, because they jeopardized government control over policy. Public demands for annexations made it difficult for the government to claim that Germany was fighting a defensive war. Zimmermann complained that "suspicion toward our efforts to create greater understanding abroad for Germany's aims is due primarily to the boundless character of Pan-German writings and speeches." Bethmann was angered by the efforts of some politicians to expand the navy and thereby affect policy toward Britain. Public discussion of these issues risked domestic dissent over war aims, particularly between Conservatives and Socialists. The government therefore reacted as it had over the reform issue—it sought to avoid the problem by a policy of procrastination, vague promises and excuses.[15]

When Erzberger submitted a memorandum demanding extensive aims, Bethmann sought to put him off with vagueness and delay: "Although all possibilities must be thought through, the final decisions still depend completely on future developments." Bethmann urged that the interest groups which might oppose economic changes in connection with *Mitteleuropa* be brought into policy discussions "as little and as late as possible." The most specific threat to government control came from Bavarian Minister President Hertling, who suggested that representatives of the Bundesstaaten meet to discuss war aims before the Imperial government dictated peace to the enemy. Imperial Minister of Interior Clemens Delbrück sought to parry Hertling's suggestion by arguing that the government was anxious to avoid all discussion both of war aims and reform. To this end, Bethmann initially planned to be absent from the December session of the Reichstag. Delbrück put Hertling off by assuring him that no decision would be made until the military situation had been clarified and by promising to discuss policy with him in a "completely academic" way. The government meanwhile sought to satisfy the public by announcing vague principles and idealizing the war. Delbrück told the Prussian parliament that Germany had been forced to fight for its existence by the "hate and malevolence" of its neighbors and that it would not stop fighting "until we have won a victory which guarantees us a lasting peace." The presidents of the two Prussian chambers repeated Delbrück's assertions, renounced expansion and idealized the war. The public pressures threatened German unity and became more dangerous when it became clear that the war would be long. The government, however, retained its control over policy for the moment.[16]

The scholarly debate over German policy raised the question of consensus between the German people and their government on war aims. Fritz Fischer asserted that Bethmann's memorandum "constitutes no isolated conception of the chancellor but represents ideas of leading persons in economics and politics as well as the military." Gerhard Ritter admitted that Bethmann advocated extensive aims in September 1914 but suggested that Bethmann did so because it was "the will of the nation" and was therefore necessary to maintain public morale and Bethmann's position. Fischer and Ritter disagreed on Bethmann's role but agreed that the German government's policy reflected the wishes of the German people. The evidence suggests that most articulate Germans favored the increase in German power which would presumably result from annexing French and Belgian territory. A number of contemporary Germans commented on the widespread public support for expansion. One of them, Minister for Colonies Solf, observed critically that "the wish for as much land as possible from our enemies is expressed with complete confidence not only by Pan-Germans but by wide circles throughout Germany." As in the case of policymakers, the German public differed on the details of war aims but was agreed that they should be extensive.[17]

The consensus between the German people and their leaders raises a question as to how policy was made. Historians sometimes make a distinction between the "old" cabinet diplomacy and the "new" democratic diplomacy represented by Wilson or the "new" totalitarian diplomacy exemplified by Lenin.[18] The "old" diplomacy suggests that policy was made largely without concern for popular aspirations. The "new" diplomacy implies that policy is influenced if not determined by the masses. Ritter's suggestion that German policy was determined by popular pressure blurs such a distinction between old and new diplomacy. Ritter's interpretation is convincing on one level. Clearly Bethmann could not have remained in power long by advocating aims unacceptable to politically powerful Germans. Ritter's interpretation, however, implies that the government opposed extensive war aims but was forced to seek them by public pressure. Actually, there was no conflict between the aspirations of the German government and the ruling classes from which the leaders were drawn. Furthermore it was both difficult and uncommon for policymakers to ascertain public aspirations in wartime. German statesmen tended instead to equate their own perceptions with public expectations and the national interest. They were inclined to ignore or overrule public resistance, just as Bethmann planned to do with the Socialists, the interest groups and the bureaucrats who were opposed to *Mitteleuropa*. "Old" cabinet diplomacy therefore remained the model and Bethmann looked back to Bismarck rather than forward to Wilson or Lenin.

BETWEEN DELIRIUM & DISILLUSION:
MAINTAINING POPULAR MORALE

The extensive popular expectations of expanded German power were the result of the popular enthusiasm for the war. As Hans Delbrück observed, "completely rational people have become crazy." While this enthusiasm threatened the government's control over policy, it also facilitated the government's task of maintaining public support for the war. The government, however, found it necessary to insure that delirium did not become disappointment because of military defeats.[19]

Many German leaders no doubt idealized the public enthusiasm for political purposes but they were also genuinely impressed by it. Bethmann and Delbrück wrote each other of the "gigantic national uplifting" and "complete enthusiasm of all parts of the population." Tirpitz praised the "immense moral exaltation with which our whole nation took up the perfidious, brutal gauntlet." Moltke's wife applauded the social and moral effects of the war but regretted the price. Hertling perceived a "marvelous patriotic wave passing over the Empire now." Even foreign observers were amazed.[20]

This excitement increased the risk of disappointment. Groener, Tirpitz and Ballin regarded the enthusiasm as excessive and premature—although they themselves shared it in August. Moltke feared that military defeat might cause a collapse of public enthusiasm. Conversely, Tirpitz was concerned that the popular enthusiasm might be jeopardized by what he perceived as the government's failure to lead. Hertling worried that the patriotism would not "develop homogeneously," i.e., affect all elements of society in the same way.[21]

The government sought to maintain morale by encouraging optimism and avoiding discouragement. Admiral Hintze believed it essential to "nurse the patriotic feelings of the German people." Government spokesmen sought to do so by reiterating both the necessity and nobility of the German war effort. The danger of discouragement became real as a result of the Marne. After Falkenhayn reestablished a stable front at the end of September, he proposed an open admission of the Marne setback but Bethmann refused on both diplomatic and domestic grounds. The government strongly denied foreign press reports that the Marne was a German defeat. Consequently, most Germans and many German leaders remained ignorant of the Marne's significance and military events thereafter were reported only vaguely to the public. In short, the government consistently opted for secrecy rather than candor.[22]

AVOIDING ECONOMIC CHAOS:
MOBILIZATION FOR A SHORT WAR

Human and economic resources were less easy to mobilize than public opinion. But, since the war was expected to be over before they could be utilized, these resources were also regarded as less important. German preparations for war were therefore haphazard.

Limited measures were implemented to produce the means of war. Since it was assumed that the war would be short and determined by military operations, the mobilization of manpower seemed critical. The German government was initially more successful than it needed to be in this area since the number of volunteers exceeded the facilities for training them. The Prussian War Ministry established a War Materials Section for Procurement and a Munitions Service to control munitions consumption. Food was not a problem during this stage of the war, but some efforts were made to extend existing food supplies, and production of alcoholic beverages was prohibited. Martial law was imposed and the Reichstag granted the government power to intervene into the economy and enact emergency legislation. Economic organizations tried to accommodate themselves to war, industrial institutions were consolidated and strikes renounced for the duration. Monetary problems were overcome to the extent that Rudolf Havenstein, President of the Imperial Bank, claimed Germany's financial position was better than any of the other belligerents. The German government issued war bonds and the Prussian parliament authorized additional funds to finance the war.[23]

The measures which were either unsuccessful or left undone were more striking than those that were accomplished. Despite the rapid mobilization the high losses incurred during initial operations caused serious manpower shortages by the end of September. Falkenhayn's efforts to alleviate these shortages with new reserve divisions created out of volunteers trained since the beginning of the war were only partially successful. The most serious shortage proved to be munitions. Prewar planners seriously underestimated the rate of expenditure and made little provision for wartime production. Despite Falkenhayn's attempts to restrict expenditure and increase wartime production, ammunition reserves were exhausted by early October. The shortages of munitions and men seriously affected Falkenhayn's operations in late September and October. No genuine effort was made to organize the supply and distribution of food. Delbrück rejected a suggestion of stockpiling reserves for the spring because the harvest was good and he opposed government intervention on principle. However, he did permit *ersatz* bread to be introduced. The government did not utilize the wide powers given it by the Reichstag to intervene in the economy. Similarly, the Army perceived martial law primarily in military terms—as a precaution against disruption of mobilization—and only later in the war used it to justify intervention into many areas of civilian life. Government efforts to improve labor-management relations were unsuccessful. The concept of an economic war against Germany's enemies was vaguely mentioned and probably motivated the discussions of *Mitteleuropa*, but little was done to translate it into a genuine weapon. German preparations for war, like those of its enemies and allies, were characterized by military mobilization and relative civil inaction.[24]

The causes of Germany's poor preparation for war are enlightening. The prewar prejudices remained and the army was initially reluctant to intervene in the civil sphere, i.e., those areas presumably beyond its competence and traditional authority. The general inefficiency of German civil and military bureaucracies was another factor. The lack of comprehensive prewar economic planning caused frequent delays. Basically, the short-war assumption was the primary explanation for German planning failures. Efforts to limit consumption of munitions, to organize food supplies, and to keep workers in factories were rejected because the war was expected to end quickly. Military strategy and economic policy were thus based on the assumption of a short war and they were consistent in that sense.[25]

The economic assumptions proved to be as fallacious as the military assumptions. Planning proceeded on the assumption that the war would be won or lost on the battlefield and that economic matters should be subordinated to military considerations. The primary economic objective was therefore to avoid a breakdown of the economy which might disrupt military operations. Prewar predictions made an economic breakdown seem to be a genuine possibility, so planning to effect a transition from peace to war without serious disruption was emphasized. The transition was accomplished so successfully that some German industrialists urged that the war be protracted. The prewar fears that the war would disrupt the economy and that economic chaos would paralyze the war effort appeared to be groundless. That success, however, tended to obscure the important fact that human and material factors such as munitions shortages seriously restricted military operations. Economic considerations could not produce victory, but they could preclude it and the war could no longer be viewed in strictly military terms.[26]

Consequently, the German government was confronted with serious domestic political problems during the first four months of the war. Partisan demands for political reform and war aims, the possibility of depressed morale, and the necessity to make the transition to a wartime economy all potentially threatened the German war effort. The government responded with procrastination and pacification. As long as the war was expected to be short, this policy was feasible, advantageous and necessary. It was feasible since the government could readily postpone or obscure problems for a short time. It was advantageous because victory could be expected to give the government greater prestige as well as booty with which to satisfy domestic demands. It was necessary since public dissent might jeopardize victory. The government's domestic policy was temporarily successful since it won popular support for the war, maintained morale, mobilized the nation, limited domestic opposition, and retained control over policy. But since German domestic policy, diplomacy and strategy were based on the short-war assumption, success depended on a rapid victory. When victory eluded Germany and the short-war assumption proved fallacious, all were jeopardized.

CONTAINMENT & ENCIRCLEMENT: THE ENTENTE'S POLICIES

THE CRITICAL VARIABLE:
THE SIGNIFICANCE OF ENTENTE BEHAVIOR

German policy cannot be understood or evaluated without reference to Entente policies. German leaders assumed that success in achieving their war aims required a short war which in turn necessitated the rapid French defeat and surrender of France. A rapid French defeat was based on the premise that French strategists would concentrate their forces and advance precipitously allowing the French army to be encircled and annihilated. The possibility of a French defeat would be enhanced if the French government limited the war rather than allowing it to become a revolutionary and popular struggle. Finally, a German success required that the French accept defeat and surrender immediately. A German success therefore was predicated on the assumption that the French would implement a specific military strategy and diplomatic policy.

French strategy and policy depended in part on the behavior of France's allies. France might be defeated only if Russian and British assistance proved ineffective. France might surrender immediately after defeat if it perceived no prospect of future aid from its allies. German success was therefore conditional upon Russian and British actions.

DETERMINATION NOT DEFEATISM:
FRENCH STRATEGY & POLICY

To win the war quickly, the Germans had to encircle the main French force. Such an encirclement required a French concentration and rapid advance at the German center. The French Plan XVII prescribed precisely such an advance in order to break through the German middle and isolate German forces advancing through Belgium. In short, Plan XVII satisfied the precondition for German success. But when Joffre recognized that his breakthrough had failed and that his left flank was threatened, he discontinued the attack and initiated a strategic withdrawal. It was still possible that the Germans might inflict high losses on the retreating French, but Joffre's decision to withdraw precluded the planned German encirclement of the French forces. The French withdrawal thus precluded German success. The French decision to stand at the Marne provided the Germans another opportunity to surround the French but their lack of superiority and their exposed strategic position prevented German forces from succeeding. During the latter half of September and early October, the Germans again tried unsuccessfully to create conditions conducive to an encircling operation. They failed for the third time due to their lack of mobility and space, and, above all, because the French were determined not to be encircled. The German Flanders offensive at the end of October imposed serious losses on both sides and threatened Entente control of the coast, but it did not seriously threaten the Anglo-French with encirclement. The German failure was therefore due to both German and French behavior. The Germans probably would have lacked sufficient superiority and mobility even if the French had behaved in a manner most conducive to German success. But the French did not; they decided to preserve their forces rather than protect their territory or pursue victory and thus rendered German success virtually unattainable.

The French strategy obviated German success, but it also led to a French disappointment. The moods of French leaders, like those of their counterparts elsewhere, were determined largely by events on the battlefield. The French began the war with characteristically exaggerated expectations. The failure of the French offensive shocked them into recognizing that their hopes had been unrealistic. During the desperate retreat of late August and early September, French leaders became alternately desperate and determined. The Marne temporarily revived French hopes for victory but eventually resulted in disappointment and frustration. Poincaré complained that "our victory has condemned us to the anguish of Sisyphus!" The maneuvering for initiative during late September and early October kept French hopes from dying completely, but there was considerable criticism of the generals and a growing recognition that the war would be longer than originally expected. The German Flanders offensive at the end of October demonstrated that the Germans were unlikely to collapse quickly. The attitudes of French leaders therefore evolved from hopes for victory through fear of defeat to perseverance.[1]

German diplomatic success depended on a French surrender immediately after its military defeat. An evaluation of German policy is dependent on an analysis of the thinking of French leaders. It is difficult to know how they would have reacted to an actual defeat, but all the available evidence and the behavior of French leaders in late August and early September suggest that they were unlikely to make peace quickly after defeat. French leaders were embittered toward Germany and thus unlikely to respond to German suggestions of reconciliation. The French Government was reconstructed at the end of August to include members of all parties in order to win broader support for the war. The new government immediately announced its determination to continue the war despite military setbacks. The appointment as foreign minister of Théophile Delcassé, who had been the architect of Anglo-French rapprochement, symbolized the policy of resistance rather than reconciliation with Germany. This policy culminated in the Declaration of London, which announced French, British and Russian determination not to conclude peace separately. The French government's decision to leave Paris was evidence of its willingness to make severe sacrifices in order to avoid surrender. French leaders anathematized German attempts to encourage defeatism. Criticism of French strategists by statesmen did not imply their willingness to accept defeat but rather their disillusionment with the soldiers' inability to produce victory as quickly as they had promised.[2]

German hopes for success introduced what was probably a false assumption about how the French would respond to defeat. German leaders hoped that the French government would make peace after military defeat in order to keep the war from expanding into a popular revolutionary struggle. In effect, they expected the French ruling class would place class above national interest, i.e., they might make a quick peace with Germany to preserve their property and avoid a revolution. But the French government reversed those priorities by proclaiming its intention to fight a popular and prolonged war even before the expected military defeat materialized. The French government recognized the possibility that revolution might follow defeat—as it had in 1870-1—but it was willing to assume that risk. French leaders therefore did not make the distinction between class and national interests as German leaders hoped. These hopes proved to be a generation premature.

The French government's domestic policies conformed with its strategic and diplomatic efforts to avoid defeat. French leaders successfully aroused popular support for the war, swept aside partisan disagreement, established a national government, and President Raymond Poincaré idealized the result as "the sacred union." For the moment, these efforts were generally though not entirely successful. As in Germany, patriotism obscured difficulties. By September it became clear that victory was not imminent and Poincaré toned down Joffre's bulletins to avoid creating unrealistic public expectations and subsequent disappointment. The government sought to discourage any demands for peace. French planners anticipated a short war and made few economic preparations for war. The financial transition from a peacetime to wartime economy was made without serious difficulties, but the shortage of munitions handicapped the French as much as it did the Germans and the French were similarly unable to alleviate it. French strategy and policy were therefore unable to produce victory but did at least avoid defeat.[3]

ERRATIC BUT ESSENTIAL:
RUSSIAN STRATEGY & POLICY

The possibility of a German success in imposing a rapid peace on France depended in part on Russian behavior. Germany could defeat France rapidly only by concentrating against France and France might then make peace if it had no prospect of Russian aid. German success therefore depended on isolating the French military operations from Russian support. The Germans pursued this objective by military and political means. They hoped to defer actual military contact with Russia as long as possible by persuading the Austro-Hungarians to attack and thus to divert the Russians. When military contact with Russia became unavoidable, the Germans sought to resist Russian military pressure in East Prussia without significant troop transfers from the west. The Germans complemented these military devices with the political tool of encouraging revolution in order to paralyze the Russian war effort. The preconditions of German success were, however, only partially a function of German strategy and policy. They also depended on the Russian actions, in particular, Russian inability or unwillingness to mobilize and attack Germany quickly. The expectation of such behavior on Russia's part was based on the assumption that Russia had no diplomatic objective which required victory over the Central Powers. Finally, the Germans could succeed only of Russia was unable or unwilling to commit itself to a popular or mass war.

Russian strategy partially fulfilled the preconditions of German success. Russian forces were divided between German and Austro-Hungarian fronts. The Russian offensive against Germany proved too weak and uncoordinated to defeat the Germans and force them to withdraw significant forces from the western front. After their defeat at Tannenberg, the Russians concentrated their uncommitted forces against Austria-Hungary rather than Germany. When they resumed their offensive toward Silesia in October, the Russians advanced so cautiously that the Germans were still not forced to alter operations on the western front. Russian strategy therefore did not prevent the Germans from pursuing their objective of military victory over France. Nonetheless, Russian strategy had a significant effect. The speed of the Russian mobilization and advance against Germany shattered German hopes that France might be defeated before Russia was actually engaged in the war. Tannenberg, ironically, was a Russian defeat in all but the most important sense. It was a disappointment to the Russians, who had hoped for a rapid breakthrough into Germany. Tannenberg also failed to divert enough German troops to the eastern front to facilitate a French breakthrough in the west. Tannenberg, however, indicated that Russia was committed to the war and that France could depend on future Russian aid. After Tannenberg the French were less inclined to surrender even following a military defeat. Russian strategy was therefore less significant strategically than diplomatically. While it could not insure achievement of Russian or French objectives, it could obviate a German success.[4]

Russian diplomacy also made German success unlikely. The Germans assumed they would succeed if the Russians exclusively pursued their own aspirations or if the Russians became discouraged. There were some signs favorable to German success. The Russian concentration on Austria-Hungary after Tannenberg reflected Russian war aims, the major part of which were to be achieved at Austro-Hungarian expense. The Marne was widely applauded in Russia because it forced Germany to remain concentrated in the west and allowed Russia to attack Austria-Hungary. Russian diplomatic policy rendered German success more unlikely. The Russian leaders committed themselves to the Declaration of London, i.e., against concluding a separate peace with Germany. The Tsar claimed that he was willing to continue the war regardless of cost. Russian antipathy toward Germany extended to the point of changing the name St. Petersburg into Petrograd. The Russian failure at Tannenberg was offset by the successes against Austria-Hungary at Lemberg in September and in the Polish campaign of October. The war aims of Russian leaders reflected their confidence and commitment to German and Austro-Hungarian defeat. Like their enemies, Russian leaders used revolutionary as well as military weapons. Russian leaders were consequently confident and committed to the war.[5]

Russian domestic policy was also unlikely to foster German success. German success would have been facilitated if the Russian government was unwilling or unable to mobilize the Russian people for a mass war. The Russian government, however, succeeded in gaining popular support for its aims by eulogizing the nobility and necessity of the war and by denying partisan differences. They accomplished the economic and financial transition to war without disrupting the military effort. Since Russia was less industrialized than the other powers, its economy was less vulnerable and the munition shortages which handicapped German and Anglo-French operations after September did not seriously affect Russian operations until December. Russian domestic policies, strategy and diplomacy thus contributed little to the possibility of a German success.[6]

THE RELUCTANT BELLIGERENT:
BRITISH STRATEGY & POLICY

The probability of a German success in imposing a rapid peace on France depended on Britain as well as Russia. The French might surrender after defeat if they perceived no prospect of British aid. The Germans therefore sought to isolate France militarily from Britain by postponing military and naval contact with Britain as long as possible. At the same time, the Germans sought to distract the British by encouraging revolt in the British Empire. Ultimately the Germans hoped that, if the British were delayed and diverted in these ways, they would accept a French defeat and thereby encourage the French to surrender.

British leaders perceived the war largely in terms of military events. Their perceptions varied from excessive optimism to extreme pessimism. Their initial confidence was shaken by the rapid German advance through Belgium in late August. Their optimism was revived at the Marne, which some of them interpreted to be the first step toward an imminent victory. But anxieties and criticism among British leaders increased during October, which was perhaps Britain's most frustrating and precarious period during the first stage of the war. British expectations of a short war were less intense and British interests less threatened by a long war than those of the other powers. Consequently, British leaders predicted a long war sooner than the leaders of other countries.[7]

The Germans could affect but not determine British behavior. British military and naval strategy eventually was precisely the reverse of what the Germans desired. British civilian leaders were at first disinclined to send a military contingent to aid the French and Belgians, and determined to limit the initial British contribution to a naval blockade. Later they were persuaded to send troops to France by Kitchener, the newly appointed minister of war. The British might have behaved according to German hopes if the British commander in France, General French, had been allowed to withdraw his forces before the Marne, but Kitchener again played a critical role and persuaded the cabinet to keep British forces in contact with the French. The British expedition in aid of Antwerp was unsuccessful but it demonstrated British military involvement in the war. The operations in Flanders during late October and early November more than previous engagements were an indication of British determination to aid the French. The British were more anxious for a naval confrontation than the Germans hoped, but they were unable to win a naval victory and feared for the safety of their fleet. The British proclamation of their intention to wage economic war and mount a naval blockade further demonstrated that they were in fact active participants. British military and naval strategy consequently disappointed German hopes.[8]

British diplomatic and domestic policies were also detrimental to German aspirations. Britain's initial reluctance to enter the war was deceptive. The central fact of Britain's diplomacy, like that of France and Russia, was the renunciation of a separate peace. The government frequently expressed its determination to continue the war and the British people supported their government. But the shock of military setbacks and the government's realization that the British public was not yet emotionally engaged convinced British leaders that it was necessary to undertake a propaganda campaign to which the public responded. British leaders also sought to mobilize the nation for war. An extensive recruiting campaign proved successful when more volunteers flocked to recruiting stations than could be trained. Parliament approved the expansion of the British army by half a million men, which was advocated by Kitchener and Churchill. The government meanwhile adjusted the economy to war and thereby avoided a financial crisis. A political moratorium was declared and bipartisan support won for the war. Prime Minister Herbert Asquith even hoped that the war might resolve some political differences. The government's actions were, however, not entirely successful. Despite the seriousness of the military situation, Parliament and the Trade Unions opposed conscription because it implied compulsion. The British efforts to alleviate munitions shortages were as fruitless as those of the other belligerents. Public support for the war was overwhelming, but there were signs of disunity both inside and outside the government. Notwithstanding bipartisan support for the war, certain prewar domestic political conflicts persisted, particularly over Ireland. But these failures did not obscure the major result of British policy, namely, that it constituted another obstacle to German success.[9]

ALLIANCE THROUGH ADVERSITY:
RELATIONS WITHIN THE ENTENTE

German success depended ultimately on isolating its enemies. Peace could be imposed on France only if it was isolated from its allies. The war against Russia and Britain could be continued successfully only if they too were isolated. The fulfillment of German aspirations thus depended on the dissolution of the Entente.

Initially there was little inclination to tighten the Entente. The requisite formalities were observed toward one another in their declarations of war, but the distinction between "allies" (Russia and France) and "friends" (the British) was retained. The Russians, Poincaré, and King George may have gently suggested formalizing the alliance but persistent frictions precluded such amiability. British suspicions of Russia ran deep and Poincaré was impatient with both of France's allies. Russian Foreign Minister Sergei Sazonov was anxious to consolidate the alliance and establish joint war aims but his suggestions only alienated the French and British. While the possibility of victory remained and they therefore were less dependent upon one another, relations among the Entente powers were characterized more by friction than friendship.[10]

Adversity altered relations. Following the setbacks of late August the Entente governments became sufficiently desperate to transform their association into an alliance. They were mainly motivated by anxiety, particularly the fear of isolation. Sazonov told the French Ambassador, Maurice Paleologue, that the Russian government was "worried again whether [France] would not allow [itself] to conclude a separate peace" with Germany. General French's desire to withdraw the British army from combat confronted the French with the prospect of fighting the Germans alone. The initiative for formalizing the alliance therefore came from Russia and France, the two most vulnerable allies. Among the French leaders who urged a formal alliance were Gaston Doumergue, Delcassé, Poincaré, Paul and Jules Cambon, and Alexandre Millerand. Russian leaders including Sazonov and Grand Duke Nicholas also favored the proposal. British leaders came around more gradually to the idea. Whatever the immediate impulses, the three governments considered a closer alliance to be necessary. Consequently on 4 September they signed the Declaration of London which committed them to discuss all peace proposals and to reject suggestions of a separate peace. The declaration was a critical turning point for Germany since it reduced the likelihood that the Entente would collapse as a result of military defeats. In effect, the Entente governments demonstrated that they preferred the risks of a longer war to an unsuccessful short war.[11]

It proved easier, however, to proclaim than to preserve harmony among the allies. The alliance had to face the test of strategic disagreements if it was to survive. The alliance was naturally affected by military events since it was forged by military setbacks. The results of the Marne and Galicia caused each ally to consider the alliance differently. Anglo-French policies tended to converge after the Marne, while they diverged from Russian policy largely because of the Russian success in Galicia. The French were worried that the Russians would concentrate against Austria-Hungary rather than Germany. Their anxiety seemed well-founded when Sazonov informed Paleologue that Russia would turn against Germany only after Austria-Hungary had been "done away with." Grand Duke Nicholas countered French doubts by claiming that the Germans were transporting troops to the east because the Anglo-French were not attacking in the west. He expressed the fear that the French might make a separate peace with Germany after French territory had been liberated or if Germany offered France the Rhine frontier. He therefore demanded a commitment that France continue to fight until Germany was defeated and "peace dictated to it" as a condition for a Russian campaign against Germany *after* Austria-Hungary had been defeated. Paleologue and the British Ambassador, George Buchanan, rejected Russian complaints and continued to insist that Russia immediately concentrate against Germany because Austria-Hungary was already defeated. Meanwhile French, British and Russian leaders publicly as well as confidentially reassured each other that they would continue to fight until Germany had been defeated. Anglo-French complaints may have altered Russian strategy slightly since Grand Duke Nicholas postponed his withdrawal of Russian forces from southern Poland because of the adverse effects it might have on his allies. The Germans inadvertently improved Entente relations by concentrating against the Russians when the Russians refused to concentrate against them. The Anglo-French nonetheless were impatient with the slow development of Russian operations.[12]

Relations among the allies were further complicated by diplomatic differences. The Russian success in Galicia augmented Russian war aims. Sazonov may have been anxious to extract commitments while the French and British were dependent on Russia and to encourage his allies with the prospect of booty. He suggested a fundamental reconstruction of central Europe in which the borders of the peripheral states (Russia, France, Belgium, Denmark and Serbia) would be shifted inward on a disunited central Europe. His suggestion implied Russian preeminence in eastern Europe, Anglo-French dominance in western Europe, and presumably joint control over central Europe and the colonial world. Sazonov described his proposal as tentative and unofficial, but he asked for allied reactions to it and later claimed that it had received their approval. Grey may have accepted some of Sazonov's less ambitious suggestions but refused a formal reply and did not take up the theme of disunifying central Europe. Nonetheless, Buchanan and Paleologue proposed a "new order" in Europe to Sazonov. This vague objective allowed each ally to project its own aspirations. The British advocated the destruction of "Prussian militarism," defense of small nations, fulfillment of treaty obligations, and a vague concept of a league of nations. The only definite objectives proposed by the French included the liberation of their own territory, the recovery of Alsace-Lorraine, and the defeat of Germany. Had the Entente powers "annihilated" German military power in 1914, they would probably have expanded these war aims.[13]

Relations among the Entente powers were therefore imperfect. Strategic and diplomatic differences persisted. The three powers could not agree on the conduct of the war or how to bring it to a conclusion but only that it should not result in German hegemony. This was appropriate since the threat of German power and not Entente policy was the critical factor in making the alliance. As in the case of the Central Powers, members of the Entente were alternately influenced by aggressive and defensive impulses, i.e., between encirclement and containment of Germany. Like German and Austro-Hungarian war aims, Entente aspirations reflected military prospects. When the military situation was propitious, war aims were increased; when military prospects were unpromising, war aims were reduced. Entente military power was insufficient to fulfill their aggressive war aims and thus to realize the objective of encirclement but it was sufficient to contain German power. The most important decisions taken by Entente leaders during the early period of the war were consequently negative and defensive. The French elected to sacrifice territory in order to avoid defeat. The French and British stopped the German advance at the Marne and in Flanders. The Russians risked Tannenberg in order to preclude French defeat but became cautious during their subsequent Polish campaign. The main point of the Declaration of London was negative in that it committed the Entente powers not to conclude a separate peace. These negative decisions critically affected the course of events. They could not produce victory but they helped the Entente avoid defeat. Since rapid Entente defeat was essential to German victory in a short war, Entente policies made a German victory unlikely.

ABSTENTION, INTERVENTION OR MEDIATION? THE NEUTRALS' POLICIES

LIMITATION OF WAR:
THE SIGNIFICANCE OF NEUTRALITY

The war was neither a genuinely European nor world war during its early stage. It included less than half Europe's states and only a fraction of the world's states. Hypothetically it might have expanded immediately to involve all European states or even all states. The fact that it did not was a significant feature of the conflict.

The short-war assumption encouraged limitation of the war since it implied that the war would end before new belligerents could mobilize. The great power system also discouraged the entry of smaller European states. Like prewar diplomacy, the war was perceived at first as a great power affair. Those small states which were involved (Belgium and Serbia) were more objects than operators. It seemed unlikely that small European states or non-European powers could influence the course of events. Like war, peace would be made by the great powers and should not be encumbered by the demands of small states. Indeed, the neutrality of some small states was more useful to some or all of the powers than their assistance and therefore their intervention was discouraged. Fear of alienating the eventual victors acted as a further deterrent. Although they sought to win new allies, the powers were neither sufficiently desperate nor convinced that it was necessary to pay the neutrals enough to warrant the risks. Consequently, no European neutral became a belligerent as long as the short-war illusion persisted. In this sense, the end of the illusion was symbolized by the entry of Turkey in early November. A short war would have reinforced great power domination by making the powerful more powerful and the weak weaker.

Conversely, the short-war assumption was based on a limitation of the war. The war could be short only if one side surrendered quickly. Either side would surrender quickly if it had no prospect of aid from its allies or from new allies. If all the European states or indeed all the world's states had entered the war immediately, the possibility of a short war would have disappeared. As it was, none of the neutral states entered while the short-war assumption persisted. Thus, neutrality and the short-war assumption were interdependent. Limitation of the war rested on the assumption of a short war and the short-war assumption depended on limiting the war to participation by the European great powers.

Limitation of the conflict to the European great powers would, however, restrict its importance. Even if one side won overwhelmingly in a short war, its victory would be incomplete. The European neutrals would probably not be a significant obstacle to the hegemony of the victor and some at least expected to be dominated if Germany won the war; such German domination would nonetheless have to be imposed and might cause practical diplomatic and political difficulties. But the non-European powers—the United States and Japan—constituted a greater potential limitation. If they perceived the victory of one side—particularly Germany—as a threat, they might become active participants in the European conflict. The prospect of American or Japanese aid might persuade European powers—particularly the Entente—to refuse surrender despite defeat. Thus the overwhelming superiority of one side was at once necessary for a short war but might ultimately preclude that result.

The neutrals nonetheless expected a short war. Since the outcome seemed to depend completely on military considerations, neutral policies were guided by events on the battlefields. Neutral statesmen foresaw the possibility of German victory, particularly after the Germans won the initiative in the west and defeated the Russians at Tannenberg. The prospect of a German victory and consequent domination over Europe was repellent to some if not all of them, but no neutral acted to resist those eventualities by joining the Entente. All preferred instead to avoid alienating the likely victors. This response illustrates that there was general acceptance of the great power system and the subordinate role of the lesser states. The Marne therefore was as important to the neutrals as it was to the great powers because it destroyed the myth of German invincibility. Italian Prime Minister Salandra concluded that "the German was not invincible after all, as had been accepted from 1870 onwards as a matter of course. The charm was broken."[1] The Marne also destroyed faith in great power omnipotence. These effects became only gradually apparent and the neutrals consequently remained cautious until the implications of the Marne were confirmed in Flanders and Poland. As the old myths died, new ones replaced them. Some of the smaller states began to act upon the belief that they now held the key to events and thereby turned the system on its head: the fate of the great power system seemed to be dependent on the small states.

FROM SECRET ALLY TO RELUCTANT BELLIGERENT:
THE OTTOMAN EMPIRE

Perhaps as much because of the habit of prewar rivalries as the recognition of its intrinsic importance, Turkey received more great power attention during the first months of the war than any other neutral. German policy toward Turkey before the Marne enjoyed mixed success. The prospect of war removed the restraints from German aspirations in Turkey and made Turkey seem a useful tool for revolutionizing the Russian and British Empires. Consequently, the Germans encouraged Turkish intervention even before war had been declared. The Turks were, however, only mildly receptive. Turkey concluded a secret alliance with Germany on 2 August, permitted two German cruisers to enter the Dardanelles, and appointed a German general commander of Turkish troops in Constantinople and European Turkey. The Germans continued to press Turkey to enter the war and assisted with military preparations. After initial disagreements, German generals and statesmen agreed that the purpose of Turkish entry was to attack Russia in the Caucasus and Britain in Egypt.[2]

These minimal successes seemed more ominous to Germany's enemies than they actually were. The Entente powers sought to discourage a Turkish entry with a combination of threats and promises. They protested the increasing German influence in Turkish military affairs as a breach of neutrality, considered operations against Turkey, and warned that Turkish entry would jeopardize the integrity of the Ottoman Empire. The British were, however, anxious to postpone an open break until the Indian army had been shipped through the Suez Canal and to allow the Turks the first move in order not to alienate Muslims in the British Empire. Eventually Entente statesmen realized that a Turkish decision depended less on diplomatic warnings or rewards than on military events in Europe.[3]

The Turks concluded the alliance with the Germans, prepared for war and actually mobilized at the beginning of September, but they declared armed neutrality and persistently rejected German pressure to intervene. The Turkish government was divided over the issue and the German ambassador to Constantinople, Hans von Wangenheim, argued that Turkey was not yet prepared for war. The Turks meanwhile exploited the distraction of the great powers to abrogate the Capitulations which granted the great powers privileges in Turkey. The Germans and Austro-Hungarians were angered and even formally joined the Entente protest but assured the Turks that they would not resist. Thus the Turks pursued a policy of watchful waiting.[4]

The Marne and Galicia altered the situation by revealing the divergence of German and Turkish interests. As the certainty of German victory diminished, the German need for a Turkish entry increased—while the Turks' desire to enter waned proportionately. Wangenheim reported that Galicia and "the gigantic impression" of the Marne had caused the Turks to "doubt whether Germany will win." A Turkish general observed that Germany could not expect Turkey to make a "suicidal offering." If Germany could "win somewhere, so that [Turkey] can believe in final German victory, then Bulgaria and [Turkey] will enter." In effect, Turkey and other neutrals were willing to join a victorious alliance when their assistance was no longer necessary.[5]

In the intense and sometimes acrimonious negotiations which followed, there was discord not only between Turks and Germans but also among factions within both governments. Turkish policy vacillated between intervention and neutrality. As Berlin became more anxious for Turkish entry, Wangenheim became more skeptical and urged patience. Events accelerated during October. The Turkish interventionists forced the decision on their colleagues and promised Wangenheim intervention in exchange for financial support. Berlin overrode Wangenheim's reservations and immediately sent the funds. Although the interventionists promised hostilities would begin with the long-planned surprise attack on the Russian Black Sea fleet, they attached conditions to Caucasian and Egyptian expeditions which partially justified Wangenheim's argument that intervention was premature. The die was virtually cast, however, when the Turkish fleet shelled several Russian ports and sank a number of Russian ships at sea. In the end, a combination of German prodding and Turkish susceptibility brought Turkey into the war after three months of negotiations.[6]

Entente influence declined as German influence increased. It appeared to the Entente that Germany already controlled the Turkish army and navy in September. Both Delcassé and Sazonov favored a harder line but British councils were divided; Churchill urged the stick whereas Grey and Kitchener preferred the carrot. Since the Entente nations favored the *status quo*, they tended to leave the initiative to the Germans. But, when they concluded that the Turks were preparing to attack Egypt, the British cabinet decided to "launch a vigorous offensive against Turkey and make every effort to bring in Bulgaria, Greece and above all Rumania." After the Turkish attack on the Russian Black Sea fleet, one brief effort was nonetheless made to avoid hostilities. When the Turkish government offered what seemed to be a conciliatory explanation, Sazonov intimated that war could be avoided if all German personnel were expelled immediately. When this condition was not accepted, he declared war on 2 November. On the next day, the Anglo-French fleet bombarded the Dardanelles and hostilities began on the southern and eastern Turkish fronts. Ironically, the dissolution of the Ottoman Empire, which Russia had sought for a century while Britain and France resisted, began on a note of Russian ambivalence and Anglo-French alacrity.[7]

Like the Ottoman entry, the Ottoman role in the war was full of paradoxes. The empire added little to German power and even reduced German strength to the extent that Germany sent supplies and personnel to the Turks.

German-Turkish relations were not harmonious and the Turks were far from being German satraps. The Turkish entry into the war nonetheless had important implications. Turkey would ultimately divert more Entente than German power and thus constitute a net gain for the Germans. Most important, Turkey blockaded Russia more efficiently than the Entente blockaded Germany and thereby cut the Russians off from their allies' arsenals. After centuries of suffering Russian threats, the Turks thereby had the satisfaction of contributing to the collapse of the Russian Empire—but only at the Pyrrhic cost of destroying their own.[8]

FROM ALIENATED ALLY TO SECRET ENEMY: ITALY

The behavior of Italy and the Balkan states was uncertain but not irrelevant to the great power struggle. If either Italy or Rumania joined the Entente, Austria-Hungary would be distracted from the Russian front, Germany would have to bear a greater share of the fighting against Russia, Turkey would become inaccessible to the Central Powers, and the Entente might be encouraged to prolong the war. Consequently, a rapid German victory partly depended on the behavior of Austria-Hungary's neighbors.

Despite prewar Austro-Italian frictions, the Central Powers pressed Italy to join them. Italy declared its neutrality instead and the subsequent German efforts to reverse the decision by claiming military success and offering bribes of Austro-Hungarian territory succeeded in alienating Vienna more than they attracted Rome. Vienna was probably correct in arguing that bribes were pointless because Italian leaders were virtually determined on a war with Austria-Hungary. Italian neutrality was therefore due more to Austro-Italian differences than Entente diplomacy. Since Italy would not move against Austria-Hungary as long as a German victory seemed possible, the Entente failed to win Italy as an ally and Italian Foreign Minister San Giuliano noted that it was "very improbable that Italy would renounce neutrality." While military prospects were uncertain, Italian policy remained cautious.[9]

The Marne marked a turning point in Italian policy. The end of the myth of German invincibility made a profound impression on Italian leaders. Since San Giuliano now feared that Italian neutrality might alienate both sides, Italian policy became more active. Rome signed an agreement with Bucharest on 23 September to consult before they renounced neutrality. Salandra gave a classic statement of *raison d'état* when he announced that Italy's policy would be "uninfluenced by any sentiment but that of an exclusive, unlimited devotion to our country, a sacred egoism for Italy." The Italian leaders had apparently decided to join the Entente during the coming spring and Salandra's announcement was designed to elicit Entente offers. Paris and London were informed that Italy might join the Entente after military preparations had been completed. The Entente nations were insufficiently responsive so Italy encouraged offers from the Central Powers in order to bid up the Entente. Italian strength did not, however, correspond with Italian aspirations. Salandra recognized that Italy could not achieve its irredentist goals without intervening, but also realized that the country was not prepared for war. Furthermore, the Italian leaders believed that a German victory was not impossible even after the Marne, and Italian Supreme Commander Luigi Cadorna argued that Italy would then be exposed to a German vendetta. Ultimately this insufficiency of power determined Italian policy.[10]

BALKAN BICKERING: RUMANIA & BULGARIA

The powers meanwhile courted Rumania and Bulgaria. The Central Powers used bribes and threats to bring Rumania in on their side and they achieved minor successes as a result. Rumania assured the Central Powers that it would not become an enemy and allowed German aid to pass through to Turkey. The Russians meanwhile offered Rumania Austro-Hungarian territory and the French suggested the Russians make concessions themselves. The Italians pressed the Rumanians not to join the Central Powers and the Turks sought an alliance with Rumania. The Rumanians declared their neutrality but negotiated with both sides.[11]

Berlin and Vienna traded prewar policies toward Bulgaria. Berlin opposed an alliance with Bulgaria before the war because it would alienate Rumania, but now sought one. Vienna formerly advocated such an alliance, but now resisted it because of Rumania. When Bulgaria refused an alliance, the Central Powers' only consolation was a Bulgarian-Turkish agreement. Sazonov characteristically led the Entente pursuit of Bulgaria by offering Turkish and even Serbian territory in exchange for a promise of Bulgarian neutrality in a Russo-Turkish war. The Bulgarians nonetheless refused and maintained their neutrality while they continued to bargain with both sides.[12]

Military events loosened the Balkan logjam. The Rumanians were impressed by Russian success in Galicia and Poland. The Russians invited the Rumanians to join them in occupying Bukovina and the French added the inducement of financial aid. Although the Rumanians refused to join the Entente, they revoked permission for passage of German aid to Turkey and on 1 October promised Russia benevolent neutrality in exchange for Transylvania. King Carol, who had sought to avoid a break with the Central Powers, died and was succeeded by his nephew Ferdinand, who was expected to be less disposed toward the Central Powers. Rumanian behavior was correspondingly ominous for the Central Powers. But, in pressing the Austro-Hungarians for concessions to Rumania, the Germans succeeded only in angering their allies.[13]

The military setbacks of the Central Powers had an unsettling effect on Bulgaria, which drew back from an alliance with Turkey, but seemed to consider joining the Central Powers in an attack on Serbia. The Turkish entry into the war allowed the Entente to offer Bulgaria larger bribes which were nonetheless rejected. The Bulgarians again decided against intervention and reaffirmed their neutrality.[14]

The leaders of both great power coalitions had two things in common: frustration and failure. In their exasperation, German leaders wrote off the Balkan states as a loss and British leaders considered neutralizing the area. The failure of the great powers to involve the Balkan states was due in part to intra-Balkan rivalries which the great powers could not erase. It was also a function of great power aspirations. The Austro-Hungarian refusal to make concessions to Italy or Rumania was both reasonable and realistic. Austria-Hungary entered the war to avoid concessions and it was unreasonable to make concessions to go on fighting. The Austro-Hungarian rejection of concessions was realistic because Italian and Rumanian decisions would probably not have been affected by them. Although the Kaiser attributed Balkan behavior to Austro-German diplomatic failures, events were probably determined less by great power diplomacy than by great power strategy and military events. Italy and the Balkan states would remain observers until a military decision had occurred. Italian and Rumanian neutrality was frustrating to the Central Powers but it was basically favorable to them. The small states did not jeopardize the possibility of a short war by expanding the conflict.[15]

THE GENUINE NEUTRALS:
THE NON-BALKAN STATES

Unlike Italy and the Balkan states, other European neutrals negotiated little over their neutrality. The Scandinavian countries, the Netherlands, Switzerland, Portugal and Spain announced their neutrality in rapid succession at the outset and most remained neutral throughout the war. Although in general not seriously questioned, their neutrality was nonetheless tested or qualified in some instances. Austria-Hungary unsuccessfully sought to win Sweden as an ally against Russia by promising Sweden concessions of Finnish territory. The Danes were compelled by the Germans to mine the Store Belt and to allow the establishment of a neutral telegraph service which provided the Germans with a mouthpiece to the neutral world. A Portuguese offer to join the Entente was refused by the British to avoid alienating Spain. The Germans sought to insure the benevolent neutrality of these states by publicizing their military successes and promising restraint after their final victory.[16]

The behavior of the non-Balkan neutrals was a result of both their own and great power policies. They, in contrast to Italy and the Balkan states, were all long-established states and therefore had fewer territorial aspirations. Their few territorial aspirations could only be realized at the expense of strong great powers (Germany and Russia) rather than against a weak one (Austria-Hungary) as in the case of Rumania and Italy. These aims therefore depended on the great power struggle. Furthermore, these states were either more valuable to the powers as neutrals or not valuable enough as allies to warrant the price of their involvement. Non-Balkan neutrality had contradictory consequences. It allowed the opposing great powers to concentrate on one another rather than divide their forces. But these neutrals were also means of unofficial communication and even mediation between the powers. Thus, they intensified the conflict but might also interrupt it.

THE UNCOMMITTED POWERS:
JAPAN & THE UNITED STATES

The policies of the non-European powers did not significantly affect the course of the expected short war. Japan took Germany's Asian possessions and thus demonstrated that Germany could not simultaneously pursue European and colonial aspirations. Japan's action also tended to confirm the European character of the war by removing colonial distractions and allowing Russia to transfer all its troops to Europe. Actual Japanese participation in the European war was feared by the Germans, sought by the French, resisted by the British and it failed to materialize. The German leaders identified Japan and Britain as their major opponents after a German hegemony had been established in Europe, but they sought for the moment to make the best of a bad situation by exploiting American fears of Japan to encourage American neutrality. German hopes that an actual Japanese-American conflict might develop were, however, disappointed when the United States declared its disinterest in the German-Japanese conflict.[17]

The German efforts to maintain American neutrality were superfluous. The vast majority of the American public was staunchly isolationist and grateful not to be involved in the war. President Woodrow Wilson claimed that he was determined to remain "absolutely neutral." Nonetheless, American policy immediately began to make qualifications which subsequently characterized its relations with the belligerents, i.e., a brittle reserve toward the Central Powers, partially concealed sympathy toward France and Britain, and a suspicion of Russia. Edward House and Robert Lansing, Wilson's main advisers, and Grey sought to reinforce Wilson's fear of a German victory. Wilson and Grey felt that an Anglo-American break would, in Wilson's words, be "a calamity." However, during the early weeks of the war Grey seems to have assumed that the war would be short enough to permit the British to employ blockade procedures which might risk Anglo-American friction. Consequently, some Anglo-American differences were resolved but others were brewing. The Germans encouraged Anglo-American tension over the British blockade and sought to reduce German-American friction. Despite these complications, neutrality remained the central fact of American policy. All of the neutral nations, whether sympathetic or unsympathetic, disinterested or self-seeking, were therefore cautious and none altered the course of events through intervention.[18]

THREATS OF PEACE:
EVADING NEUTRAL MEDIATION

Some neutrals sought, however, to affect events through mediation. This possibility first occurred at the beginning of August when the United States offered to act as mediator. This offer was politely but firmly rejected by all the belligerents. The Italians also considered mediating during the first week of war. The German leaders perceived mediation as a military, political and diplomatic threat. They seemingly believed that Russia would use the delay involved in negotiations to overcome the German advantage of a more rapid mobilization. To them mediation was politically inopportune since the German people opposed peace at the time of the American and Italian offers. It would be diplomatically disadvantageous because refusal would make Germany look aggressive. The Italians dropped the idea when the British as well as the Germans resisted. The struggle for the military initiative therefore continued without interruption.[19]

The failure of either side to win a quick victory by mid-September implied that the belligerents would have a choice between a protracted war and a compromise peace. The possibility of a compromise peace was suggested again by the Americans, who were concerned over the course of events in Europe. The American ambassador in Berlin, James Gerard, wrote House at the beginning of September and described the implications of a German victory in dire terms. Gerard, without authorization from Washington, revived Wilson's offer of mediation during conversations with Zimmermann in the first week of September. Perhaps encouraged by Austro-Hungarian Ambassador Konstantin von Dumba, House won Wilson's approval for a similar suggestion to Zimmermann. In order to avoid the odium of refusing, German Ambassador Johann von Bernstorff replied to a private sounding that Germany would consider mediation if its enemies did. American Secretary of State William Bryan immediately authorized Gerard to make an official offer of mediation to the German government with the approval of Wilson and Bernstorff. The choice between peace and war consequently confronted the belligerents.[20]

The German government tried to avoid American mediation without alienating the Americans. Zimmermann had already avoided Gerard's earlier unofficial suggestion by arguing that Germany sought "a lasting peace" which "required a reckoning with not only France [as Gerard implied] but also Russia and England. Otherwise [Germany] would have to expect a new war with the Entente powers in a few years." Zimmermann nonetheless claimed that Berlin would seriously consider Entente suggestions made via Washington. Bernstorff assumed that the Americans were anxious to end the war and recommended that Berlin "leave the odium of refusal to our enemies" in order to arouse American opinion against England, "which it holds responsible for the prolongation of the war." Zimmermann instead asked Bethmann to authorize him to parry this new offer as he had Gerard's earlier feeler. Bethmann concurred and suggested the arguments which later typified German rejections of mediatory offers, i.e., Germany was fighting a defensive war; the Entente was determined to prolong the war; any German acceptance of mediation would be interpreted by the Entente as a sign of weakness; the Entente should make the first move; the German masses opposed peace; and Germany needed guarantees for security. Bethmann's response was even less encouraging than Zimmermann's since Bethmann did not stipulate a German willingness to consider Entente conditions communicated by the Americans. The German government meanwhile denied rumors of peace in the press and Bethmann vilified British prewar policy toward Belgium in a way designed to reduce the possibility of mediation. Bethmann's opposition reflected the view prevailing at German headquarters despite the Marne. Accordingly, German leaders were not disposed to compromise. [21]

The Entente responded to mediation in a similarly negative fashion. British Ambassador Cecil Spring-Rice recommended that his government not reject the American offer out-of-hand. Grey nonetheless told American Ambassador Walter Page that a German offer would be perceived as mere propaganda and that peace could not be concluded until German militarism had been destroyed and Belgium repaired. Page interpreted Grey's answer as a threat that the United States would disqualify itself as a future mediator if it communicated inadequate German conditions. Spring-Rice meanwhile fervently appealed to House to discourage American mediation. French Ambassador J.-J. Jusserand told Bryan that the chances for successful mediation were "infinitesimal" and indignantly rejected Bryan's suggestion of a return to the *status quo ante*. The French government refused mediation which Poincaré hypothesized had been suggested by the Germans because they realized that their offensive had failed. The Russian ambassador was also ordered to discourage mediation. [22]

The belligerents' replies should have been sufficient. House initially seemed to recognize that it was hopeless to persist when he observed that "England will not stand for peace unless it also means permanent peace, and that, I think, Germany is not yet ready to concede." Page tried to reinforce House's conclusion with an impassioned presentation of the British case to House. But Gerard somehow interpreted Bethmann's answer as "an opening to mediation" and the American press buzzed with rumors of peace. House therefore decided to pursue the matter further. Bernstorff agreed to a meeting with Spring-Rice, who refused. House, however, persuaded Spring-Rice to tell Grey that the balance of power could be preserved only by a compromise peace and that Britain might alienate the United States by rejecting mediation. House presented the responses of Spring-Rice and Bernstorff to Wilson as more favorable than they actually were and sought to remove genuine obstacles by legerdemain. In reality Spring-Rice told Grey that he had left Bernstorff's sounding unanswered, while Bernstorff informed Berlin correctly that the British would do nothing without their allies. Spring-Rice became increasingly negative, denounced the German offer and warned that it would be "some time" before Grey could consult his allies. House finally realized that the Entente "intend doing nothing until what they consider a propitious time and then they will use [the United States] as a means of beginning peace conversations." [23]

Rumors of peace reverberated again in October. Reports of German willingness to mediate were repeatedly scotched by Berlin. Jagow ordered Zimmermann to deny a French claim that Germany had inspired Wilson's demarche; Germany would resist defeat and make peace only when it was guaranteed against future attacks. Clemenceau continued to needle the Germans, who tirelessly reiterated their rejection of mediation. The possibility of peace was thus postponed. [24]

Mediation failed not because of mistakes, inefficiency or poor communications but because it did not seem desirable to the belligerents. Mediation implied a compromise peace and return to the *status quo ante*. The belligerents would presumably have preferred peace on that basis to defeat or stalemate. But the antagonists all foresaw victory and a favorably revised *status quo*, so they did not anticipate defeat or stalemate and thus the need to compromise. Furthermore mediation was difficult. The July crisis demonstrated that the powers were unwilling to make concessions to preserve peace. Hostilities made them even less willing to make concessions and more anxious to make demands. Consequently, war was preferable to a peace which seemed both undesirable and impractical.

The American suggestion of mediation was an indication that neutrals and belligerents perceived the situation in fundamentally different ways and that the belligerents shared basically the same attitudes toward the war. The rejection of mediation constituted a failure for the Americans but a success for all the belligerents since they avoided the threat of premature peace. The various replies of the belligerents—particularly the British and Germans—were strikingly similar and both spoke of "permanent peace," the expectations of their public, guarantees of security, defensive war, fear of weakness, and enemy propaganda and deceit. The implications of these phrases were different within the several countries involved but their formulation revealed a basic similarity in the assumptions of the belligerents about neutral and domestic public opinion. The statements made by belligerent statesmen indicated that each side perceived its own aspirations as justifiable and its enemies' aims as unacceptable. Virtually all statesmen and soldiers assumed that the war would be short, even while their aspirations implied a long war. The belligerents therefore were disagreed on many aspects of the war but they generally agreed that a compromise peace during this early stage of the war was undesirable.

The rejection of a compromise peace had profound implications for all the powers, particularly Germany. The logic of German military and diplomatic policy for a generation was a compelling argument for making peace after the Marne. German leaders had assumed that Germany could win a short war but would lose a long one. If the Marne precluded a quick victory, they would have to choose between their assumptions and aspirations. If they continued to assume that victory was possible only in a short war, they would be forced to renounce their aspirations of victory. But, if they retained their aspirations, the assumption that Germany could win only in a short war would have to be renounced. German leaders escaped this choice by claiming that the Marne postponed but did not preclude a quick victory. They thereby adjusted their assumptions and their analysis of events to suit their aspirations.

Part II

The
Illusion
Shattered

(November-December 1914)

STABILIZATION NOT ANNIHILATION: STRATEGY & POLICY

EAST OR WEST?
DEBATE OVER STRATEGY (EARLY NOVEMBER)

The short-war illusion was shaken at the Marne and shattered in Flanders. The fighting in Flanders destroyed the old illusions and presaged subsequent problems—an encirclement was no longer possible and a German breakthrough against fortified positions seemed the only recourse. The resulting stalemate had significant implications since strategy, policy and domestic affairs had been based on the short-war assumption. It had justified the military risks involved in taking the offensive, the diplomatic disadvantage of alienating other powers, and the renunciation of party politics. The end of the short-war illusion altered all these assumptions. If the war was to be prolonged, strategy would have to be adjusted and tenacity might become as important as mobility and the defense as critical as the offense. Policy would have to be adjusted to more limited power and become more concerned with winning the war than with projecting aspirations. Domestic political differences would have to be resolved, concealed or postponed by making even larger promises. The end of the short-war illusion consequently required the participants to accommodate the long-war reality.

Their failure in Flanders caused a German strategic crisis. The basic problem which had been implicit but denied now became explicit and undeniable—their failure to win the war quickly confronted the Germans with the implications of a two-front war. In developing a strategy for this new situation, Falkenhayn had the three options of continued operations in the west with more limited goals, operations in the east, or discontinuation of operations altogether. Moltke and Falkenhayn had been pressured to transfer major operations to the east before the failure in Flanders. Conrad agitated for reinforcements in August, intensified his demands in September and early October, and made them even more frequent at the end of October. According to Hindenburg, the Russians were forcing him to withdraw from Poland and threatening an invasion of German or Austro-Hungarian territory. Conrad contended that genuine success in the west would require considerable time, whereas victory in the east could be won quickly and would allow Germany to win the decision Falkenhayn sought over France. In addition to citing these advantages, Conrad added that he might have to withdraw if Falkenhayn did not respond. These arguments, however, had little effect on Falkenhayn since he still hoped for a resounding success in Flanders and the eastern front would have to hold for the six weeks Falkenhayn estimated would be necessary to win a decision in the west.[1]

The context of the debate was altered when the German attacks in Flanders failed at the beginning of November. The failure jeopardized Falkenhayn's contention that a rapid decision in the west was necessary before significant transfers to the east could occur. It also caused general disappointment at Supreme Headquarters (OHL) and shook Falkenhayn's self-confidence and prestige. The pressure on Falkenhayn increased when Hindenburg and Ludendorff proposed a large-scale offensive requiring considerable reinforcements from the west. Falkenhayn may have considered acceding to the Hindenburg-Ludendorff proposal since the advantages of doing so were reinforced by both the entry of Turkey and the Austro-Hungarian attack on Serbia. Those events might combine with Russia's defeat to bring in Bulgaria and Rumania on the side of the Central Powers. Since Falkenhayn felt, however, that immediate withdrawal of large forces from the west would risk sacrificing considerable French territory which he equated with "a defeat," he decided that a visible success in Flanders and secure defenses in the west were necessary to avoid negative political repercussions and depressed troop morale. He nonetheless authorized plans for assuming the defensive in the west and making considerable transfers to the east.[2]

Having made his decision, Falkenhayn sought to convince Conrad and Hindenburg. Conrad was informed that Falkenhayn would transfer four corps to the east after the western front had been secured regardless of what happened in Flanders and accepted Falkenhayn's proposal. When Ludendorff meanwhile announced his intention to attack in the near future, Falkenhayn promised four corps in two weeks. Despite their apparent agreement, Falkenhayn had merely postponed the problem, whereas Hindenburg and Ludendorff committed themselves to an operation which might force Falkenhayn to send reinforcements to the east. The fundamental decision therefore was yet to be made.[3]

FINAL FAILURE & SURPRISING SUCCESS:
THE MILITARY EVENTS (EARLY NOVEMBER)

Falkenhayn's object in resuming his attack in Flanders was to gain a success for effect rather than a decisive victory—indeed a success to conceal the absence of a decision. Even that minimal object proved, however, to be unattainable. Falkenhayn provided the appropriate epitaph for the campaign to win a quick victory when he told his army commanders that "we now renounce the struggle for the decision in the west; we are satisfied with what we have." Consequently, defensive positions would have to be prepared despite extensive withdrawals to the east. The German failure was only a partial success for the French and British, who recognized that, while they had successfully deflected the major German attack, their own shortage of munitions precluded a counteroffensive. The western campaign had ended.[4]

The Flanders campaign had important ramifications. It should have demonstrated the difficulty if not the futility of frontal assaults on fortified positions, but it proved to be less a warning than a harbinger of subsequent operations on the western front since the lesson was not learned by either side. The campaign marked the end of German efforts to win the war quickly by rapidly and decisively defeating France. The Flanders campaign intensified mutual antipathy and probably committed both sides even more completely to the war by pitting German and British forces against each other for the first time in large numbers and thereby causing heavy losses for both. These results and the German failure to take the Channel coast as a base from which to strike at England marked the transition to a longer war.

While Falkenhayn was failing in Flanders, events were developing differently in Poland. The situation at the end of October was inauspicious for the Central Powers. The Germans and Austro-Hungarians were forced to withdraw from Poland, whereas Russian strength may have reached its apogee at this point—maximum troops and minimum shortages. Rumors again circulated that Japanese troops would join the Russians. The fighting ability of Austro-Hungarian troops in Poland declined and was diminished by diversions against Serbia, Rumania, and Italy. The entry of Turkey did not improve the situation markedly since it did not force Russian diversions from Poland. Hindenburg expected the Russians to exploit these favorable factors by making a bold thrust into Silesia after they secured their southern flank against the Austro-Hungarians in Galicia and their northern flank against the Germans in East Prussia. Since his response to such a Russian attack was dependent on the uncertain reinforcements from the west, Hindenburg could only project tentative goals. His minimum objective would be to protect Silesia and his maximum goal would be to deal the Russians a serious defeat.[5]

The strategy of the Central Powers depended, however, on Russian actions. Grand Duke Nicholas concluded from their rapid retreat that the Germans had been defeated and ordered preparations for precisely the "deep breakthrough into Germany between the Vistula and the Sudeten" which Hindenburg had predicted. Nicholas anticipated success for the impending operation when the Austro-Hungarian withdrawal from Galicia seemed to secure his southern flank.[6]

The Germans responded immediately. When it became clear to them that the Russian center would discontinue its advance, Hindenburg and Ludendorff made another of their characteristically bold decisions to accept risks in order to seek success. They ordered the transfer of five corps from their center in Silesia to East Prussia for an attack on the Russian northern flank. This decision had paradoxical effects on both Austro-German relations and German strategy. Hindenburg would concentrate in the north while Conrad would protect Silesia to compensate for the reinforcements Falkenhayn had refused. The net effect was therefore a clockwise-northward shift of Austro-German forces and a transferral of the encircling arm from the southern (Austro-Hungarian) wing to the northern (German) wing.[7]

The Germans won a surprising success in the initial operations. Their transfer of troops to the north went unnoticed by the Russians, who had accelerated preparations for establishing "a jumping off position for a thrust deep into Germany" in anticipation of precisely such a German maneuver. The German objective was to strike at the Russian northern flank and then break through against the Russian rear. The Germans opened a large gap in the Russian northern flank, so Grand Duke Nicholas postponed his offensive but did not withdraw. This decision surprised Hindenburg, who apparently expected that German pressure would force Grand Duke Nicholas to evacuate the Polish salient altogether. Consequently, the situation had altered. Rather than causing a deadlock, the Russian and German actions created the possibility of a decisive outcome on the eastern front. At the risk of becoming more committed in the north and less able to meet an eventual Russian thrust into Silesia, Hindenburg decided to exploit his advance in order to encircle the Russian forces. The unexpected had therefore occurred on both fronts. Falkenhayn was unable to achieve his anticipated minor success, whereas Hindenburg won an unexpected and potentially major success. Events seemed to be determining strategy rather than the reverse.[8]

ANNIHILATION OR ACCOMMODATION?
DEBATE OVER RUSSIA (MID-NOVEMBER)

During the third week of November, a second crisis occurred in German strategy and policy as a result of the events in Flanders and Poland. Falkenhayn failed to fulfill his minimal objective of winning a superficial success to conceal a fundamental failure. The stalemate in the west became increasingly obvious, while the situation in the east suddenly offered a possibility of success.

In an atmosphere of deepening depression at headquarters and recurring doubts about his abilities, Falkenhayn was pressed to discontinue his Flanders attack and turn east. Tirpitz was pessimistic and repeatedly criticized Falkenhayn. Plessen, Tirpitz and Müller observed that the Kaiser was "very depressed

[and] of the the opinion that the attack [in Flanders] was mistaken, has failed and thus [that] the campaign" had been a failure. Although he thought Falkenhayn's report that munitions would last only a week was "devastating," Plessen still agreed with Falkenhayn that "it is a moral defeat of the first class if we leave [the western front] without a decision in our favor. A very bad situation which is compounded by the recent serious losses." Groener noted that Falkenhayn had decided to send fewer troops to the east in order to be able to reinforce the western front, and criticized Falkenhayn for being "too pessimistic and not pacific"; worst of all, the static war which had been developing since the Marne precluded "the great victory." Bethmann expressed concern to Plessen about the losses in Flanders and urged that Falkenhayn be persuaded to halt the attack. Plessen agreed but doubted Falkenhayn would agree since he had become obsessed with Flanders. The Kaiser supported Bethmann's initiative and urged that troops be freed immediately for the east. The intervention by Plessen and Lyncker coincided with renewed failures and Falkenhayn finally discontinued his attack on November 18. It appeared that Falkenhayn could no longer postpone the decision to transfer the main theatre of operations to the eastern front.[9]

Falkenhayn sought, however, to escape this necessity by a recourse suggested to him in the interim by Tirpitz. Falkenhayn admitted to Tirpitz that the situation was "terribly serious" and gave Tirpitz the impression of wanting to seek "a way out more via France than Russia." But Tirpitz regarded this idea as "completely impractical since Russia and France are allies"; he therefore argued that a "way out" should be found via Russia instead. Because Tirpitz felt the defeat of Britain was the primary German objective and that it required concentrating German forces in the west, he considered the war in the east to be a diversion which should be discontinued by an "agreement" with Russia. Tirpitz claimed that Jagow and Plessen had already agreed and swept aside all practical difficulties. In his view Russia would be willing to renounce its allies, and Austria-Hungary and Turkey would make peace with Russia if the Serbian question was resolved. That was the ideal solution for which Falkenhayn had yearned. If Russia could be bought off diplomatically, Falkenhayn could not only avoid the eastern campaign which risked an Anglo-French breakthrough but he could seek victory in the west by concentrating all his forces there.[10]

Falkenhayn suggested this recourse to Bethmann immediately after he discontinued the Flanders attack on the 18th. Falkenhayn contended that Germany could not prevail as long as the Entente remained united. But, if the Entente could be split by the conclusion of a separate peace with either Russia or France, Germany could concentrate all its forces against the remaining enemies, win a decisive victory, and dictate the peace terms. Falkenhayn argued that Russia was the most likely prospect with which to seek such a separate peace and should therefore be let off lightly with an indemnity and border rectifications. He suggested that the appropriate moment for a German sounding of Russia would occur when the Germans had stopped the Russian campaign in progress. Falkenhayn showed less interest in an understanding with France than he had in the conversation with Tirpitz and therefore opposed a German initiative. He nonetheless argued that Germany should not reject a French request for a separate understanding and should grant an "honorable peace" since Germany had to reestablish relations with France after the war. In Falkenhayn's mind Britain was Germany's main enemy but could be starved out by a German U-boat blockade based in Belgium after Germany concluded a separate peace with France and defeated Russia.

Bethmann's reaction was characteristically tentative and ambivalent. He was already aware of the unpromising military situation and seems to have accepted Falkenhayn's general analysis. Bethmann wrote Zimmermann, "after the defeat of France had miscarried during the first period of the war and considering the course which our military operations are taking in the west during the present second stage of operations, [Bethmann doubted] that a military defeat of our enemies is still possible as long as the Triple Entente holds together." According to Bethmann, Falkenhayn was impressed by the "brilliant defensive power" of the French, the difficult situation in Flanders, "a momentarily very embarrassing shortage of artillery munitions," and no longer demonstrated an "outspoken martial spirit." Bethmann regarded developments in Flanders as symptomatic in that the conspicuous bravery of German troops had not produced success. He concluded that "one must describe the situation as serious despite all confidence."

The situation was acceptable if Hindenburg was successful in Poland and if the Germans were able to hold what they had occupied in the east and west. It would be disastrous if "an unfavorable turn of events" occurred, such as the arrival of Japanese troops, extensive British replacements, or "military setbacks which are never out of the question in war." The prospects would improve if military successes were won, if England were distracted by events in South Africa, Egypt and India, if Russia's power of resistance collapsed because of failures, or if French public opinion turned against the war because of fatigue and antipathy toward Britain. However one evaluated it, the situation was certainly not brilliant since the war could only end in mutual exhaustion and military inconclusiveness. The pawns taken by each side canceled each other: the German occupation of Belgium and northern France balanced the Entente's occupation of most of Galicia and the German colonies and Britain's domination over world trade. Germany's demonstration that it could defend itself against the Entente was an advantage if peace resulted on that basis. The disadvantages were that Germany would confront a reinforced Entente in the event of a subsequent war, German power relative to Britain would be low, and, perhaps worst of all, the German "people would regard [such a peace] as thoroughly unsatisfying repayment for such gigantic sacrifices."

German prospects would become brilliant, however, if the Entente could be split. If the German troops on the eastern front were concentrated against France, "a decisive *military victory*" could be won, "we could even reject a French peace offer and with luck bring France to its knees so that it would have to accept all our peace conditions." Germany could then "bend England to [its] will if the navy produced what it promised." A favorable balance sheet could thereby be achieved. "At the price of leaving things in the east generally as they were before the war, [Germany] could create attractive conditions in the west [and] the Triple Entente would thus be done away with." Bethmann's natural caution made him recognize that the defeat of France and Britain was not certain even if Russia left the war. He was also more skeptical than Falkenhayn about Russia's willingness to conclude a separate peace with Germany. Russia, he thought, might do so if Germany occupied most of Poland but would probably not after another defeat by Hindenburg in the operations then in progress. Bethmann nonetheless concluded that he could "not resist Falkenhayn's continual pressure for a separate understanding with Russia [and therefore agreed that] the possibility must be thought through at least."[11]

PROCRASTINATION NOT CONCENTRATION:
NO EASTERN DECISION (LATE NOVEMBER)

The commanders in the east meanwhile intensified their pressure for transfer of the main operations to the east. Austro-Hungarian Archduke Frederick asserted to Hindenburg that the whole eastern situation including the decisions of Rumania and Bulgaria depended on receiving enough German reinforcements to defeat Russia. Falkenhayn nonetheless gave dilatory answers to requests for reinforcements and implied that they were superfluous since the Russians had apparently discontinued their advance. Conrad, severely critical and deeply bitter, reminded Falkenhayn that a decision could be won only in the east and threatened to renounce the campaign altogether. Hindenburg warned that reinforcements would have to be larger the longer they were delayed and Ludendorff pressed for a specific deadline. These arguments were supported by Groener, Tirpitz and Hungarian Minister President Tisza.[12]

The considerations Falkenhayn raised in his discussion with Bethmann seem, however, to have confirmed his resistance. He put Conrad off by predicting that reinforcements could not arrive in time to affect the battles then in progress. Falkenhayn tried to mollify Ludendorff by claiming that considerable forces had already been sent and that more would make no fundamental difference. He argued that at best the Russians might be pushed back and forced to evacuate Galicia which would be politically desirable but not worth the risk of an Anglo-French breakthrough or a British attack on the German North Sea coast. He nonetheless promised to send reinforcements gradually as they could be released from the western front. Falkenhayn thus opposed seeking a fundamental decision in the east.[13]

The battles in Poland reached a crisis during the fourth week of November. After their early success against the Russian northern flank, the Germans sought to encircle the Russian forces there despite the advance of another Russian army from the east. It was uncertain whether the Germans would encircle one Russian army before being encircled by the other. The fluidity of the situation fostered grandiose aspirations and terrible anxieties on both sides. When the Germans discontinued their attack and managed to break out, the crisis passed. The Germans failed to win the anticipated decision, but they took many prisoners and deflected the Russian thrust into Silesia. The antagonists seem to have been more grateful to avoid defeat than disappointed to miss victory. Both consequently discontinued operations and reconstituted their forces.[14]

Hindenburg and Ludendorff now turned again on Falkenhayn. Their bitterness was probably intensified by the anxieties and unfulfilled aspirations inspired by the campaign. It was reinforced when Falkenhayn rejected their renewed request with the warning that "no further reinforcements are to be reckoned on since all victories which can be won in the east only at the cost of the west are worthless." Ludendorff angrily blamed the eastern stalemate on Falkenhayn's lack of clarity and tardy reinforcements. Falkenhayn appeared to reverse his position when he told Hindenburg that "success in the war now demands that the offensive in northern Poland not peter out and develop into a static war as in the west." He promised that further reinforcements would therefore be sent to "renew the offensive . . . at any price before the [Russians] can transfer strong forces from the south." His reversal was probably more apparent than real. In urging a "success," Falkenhayn was probably less anxious to defeat the Russians (he doubted that it was possible) than to disappoint Russian hopes for success and thereby encourage their willingness to conclude a separate peace. The conflict between Falkenhayn and Hindenburg was not resolved, but was at least concealed for the moment.[15]

Falkenhayn's behavior can probably be explained in terms of priority he gave and continued to give the western front. He believed that the eastern front was a diversion to be removed as quickly as possible with minimum risk to the western front. There are some indications that Falkenhayn genuinely intended to seek a decision in the east, but circumstantial evidence suggests he did not. He could not resume a large-scale offensive in the west for the moment because men and munitions were exhausted. Time was required to build reserves of men by extracting contingents from the existing lines and replacing them with fortifications. He could stockpile munitions only by restricting expenditures and awaiting new supplies. He therefore discontinued operations in the west and ordered preparations for a protracted defense. Falkenhayn made it clear, however, that the campaign in the west was only postponed and not renounced. As he authorized more reinforcements for the eastern front, Falkenhayn warned Ludendorff that they would be the last since he doubted that a decision could be achieved in the east. This interpretation is reinforced by Falkenhayn's suggestion to Bethmann that a separate peace be sought with Russia and by his excitement when that possibility subsequently occurred. The possibility of a separate peace with Russia may have caused him to exaggerate the importance of "a success in northern Poland [which] would decide not only the Galician question but probably the war." If that could be achieved, Falkenhayn thought Russia might be sufficiently discouraged to conclude a separate peace which would make reinforcement of the eastern front unnecessary. A success by Hindenburg would thus obviate, not justify, the need for further transfers to the east. These considerations suggest that Falkenhayn probably never intended to concentrate in the east and merely sought to win time for resuming operations in the west.[16]

The argument had paradoxical overtones. Falkenhayn, the nonadherent to the Schlieffen school, agreed with Schlieffen in doubting that a fundamental defeat of Russia was possible. Hindenburg, Ludendorff, Hoffmann and Groener —all devotees of Schlieffen—were at variance with Schlieffen when they argued that the Russians could be encircled. The open space which gave Hindenburg mobility had caused Schlieffen to conclude that the Russians could never be defeated because they could always withdraw to avoid encirclement. These contradictions had no practical results. Success rather than consistency was the object of each side in the debate.

FALKENHAYN OR HINDENBURG? STRATEGY IMPLICATES PERSONALITIES (LATE NOVEMBER–EARLY DECEMBER)

Disagreements over strategy implicated personalities and precipitated an unsuccessful attempt to replace Falkenhayn with Hindenburg. During the second half of November and beginning of December criticism of Falkenhayn became even more intense and widespread. It perhaps reflected the general frustration with the military stalemate as much as specific evaluation of Falkenhayn. The Kaiser may have shared this view of Falkenhayn at the end of the Flanders campaign. Groener was increasingly critical, felt Falkenhayn lacked support among his subordinates and younger officers, and decided that "the best arrangement is doubtless Hindenburg-Ludendorff." Falkenhayn was also condemned by Bavarian Crown Prince Rupprecht (Commander of the German Sixth Army in Flanders), the Prussian Crown Prince, the Kaiserin and Moltke. The general criticism of Falkenhayn affected Bethmann, who decided that a change in strategy and possibly a new strategist were necessary. His relations with Falkenhayn until that time were mixed but not poor. Their mutual discussions on strategy had indicated that Falkenhayn recognized the interdependence of strategy and policy. Their discussions also revealed their fundamentally similar evaluations of the military situation, i.e., that an Anglo-French defeat depended on a separate peace with Russia. But significant differences also emerged. Falkenhayn minimized the obstacles to an understanding with Russia while Bethmann maximized them. Furthermore Bethmann suspected that Falkenhayn wanted to shift responsibility for a military failure to the civilians if a separate peace with Russia was not achieved.[17]

Bethmann was probably influenced by the stronger personalities of Zimmermann, Ludendorff and Hindenburg. Zimmermann assumed that Germany's primary war aim was a peace which was "not only respectable but also lasting" which could be achieved only by "an energetic reckoning" with both England and Russia since both constituted "permanent threats" to Germany. Although this was generally accepted by German leaders in the case of England, as Bethmann's account of the conversation with Falkenhayn showed, Zimmermann felt it was not regarding Russia since he had "repeatedly" opposed suggestions of a separate peace with Russia. He thought it was essential for Germany to defeat Russia completely in order to preserve Austria-Hungary, German influence in Turkey, and ultimately its own existence. To achieve that goal Zimmermann advocated the defensive in the west and a concentration against Russia—i.e., the strategy of Hindenburg and Ludendorff. If Germany's military situation nonetheless necessitated a separate peace, Zimmermann felt it should be with France rather than Russia because France was "the least dangerous of our main enemies." If a separate peace with Russia proved unavoidable after all, Zimmermann urged that the initiative be left to Russia since a German move would imply weakness and that would solidify rather than shatter the Entente. He thought that such a Russian initiative might be encouraged by the defeat of Serbia and that it should be accepted only if Austria-Hungary and Turkey were agreeable. There is no evidence, but it is possible that Zimmermann urged Bethmann to seek the replacement of Falkenhayn by Hindenburg, as suggested to Bethmann by Hertling and Lerchenfeld.[18]

If Bethmann was not already persuaded that a change of strategy was necessary, his visit at the beginning of December to Hindenburg's headquarters seems to have convinced him. The frustration and doubt which prevailed at German headquarters in the west contrasted sharply with the confidence at headquarters on the eastern front. Hindenburg, Ludendorff and Hoffmann were impressed by Bethmann's political sophistication and thenceforth regarded him as a supporter against Falkenhayn, whose conduct of the western campaign and tardy reinforcement of the eastern front they criticized. When Bethmann informed them that Falkenhayn advocated a separate peace with Russia, they were indignant and Ludendorff regarded the proposal as tantamount to treason as long as it was still possible to defeat Russia. Bethmann returned to Berlin convinced that Russia could be dealt a severe military defeat in preparation for a separate understanding.[19]

Bethmann now sought a change of strategy and—if necessary—a new strategist. He urged a shift of the major theatre to the eastern front, but Falkenhayn refused and asserted that the army was a "worn-out tool" which could achieve no decision and would be fortunate to hold on all fronts. This response may have confirmed Bethmann's determination to seek Falkenhayn's replacement. He urged Lyncker and Plessen to have the Kaiser replace Falkenhayn with Ludendorff and limit Falkenhayn to the War Ministry. When Lyncker refused, Bethmann dropped the idea because he apparently felt that its success depended on the support of the Kaiser's most trusted and intimate advisers. Since Lyncker and Plessen seem to have sensed the Kaiser's preference for Falkenhayn and dislike of Ludendorff, they not only supported Falkenhayn's agitation for a rapid separate understanding with Russia but persuaded the Kaiser to augment Falkenhayn's authority by formalizing his appointment as Chief of General Staff. The attempt to replace Falkenhayn thereby failed.[20]

The incident produced no practical result at the moment, but it had revealing ramifications. It demonstrated that policy and strategy as well as statesmen and strategists are interdependent. The events which began with Falkenhayn's sounding of Bethmann ended paradoxically with Bethmann's seeking Falkenhayn's replacement. The incident indicated that the relative power of civil and military authorities which had tipped toward the soldiers during the early months of the war had returned to a rough balance. The incident was a preview of the subsequent pressure placed on Falkenhayn to turn east and it revealed his near-total dependence on the Kaiser. Most importantly, it was evidence of the German frustration which fostered the need for both a scapegoat and a savior.

EVENTS REINFORCE DECISIONS:
THE MILITARY EVENTS (EARLY DECEMBER)

The debate over strategy was discontinued for the moment because Falkenhayn retained his authority. The postponement was reinforced by the situation in both east and west. Events in Poland reached a dramatic climax at the end of November, but there was no decision, and subsequent operations would test whether one was still even possible. At first it seemed that no decision was likely since the German troops were exhausted and the Russian commanders were considering a withdrawal. Falkenhayn, in a meeting at the beginning of December with Conrad, nonetheless advocated seeking "political success" by pushing the Russians back but he opposed further pursuit. Conrad was more optimistic and expected a "decision" as a result of the Austro-German advance. The Germans and Austro-Hungarians therefore decided to continue operations in Poland. A success suddenly seemed possible when the Russians began to withdraw and exposed their army in Poland to encirclement. The likelihood of such an eventuality disappeared, however, when Russian resistance stiffened, Austro-Hungarian attacks in southern Poland failed, the Serbs defeated the Austro-Hungarians, and the Russians invaded Bukovina. Both sides now recognized that victory was impossible for the moment and the eastern campaign thereby ended in stalemate as had the western.[21]

In the interim the initiative in the west had been left to the French. The Germans had shortened their lines, fortified positions, and established a more efficient organization during the pause in operations. Falkenhayn's efforts to accumulate large reserves were unsuccessful, however, probably because he opposed large-scale withdrawals. Joffre meanwhile pursued contradictory objectives but men and munitions were exhausted. He pursued a strategy of attrition involving continual small attacks although it was necessary to accumulate reserves by restricting operations. Despite the fact that German transfers to the eastern front would facilitate a French breakthrough, he sought to deter them since a German reinforcement might cause the Russians to discontinue their offensive. A French breakthrough required concentration, munitions, and Anglo-French-Russian coordination but all these prerequisites were lacking in the French attacks during December. The Germans recognized that the French were seeking to deter withdrawals rather than break through and the French achieved no significant results.[22]

These operations produced no decision on either front but they had important implications. Falkenhayn's fears that the French would capitalize on German withdrawals and achieve a breakthrough were groundless. The efficiency of the German defenses revived German morale on the western front. If they could not defeat their enemies, the Germans could at least repel them. Conversely, the French attacks demonstrated that the French were far from being defeated but that they could not defeat the Germans. It became even more evident that a successful breakthrough by either side required tremendous reserves of men and munitions which would take considerable time to accumulate. The lack of a decision on the eastern front implied a longer war rather than a separate peace with Russia. Events on both fronts reinforced the military stalemate which had been evolving since early November.[23]

WEST NOT EAST:

FALKENHAYN'S APPARENT VICTORY (LATE DECEMBER)

Falkenhayn retained his post and the debate over strategy abated during the intensified operations of mid-December, but he had not resolved the differences over strategy with his critics. He was nonetheless determined to reimpose his authority and sought to fix the course of future operations.

Falkenhayn again agreed with Conrad that the Russians should be pushed farther back but he opposed Conrad's suggestion of a large, double encirclement since the Central powers lacked the means and Russia could withdraw too quickly. Conrad personally rejected Falkenhayn's suggestion of a combined Austro-German attack on Serbia as a diversion. Confronted with Falkenhayn's renewed resistance, Conrad again sought support from Hindenburg and Ludendorff for a large offensive in Poland. Falkenhayn's exchanges with Hindenburg and Ludendorff seemed less bitter during this period than they had a month before. Ludendorff and Falkenhayn agreed that the Russians should be pushed back and that a combined Austro-German attack of Serbia should then be launched. But Falkenhayn warned Hindenburg that he would have to give up rather than receive forces. Falkenhayn rejected Conrad's proposed offensive into Poland as impractical because of Austro-Hungarian weakness, winter conditions, and the threat of a Russian attack on its northern flank. Even if such a campaign were feasible, he doubted it could ever encircle the Russians in Poland because they could always withdraw.[24]

Falkenhayn's critical consideration remained the achievement of his objectives in the west and not the German difficulties in the east. As soon as the Russians were thrown back, Falkenhayn recommended a "more restricted conduct of war in the east" so that "considerable forces can be made ready for transport to the western front in the second half of January." He planned to resume the offensive there when the shortages of men and munitions were alleviated and the problems on the eastern front were stabilized or even removed through a separate peace with Russia. His projected operations in the west were to be a "strong offensive" which he hoped would defeat the Anglo-French. Falkenhayn apparently had survived failure and prevailed over his critics.[25]

It appeared that the pattern of operations in 1914 would continue in 1915. The western front would apparently remain primary and the eastern front secondary. Had this been the case, the history of the war might have been significantly different. Falkenhayn might have launched an offensive in 1915 like his attack on Verdun in 1916. Germany might have either prevailed on the western front or exhausted itself and its western opponents. Russia might then have dominated the eastern front, caused the collapse of Austria-Hungary, and even determined the course of the conflict.

All this, however, did not come to pass. A revolt was already brewing against Falkenhayn, who was eventually forced to renounce his offensive on the western front and accept a campaign first against Russia and then against Serbia. He was ultimately to postpone his western campaign for a year. Operations during 1915 became a test of the propositions advocated by Hindenburg, Ludendorff and Conrad rather than Falkenhayn. As a result, the Anglo-French had the initiative in the west, the Germans dominated in the east, Austria-

Hungary was preserved, Russia weakened, and the Balkan states and Turkey increasingly drawn in. The redirection of German strategy affected the subsequent character of the war.[26]

THE EASTERN DISTRACTION:
AUSTRIA-HUNGARY &
THE BALKANS

THE BITTER NECESSITY: AUSTRO-GERMAN RELATIONS

The debate over strategy during November and December 1914 involved political considerations. Falkenhayn's argument that Germany could win only if it concentrated on one front implied that it was necessary to renounce military and political objectives on the other. He advocated seeking victory in the west partly because of military considerations, i.e., his conviction that France could be defeated more easily than Russia. But he was also motivated by the political concerns that Russia seemed more inclined to conclude a separate peace and Britain was Germany's main opponent. Falkenhayn believed therefore that military victory and political aspirations in the east had to be subordinated to a victory and achievement of German aspirations in the west. In this sense, he considered the east to be an unfortunate distraction. His view seemed to have prevailed at the end of December 1914. Military victory in the west and a separate peace with Russia seemed to be the guiding principles of German strategy and policy.

Pressures were already building up, however, to alter these priorities. The demands for a reversal of German strategy were immediately successful, and accompanied by proposals to give political objectives in the east equal if not greater consideration. Some of the suggestions were made by members of the German government, most notably Zimmermann.[1] Germany's allies and the Balkan neutrals consistently tried to influence the strategic planning. As long as a quick victory seemed possible, these pressures were largely ignored by German leaders who maintained only the minimum necessary communication and coordination as an operating procedure toward the east. But when the short-war illusion was shattered by the reality of military stalemate and the prospect of a longer conflict, eastern questions became more difficult to negate.

The alliance between Germany and Austria-Hungary began to come full circle at the end of 1914. The July crisis demonstrated greater interdependence than the alliance had revealed during the previous years but it was followed by several months of relative independence. Austria-Hungary demanded increasing attention, however, at the end of 1914 and forced a reluctant revival of German interest in the east. This intensified communication was motivated more by necessity than by intimacy or common interest, less by conscious policy than by threatening problems.

The most serious problem of the alliance was the mutual antipathy which developed during the autumn because of differences over strategy. German leaders became increasingly critical. Tirpitz blamed the failures of November on Austro-Hungarian military weakness. Groener concluded that Austria-Hungary was a "corset-ribbed" system whose failures were due to unalterable character traits and lack of "strong will." The most damning criticism was leveled by the German military in the east. Ludendorff claimed that the Austro-Hungarians were useless because their "power of resistance [was] completely broken" and were a detriment to operations. He therefore urged Berlin to counter the extreme pessimism he felt was rife in Vienna. Ludendorff's relations with Conrad became so acrimonious early in November that Falkenhayn felt compelled to intercede. Hugo von Freytag-Loringhoven, the German liaison officer at Austro-Hungarian headquarters, reported early in November that Austro-Hungarian weakness precluded an offensive and required the establishment of a narrow defensive front. Freytag reaffirmed his estimate of Austro-Hungarian weakness in December, but he was sympathetic toward Conrad and critical of Ludendorff. Hindenburg concluded at the end of December that "the Austro-Hungarian command and troops are no longer factors with which a large-scale operation can be undertaken." These complaints are understandable but they reflected a contradiction in German thinking. On the one hand, the Germans went to war in part to deter the dissolution of Austria-Hungary, and they frequently dismissed the expansive aspirations of their ally as unrealistic because of Austro-Hungarian weakness. On the other hand, the Germans were impatient when the Austro-Hungarians demonstrated military weakness.[2]

German complaints were matched by Austro-Hungarian bitterness of which Conrad was the most articulate spokesman. He was alienated at the beginning of November by Ludendorff's strategy and the German efforts to dominate operations on the eastern front. Conrad regarded Falkenhayn's refusal to designate the eastern front as the main theatre as both shortsighted and disloyal. His anger was intensified in mid-December when he learned of Falkenhayn's plans to return to the western front. Thus the attempt to cooperate militarily caused tension instead.[3]

The tension was not limited to disagreements over strategy, and affected policy as well. The end of the short-war illusion forced the allies into greater military interdependence which required policy reevaluations potentially prejudicial to the alliance. The most serious threat in this respect was a separate peace by one of the allies. The separate peace with Russia suggested by Falkenhayn raised fundamental questions. In one sense, a separate peace was the most logical escape for both Germany and Austria-Hungary since Russia was the common denominator of an alliance which could be preserved only by jointly making war or peace with Russia. Conversely, Russia could prove to be the alliance's undoing if the allies concluded separate understandings with Russia. The possibility of peace with Russia consequently implicated the Austro-German alliance.

Rumors of a separate understanding between Austria-Hungary and Russia began circulating just as the Germans started to consider the possibility of a separate peace with Russia at the end of 1914. The Italians were worried that Russia and Austria-Hungary might come to terms at Italy's expense. It was reported that the King of Spain was anxious to mediate such an understanding. High officials in the Austro-Hungarian Foreign Ministry were reputed to favor it even at the expense of other interests. The British and French were distinctly interested in such an escape from the emerging stalemate, but the Russians brusquely rejected it. The possibility was raised by some Austro-Hungarian officials at the end of December but it is unlikely that serious contacts were made at this time or indeed that Vienna wanted them. The Germans were aware of this possibility. Ludendorff relayed the reports to Jagow, Tschirschky, Falkenhayn and Bethmann in November and all agreed that Vienna was unlikely to make peace with Russia because Austria-Hungary would have to sacrifice both territory and its limited remaining prestige in the Balkans.[4]

German leaders meanwhile sought to insure that their own efforts to achieve a separate peace with Russia would not induce Austria-Hungary to leave the alliance. Both Tirpitz and Falkenhayn were aware of this possibility. In their discussion of 18 November, Falkenhayn and Bethmann recognized "the serious danger that Austria would bolt" unless Vienna was informed that Germany was seeking peace with Russia. Falkenhayn reversed himself, however, when a possible channel to Russia was subsequently reported, and argued against concluding a prior agreement with Vienna, whose perseverance he doubted. Bethmann remained convinced that Vienna should be informed and the Austro-Hungarians were told in vague terms which minimized the possibility of a peace with Russia. Vienna approved, but the sounding caused a revealing misunderstanding between the allies. Berchtold did not inform either Hohenlohe or Conrad, who heard about the move through his liaison officer. Conrad immediately concluded that the Germans were anxious to desert Austria-Hungary and demanded an explanation from Berlin. Berchtold reassured Conrad but transmitted the query to Hohenlohe, who denied that Berlin would betray Vienna. Conrad personally informed Falkenhayn that he was opposed to a separate peace with Russia. Rumors nonetheless continued to circulate that both Vienna and Budapest were in contact with members of the Entente. German efforts to conclude a separate peace with Russia therefore threatened their alliance with Austria-Hungary.[5]

The war aims of the two allies also created tension between Vienna and Berlin. The annexation and division of Polish territory following the peace with Russia was the worst obstacle. In their discussions of a separate peace with Russia, German leaders discounted the possibility of annexing Polish territory. But when it seemed possible that the Russians might be pushed beyond the Vistula, Zimmermann suggested to Hohenlohe that occupied Polish territory be divided between the allies. The question precipitated a blowup between Falkenhayn and Conrad because Falkenhayn demanded some of the richer areas. Conrad rejected Falkenhayn's suggestion of an expedition against Serbia with mostly Austro-Hungarian troops because he perceived it as a German ruse to distract Vienna from Poland. The German war aims in the west, particularly with regard to Belgium, were another area of friction. Austro-Hungarian leaders condemned the German attack on Belgium (which they contended had brought England into the war) and the German plans to annex it while Austria-Hungary was fighting for survival against Russia. The Germans seem to have been more favorably disposed toward Austro-Hungarian aims outside Poland. German leaders insisted that a separate peace with Russia should include an Austro-Hungarian reckoning with Serbia, which was an important concern of Berchtold. German leaders also apparently expected that Austria-Hungary would get a large if not the largest share of an indemnity from Russia. The *Mitteleuropa* project and a customs union with Austria-Hungary which was discussed earlier in the autumn received only unofficial attention at the end of 1914.[6]

Despite these specific areas of agreement, Berlin refused a general discussion with Vienna on war aims and was less inclined than its ally to conclude a compromise peace. Berchtold made all the required concessions to caution and then urged Bethmann to accept the American offer of peace mediation providing that it satisfied the aspirations of the Central Powers. Berchtold argued that mediation would allow the Central Powers to influence neutral public opinion favorably and that American mediation might later be desirable. Whether or not the Central Powers responded to the American offer, Berchtold urged a "confidential exchange of ideas between Berlin and Vienna on desirable and feasible war aims, in order to compare them with the price which we must pay for their realization and to estimate the dangers which rigid commitment to overly ambitious aims could involve." Berchtold thought this all the more necessary because of what he believed was "continuous contact" between the Entente, which pursued "a common program at the expense of [the Central Powers] in expectation of a final reckoning." Bethmann, however, emphasized the disadvantages of American mediation and entirely disregarded

Berchtold's suggestion that war aims be discussed with Vienna. Bethmann claimed, perhaps as consolation, that he had assured Tisza that Germany would stand by Austria-Hungary until they had achieved their "common goal." As in domestic politics, Bethmann preferred to sublimate rather than solve alliance problems.[7]

These problems caused German and Austro-Hungarian leaders to make a conspicuous effort at the end of 1914 to reaffirm their alliance publicly. The Kaiser awarded military decorations to the Austro-Hungarian Crown Prince. The alliances with Germany and Turkey were extolled in the Hungarian Parliament. The Kaiser praised both armies publicly after German and Austro-Hungarian military leaders met in early December. Bethmann made what may have been designed as a fundamental reaffirmation of the alliance in his December speech to the Reichstag. The Reichstag sent similar reassurances to the Austrian and Hungarian Parliaments, and the telegrams between Bethmann and Berchtold were published. As is so frequently the case in relations between allies, an increase in private enmity produced more public expressions of amity.[8]

The proclamations concealed but they did not resolve problems. Military setbacks caused deep pessimism in Vienna at the end of 1914. The Austro-Hungarian campaign against Serbia collapsed early in December after a promising beginning in November. The Polish campaign demonstrated that the Russians could not be decisively defeated even though they had divided their forces. Tisza shared the pessimism underlying a Foreign Ministry study on the eventuality of a "minimal peace" which Berchtold defined as the demonstration by Austria-Hungary that Russia could not protect the Serbs. Berchtold espoused the German argument that Italy might be kept neutral by Austro-Hungarian concessions in a discussion with Conrad and Hohenlohe. Internal stresses were added to Hungarian military and diplomatic problems. The Hapsburg Empire needed victory for domestic reasons more than any other power but it was less able to win precisely because of those domestic problems. Yet the empire seems to have made economic adjustments as successfully as the other belligerents. Vienna consequently had genuine and serious problems.[9]

These problems affected the attitudes of Austro-Hungarian leaders. Their pessimism frequently took the form of bitterness toward Germany, which they blamed for Austria-Hungary's difficulties. Viennese rancor toward Berlin may have been crystallized by the appointment of Prince Bülow as German emissary to Rome since Bülow was known to favor Austro-Hungarian concessions to keep Italy neutral. Conrad was embittered by Falkenhayn's advocacy of a separate peace with Russia and he suspected that Falkenhayn's suggestion of an expedition against Serbia was a device to distract Austria-Hungary from Poland. Joseph Baernreither insinuated that Germany had dragged Austria-Hungary into the war. Johann Forgách, Secretary of the Austro-Hungarian Foreign Ministry, asserted that "Germany is politically and militarily to blame for the unfortunate circumstances." Karl von Stürgkh, Austrian Minister President, concluded that it would be "ruinous" for Austria-Hungary to continue fighting only because Germany wanted to achieve its war aims. Hoyos concluded that "there was no organic necessity for . . . Germany to dominate not only Europe but also the world." Conrad mixed hyperbole with honesty when he complained that "one must nonetheless swallow all of the [German disloyalty] and assume before the world the pose of the most intimate agreement and loyalty to the alliance. But in my soul I am fed up with the association." The alliance was no less bitter for being necessary.[10]

Austro-Hungarian statesmen reacted in contradictory ways to these unpromising prospects. In a general sense, they sought "self-preservation by virtue of annexation and hegemony over the Balkans," and they had several hypothetical options. They could accept the fact of their limited power and leave the war by concluding a compromise peace. They could adjust their aspirations to their limited power and continue the war against some opponents by granting concessions to others. They could maintain their aspirations and try to force Germany to help achieve them by concentrating in the east. The first two courses were apparently favored by less optimistic leaders like Berchtold, whereas the last was advocated by the more confident Conrad and Tisza. The collision of these views resulted in a harder line in January 1915. Berchtold was replaced by Tisza's man, Stephan Burian, who resisted German pressures for concessions to Italy and took a generally more independent tack. This change of Austro-Hungarian policy and personnel pushed German policy and strategy toward the east at the beginning of 1915.[11]

THE RIVAL ALLIES: OTTOMAN-GERMAN RELATIONS

German interest in Turkey lapsed curiously after the Turks had been brought into the war early in November. The Turkish entry was an important gain for Germany because it isolated Russia, distracted Anglo-French troops, favorably influenced Balkan politics and supplied the Central Powers a few additional troops in Europe. During the course of the war, the Germans paid for these advantages with considerable financial assistance, military materiel and personnel. But relations were still far from amicable. German-Turkish relations, like all alliances and perhaps more than most, were a patchwork of mostly frustrated efforts by each ally to persuade the other to serve its interests. Despite their relative weakness, the Turks were not noticeably less successful in this sparring. As a result, the alliance was characterized by equal measures of rivalry and reciprocity.[12]

German expectations vis-à-vis the Turks were high but generally frustrated. They hoped to dominate the Turkish army and subordinate Turkish strategy to their own objectives but the Turks retained control of both. The Germans tried from the beginning of the war to incite revolution among the Muslim peoples in the Russian and British Empires but they had made little progress by November 1914. They therefore pressured the Turks to mount an expedition against Egypt in anticipation of significant results but they were disappointed. The Germans also encouraged a Turkish proclamation of a holy war but they were again thwarted. The Turkish offensive operations against Egypt were disappointing and threatened to cause Turkish-Italian frictions. As a result of Turkish suspicions and practical difficulties, German aspirations to extend their economic penetration in the Ottoman Empire during the war were limited. Indeed, it is arguable whether the Germans could have dominated Turkey even if they had won the war.[13]

Turkish domestic problems meanwhile increased. The Turkish treasury was empty by November 1914 and German efforts to aid the Turks were financially expensive and frustrating. The Turkish army still suffered from its earlier wars with Italy and the Balkan states. The Rumanians resisted the passage of goods to Turkey and made it difficult for Germany to supply materiel. The German leaders who valued Turkey highly—particularly Ambassador Wangenheim and Zimmermann—consequently argued in vain for an expedition against Serbia to clear the passage. The Turkish war effort also suffered from internal political problems and a primitive transportation system. Despite these drawbacks, Turkey's military accomplishments were considerable though primarily defensive, most notably at the Straits.[14]

Relations between Germany and Turkey were best illustrated during the renegotiation of their alliance at the end of 1914. In the final discussions before Turkish entry, the Turks asked that certain conditions of their August alliance be adjusted. Bethmann claimed "the preservation and protection of Turkey correspond with our interests and the basic principles of the policy we *must* follow," although Germany had "decided only with great reluctance to conclude a formal alliance with Turkey and considered a further extension of it basically undesirable." He argued that Turkey's future depended less on treaty conditions than on military events: if their alliance won, Turkey would be safe; if it lost, no alliance could save it. Bethmann's logic was impeccable but unpersuasive to the Turks. Bethmann reluctantly authorized open discussions when Ambassador Wangenheim warned that German refusal would cause the pro-intervention Turkish ministers serious difficulties. After difficult negotiations, a draft agreement was reached but Berlin demanded a reduction of liabilities. Berchtold was even more opposed to expanding the alliance but Zimmermann dismissed his objections by warning that a fundamental reconsideration of the alliance might jeopardize Turkey's participation since there was strong opposition to the war in Constantinople. The new German-Turkish treaty was signed at the beginning of January and reflected the hard bargaining. The German guarantee of Turkish territorial integrity was dropped but the treaty extended German obligations and reduced German influence. The Turks would not renew their commitment to allow the German military mission an "effective influence on the general direction of the army." The Austro-Hungarians belatedly declared their adherence to the treaty in March 1915.[15]

The German reservations about the treaty may have been due in part to skepticism about Turkish strength and a desire to avoid diverting scarce German war materiel. The more immediate German consideration, however, was probably the military stalemate. The stalemate made a separate understanding with Russia seem desirable and that affected the German perception of Turkey. Bethmann showed definite reserve toward Turkey in discussing the implication of separate peace with Russia and recognized that Turkey "traditionally had a weak voice at peace conferences." Jagow opposed informing the Turks of the possibility of a separate peace with Russia because the Turks might then conduct the war less vigorously against the British. Zimmermann initially assumed an air of disinterest regarding Turkey, perhaps as a tactic to shock Falkenhayn into ordering an expedition against Serbia. But Falkenhayn called Zimmermann's bluff by advocating a separate peace with Russia. Zimmermann immediately opposed that step because he thought it might jeopardize Germany's alliance with Turkey or at least Turkish operations against the British. Zimmermann felt that if a separate peace with Russia nonetheless proved unavoidable, it should be made acceptable to Turkey and not restrict Turkey's prosecution of the war against Britain. Instead of a separate peace with Russia, Zimmermann recommended a rapid expedition against Serbia to insure communication with Turkey. The choice did not have to be faced directly before the end of 1914, but German efforts to conclude a separate peace with Russia would clearly implicate the German-Turkish alliance in 1915.[16]

The Turkish entry into the war caused neither a significant immediate military reaction from the Entente nor an alteration in the course of operations already in progress. The great powers were too involved in their own struggle to divert large forces either to attack or protect Turkey. Like the Turkish naval expedition against Russia, the Anglo-French bombardment of the Turkish forts at the Dardanelles at the beginning of November was an isolated gesture intended to provoke war. The Germans were concerned about the possibility of an Anglo-French expedition against the Straits. Churchill had already agitated for such a move but the opposition of Kitchener and Grey caused it to be postponed. Entente military activities against Turkey were restricted primarily to repulsing Turkish attacks against the Caucasus and Suez. The only offensive operation undertaken by the Entente was the Indian army expedition into Persia, but even that had the primarily political purpose of encouraging Arab antipathy against their Turkish rulers.[17]

Entente activity was greatest in the area of political questions at the end of 1914. The British had long been aware that it was possible to exploit Arab hostility if the Turks became Britain's enemies. Kitchener, like his German counterparts, was anxious to use revolution to achieve political-military objectives, and he encouraged the Arabs to revolt against the Turks. The British meanwhile declared a protectorate over Egypt and took Cyprus. The discussions between the Entente powers over the future of the Straits were most important although most hypothetical. Ironically, the Straits became available as a desirable strategic prize only after the war was so deadlocked that neither side could take them. The Turkish entry into the war consequently shifted attention from the stalemated west to the apparently mobile east. The efforts of exponents of increased operations in the east were resisted at the end of 1914 but they would succeed at the beginning of 1915.[18]

THE INFERNAL TRIANGLE: BERLIN-VIENNA-ROME

The greatest threats to Austria-Hungary's continued participation in the war were the danger of defeat by Russia and an Italian entry on the side of the Entente. If Italy entered, the Central Powers would face the double disadvantage of a military diversion and diplomatic repercussions in the Balkans which might produce additional enemies. Berlin sought to prevent an Italian entry by appeasing Italy with promises of enemy and Austro-Hungarian territory. The Germans were confronted with choices between two unattractive eventualities: Italy might enter the war if it was unsatisfied with German concessions but Austria-Hungary might withdraw if alienated. The Italians increased their pressure on Berlin at the end of 1914 and the Germans chose to appease the Italians at the risk of alienating the Austro-Hungarians.

The Germans reluctantly put pressure on Vienna. Berlin naturally sought to satisfy the Italians first with promises of Entente territory and their efforts in this direction continued. The Germans already assumed, however, that Italian neutrality required Austro-Hungarian concessions. Zimmermann and Bethmann therefore offered the Trentino to Italy but the offer was refused. The combination of military stalemate and Italian pressure caused a shift in German policy at the end of 1914. Bethmann and Jagow initially resisted but finally agreed to the appointment of Bülow as a special emissary to Rome. The Bülow mission was correctly interpreted as a German decision to exert greater pressure on Vienna although it was officially designated as an effort to achieve a compromise between Rome and Vienna.[19]

Italian policy was the effect as well as the cause of German policy. Minister of Foreign Affairs Giorgio Sonnino agreed with Prime Minister Salandra that Italy could fulfill its aspirations only by going to war against Austria-Hungary. The signs of Italian preparations for war resulted in cooling reactions with Vienna. Salandra announced in the Italian Chamber that Italy would seek to maintain its great power status through a policy of neutrality. He felicitously described the policy as "sacred egotism" and noted that it would be characterized by "Silence and Negotiation." The Italian diplomatic offensive may have been encouraged by Bülow's appointment and the Austro-Hungarian defeat in Serbia. Austria-Hungary's adversity was Italy's opportunity.[20]

Rome's offensive was launched simultaneously in Vienna and Berlin. Sonnino suggested that he and Berchtold begin to discuss their differences and announced his intention to Berlin in the hope that it would put pressure on Vienna. The Italian demarche arrived at a moment of extreme Austro-Hungarian pessimism. Berchtold consistently refused to make concessions in the Trentino in the hope that Italy would do nothing until Italian military preparations were completed in 1915. His refusal was based on the assumption that Italian aspirations were in any case insatiable and that concessions were thus irrelevant. The military setbacks of December, however, made Austria-Hungary more inclined to make concessions in order to avoid or postpone greater evils. Berchtold consequently agreed to discuss concessions. Bülow meanwhile told Sonnino that Italian demands were justified and would be fulfilled. Berchtold gave Tisza, Conrad and others the impression that he had unnecessarily acceded to German pressures. This conclusion, whether true or not, reinforced the conviction of Conrad and Tisza that a stronger personality was required to defend Austro-Hungarian interests and they therefore replaced Berchtold with Burian at the beginning of January. German policy may thus have contributed to a change in Italian policy as well as in Austro-Hungarian policy and personnel. These changes increased Austro-Italian tension and the strains on the Austro-German alliance.[21]

The Italian question primarily concerned the Central Powers at this juncture. Italian statesmen may have decided by the end of 1914 on war with Austria-Hungary. The negotiations in Berlin and Vienna were therefore probably designed as a tactic to elicit offers which could be used to raise the price of an Italian entry with the Entente. Serious Italian negotiations with the Entente were consequently postponed, but Rome nonetheless kept channels open with the Entente. The Entente powers were aware of these events but they were not particularly interested since it was generally assumed that Italy would eventually join the Entente in any case. On the contrary, the Entente powers were seemingly less anxious to encourage Italian aspirations against Austria-Hungary than to discourage them against Turkey. The Entente efforts to effect an alliance with Italy may have been further deterred by the possibility of a separate peace with Austria-Hungary which would be even more useful in defeating Germany. Italy's efforts to auction its services had to wait until the Central Powers were more concerned and the Entente more desperate. The pressures were nonetheless building up already to make Italy another factor in shifting the war away from the western front in 1915.[22]

THE BALKAN LOOKING-GLASS: BULGARIA & RUMANIA

The great power military stalemate at the end of 1914 caused the competition for new allies to assume an unprecedented importance for the great power diplomats. It seemed to them that the small increment of power provided by a new ally might tip the delicate balance toward a decision. Until the beginning of November, the crucial issue of great power diplomacy in the Balkans was the Turkish entry into the war which in turn influenced the policies of the powers toward the Balkan states. The Turkish entry changed the pattern and acted as a catalyst in the Balkan chemistry.[23]

Bulgaria replaced Turkey as the critical question mark in the Balkans. The initial assumption that Bulgaria might exploit the Balkan situation and seize the opportunity to attack Serbia was disproven. Bulgarian Premier Vasil Radoslavoff reaffirmed Bulgarian neutrality since he apparently assumed that an attack on Serbia would risk a Rumanian reprisal. The Entente launched a diplomatic offensive either to insure Bulgarian neutrality or to win its association. Delcassé, Sazonov, and Grey tried but all failed, and Poincaré concluded that Bulgaria might even be slipping into the enemy camp.[24]

Bulgaria was in fact moving slightly toward the Central Powers, which regarded Bulgarian entry as pivotal since Austria-Hungary seemed unable to defeat Serbia without Bulgarian assistance. Bulgaria refused, however, to enter before Serbia had been defeated and also demanded a written guarantee that all Serbian territory it occupied or to which it had historical and ethnic claim would be conceded. Since Bulgarian aid after a Serbian defeat would be superfluous, the Central Powers were at first uninterested. But failure of the Austro-Hungarian campaign against Serbia made the Central Powers more amenable and they finally acceded to Bulgaria's demands at the beginning of 1915. The Central Powers thereby sought to insure at least Bulgarian neutrality if not support. As it turned out, Bulgaria remained quiescent until the spring when the eastern European situation altered radically. The arrangement with Bulgaria increased the likelihood that the war would move east in 1915.[25]

The great power efforts to move Rumania were even less successful. Rumania felt little compulsion to assume the risks of war since it had received concessions from Russia in October to remain neutral. Rumanian policy was strongly influenced, however, by Bulgarian behavior. The competition over Bulgaria caused Rumania to hint that it might join the Entente providing there were guarantees against Bulgaria. The Central Powers knew that Rumania had an agreement with Italy and would probably never join them because of the Hungarian refusal to make concessions to Rumania in Transylvania. But when Bulgaria elected to remain neutral, the Rumanian entry into the war became unlikely.[26]

The fluid situation in the Balkans which apparently resulted from Turkey's entry at the beginning of November became as rigid as the great power stalemate by the end of December. The rigidity of Balkan politics was caused in part by the Balkan balance of power and in part by the great power balance demonstrated by the military stalemate. Neutrality was more appealing than war to the Balkan states until the results of the great power struggle were clearer and thus made the rewards increase and the risks decline. Soldiers and statesmen on both sides recognized that the decisions of the Balkan states were dependent on the great power struggle. Falkenhayn thought success in Flanders would bring in Rumania. Wangenheim asserted that an Austro-German military success in the east was the precondition of Bulgarian entry. Hindenburg agreed with Austro-Hungarian Archduke Frederick that the attitudes of Rumania and Bulgaria depended on how many German troops were on the eastern front. Zimmermann asserted that Bulgaria, Rumania (and even Sweden) might be won over by defeating Russia in Poland. Poincaré condemned the attempts to bribe the Balkan states and concluded that "it is not in the chancelleries but on the French and Russian fronts that we shall win allies."[27]

Stalemate made it difficult, however, to win new allies by demonstrating military superiority and so the great powers faced a dilemma. The stalemate could be broken with the aid of new allies but winning new allies required a military superiority which the stalemate made unlikely. Conversely, the success of one side and an end to the stalemate would make new alliances unnecessary. The great powers were in a quandary—new allies were necessary when they were unlikely to be found but likely only when they would be unnecessary. The Balkans mirrored and could not resolve the great power dilemma. At the end of 1914 all things had conspired to reinforce the great power stalemate.

BRIDGE OR BARRIER? THE SERBIAN PROBLEM

The Serbian problem, like those of other states in the Balkan complex, illustrated the interdependence of strategy and politics. By distracting Austria-Hungary and isolating Turkey, Serbia gave another impulse for Germany to turn away from the western front. Because of Turkey's entry, Serbia became either a bridge or a barrier between the Central Powers and Turkey. When the Turks reported munitions shortages and the threat of Entente attacks on the Dardanelles, it seemed mandatory for Germany to insure that supplies could be sent to Turkey if it were to be kept in the war. Rumanian refusal to allow the passage of shipments to Turkey left the Danube as the only alternative route, but an Austro-German expedition against Serbia was required because the Danube passed through the northeast corner of Serbia.[28]

Such an expedition was consequently debated by German leaders. Zimmermann, consistent with his general interest in the east and his opposition to a separate peace with Russia, was a leading advocate of the proposed campaign. Believing that the fate of Turkey and the whole Balkans was involved, he argued in mid-November that "all other military tasks should therefore be subordinated to the opening of a passage through Serbia." That seemed likely until the Austro-Hungarian campaign against Serbia collapsed at the beginning of

December. The crisis in Poland and Falkenhayn's growing reluctance to transfer more forces to the east caused Falkenhayn to reject the demands of Zimmermann, Bethmann and Jagow for the Serbian expedition. As a result of Zimmermann's prodding, Bethmann sought unsuccessfully to win over the Kaiser. The expedition against Serbia was, however, supported by General Colmar von der Goltz, who asserted that the Turkish situation would not improve unless a passage was quickly guaranteed. Goltz forecast exceptional results possibly to enhance his minority position: he suggested that, if the expedition against Serbia was successful, Turkey would be preserved, Bulgaria and Rumania would join the Central Powers, and a critical advantage in the whole war would be won. Falkenhayn, Bethmann and Ludendorff finally agreed in December that the Central Powers should attack Serbia after the Russians had been pushed beyond the Vistula. When Conrad refused to supply forces, Falkenhayn dropped the idea since he himself was not prepared to give up troops in large numbers for the project. Bethmann concluded at the end of December that any attempt to insure passage to Turkey would be impossible for a considerable period.[29]

The leaders of the Central Powers were not unanimous on the significance of Serbia. Berchtold and Johann von Pallavicini, the Austro-Hungarian ambassador in Constantinople, felt that the primary Austro-Hungarian aim should be what it had been during the July crisis, i.e., to prove that Russia could not protect Serbia against Austria-Hungary. Tisza was, however, less concerned with Serbia and Conrad believed Berchtold was excessively interested in Serbia. These divergences may have contributed to the decision made by Tisza and Conrad to replace Berchtold with Burian. Differences of emphasis also existed between Berlin and Vienna. Serbia was perceived as a war aim by the Austro-Hungarian leaders; it was a means of war for German leaders. [30]

The Germans decided at the end of 1914 to leave Serbia as a barrier rather than transform it into a bridge to Turkey or use it as a bribe to the Balkan states. The Serbian problem was thereby postponed just as the eastern question in general had been. It seemed that the Turks and the Austro-Hungarians would have to fend largely for themselves. But appearances were again deceiving and pressures to march east were already mounting in the German capital. As it turned out, the postponed campaign against Serbia materialized before Falkenhayn's projected campaign against France. The east, which was considered to be an unfortunate distraction at the end of 1914, became the major attraction in 1915.

IMPLACABLE BUT INVULNERABLE: GERMANY & ENGLAND

THE MAIN ENEMY: GERMANY PERCEIVES ENGLAND

The military stalemate at the end of 1914 completed a metamorphosis in the German government's attitude toward its opponents. In July and August the government perceived France and especially Russia as Germany's main enemies, whereas Britain was envisaged as the potential mediator and a passive bystander. But the roles were gradually reversed so that by the end of 1914 Britain was viewed as the main obstacle to a German victory, while Russia and France were seen as British tools.

The increasing contradictions of German policy which emerged as the result of the military stalemate were most evident in connection with Britain. German success was dependent on a short war and rapid victory, but the stalemate promised a longer war potentially advantageous to Britain. Germany had tried to destroy the balance of power but the stalemate implied that the British balance of power policy more closely conformed to the actual distribution of strength. Germany's objective was a continental hegemony, but Britain, the only noncontinental power, was perceived as the main opponent. The Franco-Russian armies played the greatest role in precluding a rapid German victory, but the Germans regarded Britain as their main obstacle. Britain went to war more reluctantly than the other powers and reticently formalized its alliance, but it was regarded as the leader of the enemy alliance. Germany perceived Britain as the most obstinate opponent, but Britain was least susceptible to German pressure. German policy was therefore in a dilemma: Britain would have to renounce its allies if Germany was to win, but Germany would have to defeat Britain's allies before Britain would renounce them. Germany's rising antipathy toward Britain was reflected in the confidential statements of German leaders at the end of 1914. German bitterness was probably motivated in part by a desire to alleviate frustration and explain failure by seeking a scapegoat. It may also have been expressed in an effort to distract attention—particularly of the German public—from the real problems of defeating France and Russia. On another level, German rancor toward the British was perhaps a calculated policy intended to encourage France and Russia to conclude a separate peace.

Tirpitz's motive in suggesting to Falkenhayn that Germany conclude a separate peace with Russia was Tirpitz's ubiquitous anglophobia. He believed Germany's enemy was England, and that the war against Russia should be discontinued. Falkenhayn made the same assumption in his discussion with Bethmann: "in this defeat of England, . . . Falkenhayn perceives the sole and sufficient guarantee against renewed wars." Falkenhayn argued that the German goal could be achieved by concluding a separate peace with Russia and concentrating "to defeat France and England so thoroughly that we could dictate peace." Once France had been defeated, "we would crush England, if it did not submit completely to our will, by starving it out with a blockade from Belgium, even if months were necessary to do so." In refusing Hindenburg's request for reinforcements, Falkenhayn asserted that "our most dangerous enemy is not in the east but England, with which the conspiracy against Germany stands and falls. [Since] we can injure [England] only if we maintain contact with the sea," he did not want to risk an Anglo-French counteroffensive which would drive the German army away from the Channel.[1]

Bethmann was somewhat less sanguine than Falkenhayn, but he nonetheless recognized that a separate peace with Russia would allow Germany to crush France and then "we can compel England to bend to our will if the navy does what it promises." If a separate peace was not concluded with Russia, Bethmann believed the war was likely to drag on until both sides were exhausted. That outcome, he felt, would favor England more than Germany since England would dominate world trade and play off France and Russia against Germany. Despite his reservations, Bethmann seems to have shared the views of Falkenhayn and Tirpitz that Britain was the main opponent. Bethmann told the Turks that "the stakes of the struggle are destruction of England's world supremacy." He wrote Berchtold that "England is our most obstinate enemy."[2]

This view was shared by other German leaders. Zimmermann felt it was widely held: "Determination to carry the battle with England to the ultimate seems to me so general and firm that one may well dispense with further discussion to justify it at this point." Tirpitz advocated the use of all available means, including large-scale bombing raids on London, to defeat England. The German commanders in the Flanders campaign expressed hatred of England in their exhortations to their troops. Groener shared the view that England was exploiting France to destroy German commerce and was the "soul of French resistance." The importance of the Anglo-German conflict had become virtually an unquestioned faith among German leaders.[3]

German leaders apparently believed that the German people shared their antipathy toward England. Bethmann asserted to Zimmermann that the defeat of England was "demanded by popular sentiment." Groener wrote that

Swabians, Prussians, Bavarians and Saxons were united in their hate of the English. Gerard reported to House that "the hate [in Germany] against England is phenomenal—actual odes of hate are recited in the music-halls."[4]

Nonetheless, German leaders felt the compulsion to reinforce this sentiment in the German public. Commanders encouraged it among their troops. Hertling told Italian journalists that England had started the war to destroy the German economy, was "misusing" France, Belgium and Russia, and disdaining neutral rights. Bethmann made hatred of England the major theme of his Reichstag speech in December, his first public appearance since the beginning of the war. He claimed that although the "superficial responsibility" for the war was the Russian government's, "the fundamental responsibility belongs to the British government" since it "let this world war come in order to cut the life's blood of its greatest European competitor in the world market." To this end, Britain exploited "its political allies in the Entente," which had been "the work of England" and was its "strongest tool." Consequently, "the first and foremost principle of English policy remains to check the free development of German power by means of the balance of power." Bethmann concluded that "the ring was closed" around Germany by England. In response to the British claim that they would fight on "until Germany is defeated economically and militarily," Bethmann announced that *"Germany will not let itself be defeated."* He apparently struck the prevailing note since his attacks on Britain received "stormy applause" from all parties. The German government meanwhile sought to demonstrate that England had planned the war by publishing Russian documents on the Anglo-Russian negotiations during the spring of 1914 for a naval agreement.[5]

Britain thus seemed to embody all the obstacles to the achievement of German aspirations. Since Germany perceived the existing balance of power and the prewar European state system as being antithetical to a German victory, they were alleged to be the goals of British policy. British and German objectives were mutually exclusive: the success of the one required the failure of the other. A compromise would imply a defeat for Germany since it would perpetuate the system on which British policy was based. Consequently, German success required destruction of the state system, the balance of power and above all the Entente.

German leaders recognized that the defeat of Britain would be difficult to achieve. Groener begrudgingly acknowledged British tenacity, while Bethmann and Jagow doubted Admiral Capelle's assertion that Britain was becoming tired. The separate peace with Russia was one possible means for defeating the British, since it would shatter the Entente and might discourage France sufficiently to make it conclude peace. If Britain did not seek peace as a result of having lost its allies, a U-boat war would be conducted against British commerce until Britain succumbed. German leaders meanwhile hoped that Britain might be diverted from the war in Europe by threatening its colonies, in particular an attack on Egypt or revolt of Muslims in the British Empire. Alternatively, the British might be bribed to accept German continental domination by offering them pawns such as Belgium. Unfortunately for the Germans none of these recourses was even as promising as the military means which had already failed. Britain was invulnerable to Germany at the end of 1914.[6]

British invulnerability was reflected in the relative absence of German war aims which could be achieved at British expense. Like other aspects of Germany's behavior toward Britain, German war aims policy regarding Britain involved a paradox—Germany perceived Britain as its most vicious enemy, but Britain would suffer least because it was least vulnerable. The German war aims policy toward Russia and France reversed this situation—although they were considered to be less dangerous than Britain and Germany sought separate understandings with both, they would be expected to suffer because they were vulnerable.

German war aims policy nonetheless implicated Britain indirectly, particularly in the case of Belgium. Bethmann's policy on Belgium was as ambivalent as his evaluation of Germany's military prospects against Britain. At one extreme, he implied that there was a possibility of an understanding with Britain when he opposed the outright annexation of Belgium because it would force Britain to continue the war. At the other, he implied that agreement with England was impossible by reinforcing the general sentiment against Belgium by publicly rejecting the reestablishment of Belgian neutrality because Belgium was an ally of Britain. Bethmann tried to establish *de facto* German military and economic domination over Belgium, but apparently wanted to do so without alienating Britain, which was unlikely. Bethmann's policy was based on a contradiction: the British might have accepted German domination of Belgium if they could not prevent it; but then British acceptance would have been irrelevant. Conversely, the British would not accept German domination of Belgium as long as they had the power to resist it; but those were the circumstances when it was desirable. Thus, an Anglo-German reconciliation over Belgium would have been most useful when least likely and least useful when most likely. The pursuit of these contradictory objectives made Belgium a "frightful problem".for Bethmann, who could "seek only the least bad among all the solutions."[7]

Other German leaders were less ambivalent. Delbrück and Zimmermann favored a harder and more consistent line toward Belgium and they advocated announcing the end of Belgian autonomy, administering Belgium in "more or less dictatorial fashion" and promising that Belgium would become a German crown colony if it behaved. Falkenhayn wanted to maintain German control over the North Sea coast as a base for subsequent U-boat operations against Britain. The Kaiser apparently agreed with Tirpitz's argument for keeping the Flemish coast. Groener advocated a degree of domination equivalent to annexation in all but name. The construction of a *Mitteleuropa* as a base from which to continue the struggle against Britain was implied by the German objectives but these goals were not specifically discussed at the end of 1914. German policy and its war aims toward Britain may have been affected by the military stalemate. The immediate problem of winning was of greater concern to the German leaders than the problem of determining how to exploit their as yet unrealized gains.[8]

REJECTION OF COMPROMISE:
POLICIES PRECLUDE PEACE

The antipathy between England and Germany was demonstrated by their instantaneous and simultaneous rejection of compromise despite their mutual assumption that a stalemate would result in compromise. German strategic thinking was based on the assumption that Germany could not win a long war, and that assumption justified the risks and disadvantages the German strategists accepted by seeking a short war. The assumption also implied that a compromise peace was preferable to a long war once a short war was proven to be impractical. British policy traditionally sought to establish and defend a balance of power in Europe. The stalemate demonstrated that this balance existed, however precariously. But both Germany and Britain rejected the recourse of compromise which they regarded as dangerous rather than desirable. To the Germans, compromise would perpetuate a balance of power which seemed a threat to their self-preservation and aspirations. To the British, compromise would leave a strong Germany facing a tenuous Entente. To both nations compromise implied only a temporary peace and the likelihood of new wars. Consequently, both preferred the risks involved in continuing the war rather than compromising. A continuation of the war could result in either a German victory and reconstitution of the existing state system or an Entente victory and removal of the German threat. The stalemate, however, made victory by either side unlikely. The Germans and British were therefore in a trap much like the other powers. The stalemate made compromise undesirable but logical, and made continuation of the war desirable but illogical.

The growing awareness of military stalemate on both sides was hypo-thetically conducive to neutral mediation for a compromise peace. The Papacy or Italy might have taken the initiative but other neutral observers regarded mediation as premature. Although German leaders were opposed to a compro-mise peace or peace conference, Jagow suggested preparing for the possibility and Lerchenfeld retrospectively regarded November 1914 as the most opportune moment for peace.[9]

Soundings for an Anglo-German understanding came from two sources of which the United States was the more persistent and important. The possibility of American mediation recurred when House approached Dumba, the Austro-Hungarian ambassador in Washington, at the beginning of October. According to Dumba, House gave him a confidential outline of Wilson's "projected mediation," the first stage of which would be "an unbinding exchange of ideas" on three points which would constitute "the basis for later peace negotiations: no large territorial demands, mutual territorial guarantees, and partial disarmament as a guarantee against militarism." When he forwarded Dumba's report to Bethmann at the beginning of November, Berchtold granted the usual reservations but was basically sympathetic. He proposed that if the Central Powers could achieve their vital interests and necessary compensation, they should not prolong the war. Even if peace under those terms was unlikely, Berchtold argued that American mediation should not be rejected out of hand since it provided the Central Powers an opportunity to make their case to the neutrals.[10]

The reaction of German leaders was the best indication of their attitude toward a compromise peace at this juncture. Bethmann replied that no analogous American sounding had reached Berlin. He agreed with Berchtold that outright rejection would not be "opportune" since it would imply that the Central Powers were committed to a war *à outrance*. Bethmann also felt that the offer was impractical since the Anglo-German understanding which the Americans sought because of commercial considerations was "the most difficult to achieve." Perhaps in order to shame Berchtold out of defending Wilson's proposals, Bethmann denigrated them as so "utopian," "do-goodish," "empty" and "panting for peace" that "it was difficult for a *Realpolitiker* to give a precise answer to them." Furthermore, the American proposal constituted a "definite danger" since it implied the possibility of a peace conference at which the Central Powers would have a two against three disadvantage. His more positive reason for rejecting the offer was the possibility that the Central Powers could do better by continuing the war than by compromising. "If the fortune of arms is favorable to us, we shall hardly be able to renounce all the prizes of victory." Bethmann's main consideration may have been a point he deleted from his reply to Berchtold. "A poor [i.e., compromise] peace with England would mean only the perpetuation of a state of war" since "England is our most obstinate enemy and mediation could hardly produce an acceptable result." A compromise peace would only sublimate but not solve Germany's conflict with Britain. Bethmann therefore concluded that House's mediation offer should be discouraged with the standard argument that the Central Powers were only defending themselves.[11]

Having parried the offer of American mediation, the German government was immediately approached by the Danes. On the day following Bethmann's reply to Berchtold, the Kaiser received a report from Ballin on his conversation with a Danish official, Hans Andersen. Andersen claimed that he was sent at the beginning of November by Danish King Christian to sound the British government on peace and found Grey sympathetic toward Germany. Andersen was anxious to ascertain the German reaction to a "firm and extensive alliance" between Britain and Germany. Such an Anglo-German alliance was described by the Kaiser as "utopian" and it was rejected out of hand. Bethmann favored rejection after the military situation on the eastern front had been clarified. But Falkenhayn was anxious to convert the offer into a means of making contact with the Russians. Ballin was therefore ordered to advocate a Russo-German rather than an Anglo-German reconciliation. After a brief discussion of the prospects for a Russo-German peace, Ballin and Andersen, however, returned to the Anglo-German understanding which both desired. Andersen claimed that the British were prepared to make "quite considerable concessions," including a share of their world power. Ballin expressed doubts about British willingness to make concessions and insisted that Britain not only renounce its balance of power policy but also make an "iron-clad agreement" to share the control of the seas with Germany. Although they hoped the Danish sounding might precipitate a Russian offer, German leaders had done their best to squelch an Anglo-German understanding.[12]

The Germans had no sooner deflected the Danish probe when House revived the American effort. The reasons for House's move were not clear since he was encouraged neither by the belligerents nor by Wilson. Whatever his motive, House offered to sound the Germans if Grey assured him that the Entente would negotiate on the basis of a renunciation of militarism and the evacuation and reparation of Belgium. Grey replied that Britain would fight until it was secure. American Ambassador Page predicted that the British would negotiate on the terms suggested by House but he foresaw two stumbling blocks. Page felt that Russia would insist on a guarantee of Constantinople and that Germany would not renounce its military superiority since Britain would not give up its naval supremacy. The Germans were equally discouraging. Bethmann attacked the British in his Reichstag speech and told American Ambassador Gerard that he saw "no chance of peace now." Zimmermann slightly qualified his rejection of mediation with the suggestion that House sound the Entente. Despite the discouraging response, House reopened the question by informing German Ambassador Bernstorff that he was sounding the British. Without authorization, Bernstorff assured House that Berlin would accept American mediation if the Entente agreed and would oppose neither the reestablishment and reparation of Belgium nor disarmament. Bernstorff informed Berlin that House wanted to sound London and Berlin personally if Grey agreed. Thus House's move seemingly depended on the British reaction.[13]

The British sought to avoid alienating while not encouraging House. British Ambassador Spring-Rice told House that the Entente would not reject negotiations which included the reestablishment and reparation of Belgium as well as disarmament. House claimed that Wilson was "much elated" with this response and wanted House to leave at once for London and Berlin. Grey augmented Spring-Rice's conditions when he stipulated that the "two objects to be secured" were Entente security and Belgian independence. He correctly predicted that the German interpretation of its own security would preclude the security of other states since the Germans "aim at a durable peace by placing the west of Europe under German domination." He, however, considered the alternative of crushing Germany as probably neither practical nor conducive to a secure peace. Grey thought that the end of Prussian militarism and the subsequent democratization of Germany might follow a German defeat but that these results could not be imposed from outside. He suggested that peace might be maintained by the establishment of an international system including the United States. Grey added that serious negotiations required consultation with his allies whose aims he warned would "depend largely upon the progress of the war." House, Spring-Rice and Grey doubted that either the German people or the military would want to make peace after their initial successes. House and Grey nonetheless hoped that German civilian leaders would recognize that the war could not be won. Spring-Rice reported that Bernstorff and Dumba were working for peace and that Wilson believed the Germans would evacuate, compensate and guarantee Belgium. Asquith doubted these conditions would satisfy France and Russia but felt they were "significant as showing how the wind is blowing." Grey was less encouraging and raised serious difficulties in his reply to Spring-Rice. Since the United States was unlikely to guarantee a settlement, Grey doubted negotiations would be successful. Furthermore, he was convinced by statements of the German government in the interim—particularly Bethmann's Reichstag speech—that Germany desired neither a settlement with Britain nor restoration of Belgium. He virtually precluded negotiations by stipulating that he would not consult his allies until Germany demonstrated greater inclination to peace. The British consequently sought to satisfy American requests for conditions without encouraging a mediatory offer.[14]

The German government meanwhile discouraged an American move. Zimmermann's letter which described mediation as premature was received by House at the end of December. Zimmermann was impatient over the persistent possibility of American mediation and told Bernstorff that "we wish to conclude peace directly with our enemies and to avoid a conference." Zimmermann meanwhile tried to discourage American mediation in the German press while scrupulously avoiding the appearance of an official initiative. The Germans also wanted to avoid the American move without alienating them. At the end of 1914, it appeared that both the Germans and the British had successfully avoided American mediation; thus, a move which might have altered or ended the stalemate seemed to have been deflected. Other initiatives being taken, however, revealed that the appearance was deceptive. House would decide at the beginning of January to embark on a mediatory venture despite a lack of encouragement from the belligerents.[15]

The hypothetical possibility of mediation at the end of 1914 clearly demonstrated the opposing logic of belligerent and mediator. All of the belligerents opposed mediation and their opposition reflected the emotional as well as military stalemate. To the belligerents mediation implied the acceptance of compromises which they equated with defeat. These compromises were, however, precisely the conditions which House and other mediators interpreted as necessary for mediation. House furthermore concluded that the military stalemate implied that there was a balance of power which prevented either side from achieving victory and required a compromise peace. Since the belligerents could therefore have no interest in continuing the war, House concluded that no insurmountable issues were involved in the conflict. According to House, the war had been caused by mistake and continued by misunderstanding—a popular view among liberal Anglo-Saxons. For House and many would-be mediators, the problem was therefore one of communication. The belligerents' wariness about entering discussions probably confirmed his conviction and encouraged the belief that a catalyst was necessary to initiate negotiations. He hoped that, once begun, negotiations would reveal that problems were semantic and consequently surmountable. This interpretation was reinforced by the belligerents, who claimed that they were fighting only to establish a system which would preserve peace and their own national existence. The nature of this system was, however, the precise subject on which the British and Germans could not agree. The British sought a system which would balance rather than reflect power, so a stable peace required an adjustment of the system to contain inordinate German power. The British wanted to preserve the balance of power, maintain the Entente, and incorporate the United States into the system. The Germans, however, projected a system which would reflect rather than balance power, so a permanent peace required an adjustment of the system to allow their power to develop. The Germans therefore wanted to renounce the existing balance of power, dismantle the Entente, and exclude the United States from the system. In effect, the British favored stability whereas the Germans advocated change.

The disagreement between mediators and belligerents came down ultimately to the distinction between their aspirations and the war situation. The mediators regarded the stalemate as significant and the aspirations of the belligerents as renounciable. The belligerents interpreted the issues which divided them as significant and stalemate as surmountable. Consequently, the offer of American mediation was unacceptable to both the Germans and British at the end of 1914. Both belligerents might have accepted mediation by force but that would have constituted intervention rather than mediation. Mediation might also have been accepted if a military decision had been achieved by either side, but in that case if would have been unnecessary. Thus, the offer of American mediation was necessary but was unacceptable to the belligerents. It might have been acceptable only when it would have been unnecessary.

FRUSTRATION & PREPARATION:
BRITISH STRATEGY & POLICY

The British and the other belligerents only gradually recognized the implications of military stalemate. They all tended to fumble with familiar problems rather than seek innovative solutions to the major problem of continuing the war.

The British continued to concentrate on the western front despite failure and frustration. The British and French could not agree on the details of operations during December, but their strategy was directed at the same objective, namely, response to Russian demands for a diversion rather than to achievement of a decisive military success. As it turned out, operations on the western front merely demonstrated that the Germans could hold with limited forces and thus confirmed the stalemate. British leaders were more concerned with defensive considerations than defeating the Germans. Kitchener and the cabinet feared the possibility of a German invasion of Britain, a breakthrough on the western front, and a Russian collapse but they were reassured by Generals French and Joffre that the situation was not as critical as it seemed. It therefore seemed that the prevailing pattern of frontal attacks on the western front would persist.[16]

This impression was somewhat misleading. The previous failures of this approach caused several British leaders to begin agitating for an entirely different conception at the end of December. Lloyd George, Churchill and the Secretary of the Committee of Imperial Defense, Maurice Hankey, were all concerned about the stalemate, criticized the strategists and advocated new approaches, including campaigns in the Balkans and the Baltic. Some of these impulses would subsequently alter the course of the war and reinforce the general eastward shift of operations during 1915.[17]

The British government and the other belligerents found it necessary to accommodate themselves to an unexpectedly long and difficult war. Britain's relatively secure geographic position rendered it least prepared for a long war in military and social terms but gave Britain the most time to adjust. The adjustment was made gradually but sporadically.

Britain found political accommodation was in many ways the easiest adjustment to make. The politicians renounced party politics and deferred the discussion of significant questions in parliament until May 1915. A general sense of immediacy was nonetheless lacking and leading politicians were notably unwilling to make important decisions. Following the crisis in Flanders the government and opposition tried to persuade the British people that the allied position was secure although serious. German air and coastal bombardment and rumors of a possible German invasion brought the war home and aroused public indignation. The press moved into the political vacuum created by the party truce and the opposition role renounced by the Conservatives was assumed by radicals. The cabinet, recognizing that numbers reduced efficiency, appointed a smaller Committee of Imperial Defense, which, however, met infrequently and acted slowly. The parliament passed legislation giving the government extensive powers for the duration of the war, which was publicly criticized.[18]

The British mobilization was successful in human and financial, but not industrial, terms. Men volunteered for military service in numbers larger than the training facilities could handle but the high level of resistance to conscription indicated that many Englishmen were still anxious to reconcile individual liberty with national security. Despite the opposition to conscription, the British army was probably altered more than any other because the old professional army was decimated in Flanders and the "New Army" was rapidly expanded. Rather than breaking the deadlock as it was supposed to do, the expansion of the British army insured that the war would last at least until the new forces could be tested in the spring. The predictions of a long war by British leaders may therefore have functioned as self-fulfilling prophecies since they wanted the war to last long enough to exert maximum British power. The government was meanwhile less successful in solving the munitions problem but it did mobilize Britain's economic resources and stabilize its finances.[19]

The British reaction to the war situation was therefore mixed. The British response was rapid enough to preclude a German victory and the British commitment was sufficiently great to insure against a British withdrawal. But British adjustment to the possibility of a long war was too slow to insure an Entente victory, and British plans would require considerable time to materialize. British behavior accordingly tended to reinforce the stalemate.

BLOCKADE NOT BATTLE:
ANGLO-GERMAN NAVAL POLICIES

In their search for a strategy to break the stalemate, some British leaders sought means of attacking the exposed enemy flanks in the Balkans and the Baltic. Both involved amphibious operations and depended on Britain's control of the seas; indeed the British navy was a critical element since operations in either area might succeed only if the navy could transport troops more quickly than the Germans could respond. Britain had two other hypothetically feasible options for employing the navy. It could seek a large-scale naval battle against the German fleet with an objective analogous to that of the Schlieffen plan, i.e., a battle of annihilation which would presumably shorten the war. The navy could also be used as the primary means of blockading Germany and its allies. This strategy, like the land war of attrition which emerged at the end of 1914, implied a longer war. The choice between a battle of annihilation and a blockade of attrition would influence the course of the war since the battle might break the stalemate whereas the blockade would reinforce it.[20]

The great fleet action which both the German and British navies expected during the early months of the war still seemed possible at the end of 1914. Such a battle required that both fleets seek contact or that one force battle on the other. The German naval options were analogous to their choice on the eastern front. They might have chosen battle if their inferiority in numbers was compensated by superiority in materiel and mobility. As on the eastern front, the Germans could do so only if the British divided their navy (as the Russians had divided their army before Tannenberg). The British had naval superiority so they were more likely to seek battle. But unlike the Russians, they were sufficiently cautious not to divide their forces. Consequently, it was unlikely that the Germans would accept battle. Since the German fleet had a safe sanctuary, it was difficult for the British to force battle upon it. Thus, the situation militated against a naval battle of annihilation.

A battle might nonetheless have ensued if the Germans could have induced the British to divide their forces. The Germans provided such an inducement when they took the initiative in the peripheral aspects of the naval war. These German activities came to a climax at the end of 1914. In the process of moving the British fleet to the security of Irish waters against the threat of German U-boat attacks, one battleship (the *Audacious*) struck a German mine; the Germans did not discover their success for some time, but nonetheless intensified their mine-laying. Individual German cruisers and small naval contingents meanwhile diverted British naval forces to extra-European waters. The best German opportunity to improve conditions for a large naval battle in European waters was provided by the operations of Admiral Spee off the coast of South America. Spee confronted the British with an awkward choice. They could risk failure by seeking to defeat Spee with limited forces or they could reduce their own forces elsewhere (possibly in Europe) to engage Spee with larger forces. The British elected to send contingents from Europe, and thereby improved the odds for a German naval success in Europe.

The great naval confrontation did not occur, however. As a result of Spee's success and perhaps their military failure in Flanders, the Germans decided to make a naval strike against the British coast. Before the strike could be launched, Spee was sunk with most of his squadron off the Falkland Islands at the beginning of December and the Germans thereby lost their best diversion. They might nonetheless have exploited their small advantage if they moved against the British in the North Atlantic before the British contingents sent against Spee returned. The German foray against the British coast in December attracted large forces on both sides and the Germans may have had favorable odds, but the expedition did not produce a major confrontation. This operation demonstrated that the Germans could harass the British coast without reprisal and was therefore a short-run, psychological success for the Germans. However, it implied an eventual failure for the Germans since they probably missed their best opportunity for a decisive naval battle.[21]

The British prospects in the naval war were the reverse of German prospects. British superiority increased the chance of victory but could be lost, whereas German inferiority reduced the likelihood of success but implied less loss. The circumstances which offered the Germans an opportunity at the end of 1914 therefore caused the British corresponding concern. Conflicting demands produced "great strain" and depressed the navy and Churchill. The situation seemed to favor the Germans but it improved for the British when John Fisher's appointment to succeed Prince Louis Battenberg as First Sea Lord revived Churchill's prestige and the navy's confidence. Several German ships were sunk in quick succession and the difficult decision to divert forces against Spee was a success. The British therefore confronted the prospect of a large-scale battle in the North Sea with greater confidence.[22]

British naval leaders did not unanimously agree on how the great battle should be fought. Fisher and Churchill were seemingly more anxious for a confrontation than John Jellicoe, Commander of the Grand Fleet. The British fleet sortied into the North Sea to draw the Germans out of their sanctuary and responded to the German foray against the British coast. But even Churchill imposed conditions on the fleet which permitted it to operate only if British victory was assured, and thereby virtually precluded a battle. British and German naval leaders were both more anxious to avoid a naval disaster than to seek a naval decision. Their responses were typical of belligerent policies in general at the end of 1914 and tended to reinforce the stalemate.[23]

The effective rejection of a naval battle was consistent with the prerequisites for a naval blockade. A decisive naval battle implied a short war which would render a naval blockade both unnecessary and unsuccessful. It was therefore appropriate that the British blockade became more intense as a battle became less likely. This choice likewise reflected the military stalemate and a longer war which required adjustments of economic warfare as it did of warfare in general.

The British imposed a strictly naval blockade in August when the war was generally expected to be short and sought to restrict German access to articles of war, i.e,, contraband. The designation of contraband and noncontraband materiel was derived from the distinction made between combatant and noncombatant personnel. Those distinctions reflected the basic assumption of a short war, i.e., that nations surrender when their armies are defeated. The British naval blockade could therefore have been effective only if military operations had been immediately sensitive to the deprivation of materials designated as contraband. Actually, the belligerent governments paid little attention before November to the materials which the blockade could control. The shortages which affected military operations—particularly munitions and men—were more the result of deficient prewar planning than wartime stoppages.

The prospect of a protracted conflict reversed many propositions about economic warfare. Whereas a war of annihilation depended almost exclusively on the men and materiel at the front, a war of attrition increasingly involved the whole nation. The distinction between combatant and noncombatant personnel therefore diminished and extension of the definition of contraband and intensification of the blockade were a logical result. Less logical considerations may also have affected the British decision since the blockade provided them with a means of striking back at the Germans. A more practical impulse was the British realization that the blockade was inefficient as previously applied. Furthermore, the British could now justify intensification of the blockade as a response to German measures. Despite these reasons for intensifying the naval blockade rapidly, it was imposed gradually and did not become total until the United States entered the war.

This gradualism had several causes. It was due in part to Entente—primarily British—concern for neutral sensitivities. There was also the practical necessity for testing various approaches, but above all it resulted from the reservations of Entente statesmen. The blockade might have significantly affected the course of the war only if it had been total. Entente statesmen desired the benefits of a total blockade, but did not want to accept its high risks and sacrifices. Instead they imposed the blockade bit by bit in a vain attempt to cause maximum harm to the enemy with minimum cost to themselves. Thus, British leaders chose the conservative alternative in regard to both the battle and blockade questions. By trying to avoid a long war, they made it more likely.

The blockade was primarily a British concern. Maritime commerce was more important for the blockade than the land trade between adjacent states which was less controllable and usually involved goods which were less critical because they were replaceable. The British tried to intensify the contraband blockade at the end of 1914 by rectifying three weaknesses in their previous practice. To reduce the number of ships which reached continental ports without being searched, they declared the North Sea a war zone and assigned more ships to patrol duty as diversions like Spee were removed. They broadened the definition of contraband and improved the organization for dealing with it. Finally, the British insisted on agreements with the northern neutrals in order to insure that vastly increased wartime imports into those countries did not reach the enemy. By pursuing these policies, the British sought to impose maximum control on the German economy compatible with good relations with the neutrals, particularly the United States. In fact, Grey attached higher priority to Anglo-American relations than to an intensified blockade. Fortunately for the Entente, the American government defended only its own rights and did so flexibly enough to allow the Entente to maintain both the blockade and American benevolence. Consequently, the British efforts to intensify the blockade, isolate the problems, and solve some of them had only begun by the end of 1914.[24]

The Germans responded to the British blockade in several ways. They pressed the neutrals to reject Entente demands. They tried to circumvent the blockade by finding substitutes for restricted items. Their best recourse proved to be the self-interest of the neutrals which caused the Entente to move slowly. The Germans also reacted with reprisals against British commerce. The U-boat appropriately appeared just as the likelihood of a naval battle was about to disappear.[25]

The British declared the North Sea to be a war zone at the beginning of November and thus stimulated German use of the U-boat. The Germans immediately investigated the feasibility of a counterblockade with U-boats and mines but concluded that it should be deferred until the military situation was more secure since the U-boat might provoke neutrals into joining the Entente. A thorough discussion of a U-boat blockade followed. Admiral Reinhold Scheer, a commander of one fleet, and Admiral Friedrich von Ingenohl, Commander of the High Seas Fleet, favored it. Tirpitz, after first displaying an uncharacteristic caution, supported the idea and became its public symbol when some of his statements reached the press. Falkenhayn was favorably disposed but Bethmann remained typically reserved and Zimmermann accepted the Admiralty's argument that U-boat operations should be deferred. Admiral Hugo Pohl, Chief of the Admiralty Staff, urged the Foreign Office to declare the Channel and British Isles a war zone in reprisal for the British declaration. He persisted despite Tirpitz's argument for a blockade instead. Bethmann still demurred. Since a U-boat blockade might prove counterproductive by cutting off trade with Scandinavia and isolating the Central Powers completely from world trade, he thought the U-boat might become useful only if the military situation improved. Thus Bethmann, Zimmermann and the Admiralty contended that U-boat warfare could be a result rather than a cause of breaking the stalemate. But if the stalemate was broken, the U-boat would probably become unnecessary. The Germans were again trapped in a dilemma: the U-boat was necessary when it was too risky to use but would probably be unnecessary when it became safe.[26]

The German U-boat policy was conservative and defensive like the British decision against a more aggressive blockade. British and German leaders were more anxious to avoid new enemies than to defeat their existing ones. The decisions of both therefore reinforced the stalemate and lengthened the war. At the end of 1914 it appeared that these conservative considerations would continue to determine German and British policy. The impulses for intensifying U-boat warfare and the blockade, however, existed already. Like the other efforts to break the stalemate, these would alter the subsequent course of the war.[27]

DIVIDE & CONQUER:
GERMANY, RUSSIA & FRANCE

SEEKING SEPARATE PEACE:
GERMAN POLICY TOWARD RUSSIA

The stalemate revolutionized the military and diplomatic policies of both sides. More specifically, it revived diplomacy. Diplomacy took precedence over strategy until diplomacy failed during the July crisis. Diplomacy was then subordinated to strategy as long as there was a chance that strategy would produce victory quickly. The importance of diplomacy revived when victory eluded German strategy at the end of 1914, but it did not replace strategy, which it could have done only if peace had resulted. It now became clear that diplomacy and strategy were complementary rather than contradictory.

The stalemate demonstrated that a German victory was unlikely as long as the Entente existed. The Entente therefore had to be shattered by the conclusion of a separate peace with either Russia or France. The choice of Russia or France instead of Britain reflected the change which occurred in German policy toward the enemy powers. Russia and France were perceived as the most dangerous enemies in July and August, whereas Britain was regarded as least threatening. The roles reversed in the interim and Britain emerged as the main opponent by November, whereas Russia and France were regarded as British tools. German objectives changed accordingly. The defeat of France, expulsion of Russia from Europe and avoidance of Britain were the German objectives in August. By the end of 1914 a "reckoning" with Britain assumed central importance and France and Russia became secondary. The means of achieving German objectives also changed. The military means initially seemed sufficient but by November it became clear that diplomatic assistance was required. The nature of diplomatic activity also altered. Prior to November

117

German diplomacy was concerned with the shape of a hypothetical victory and war aims; now it was called upon to produce the practical reality of a separate peace. Thus, war diplomacy began in earnest at the end of 1914.

The altered relationship between strategy and policy and the change in German policy toward Russia and France was evident in mid-November. During the critical discussion with Bethmann on 18 November, Falkenhayn contended that Germany could not achieve a decisive victory as long as the Entente existed. The Entente would collapse only if Germany concluded a separate peace with Russia or France. If the Entente split, Germany could defeat the remaining continental enemy and then Britain could be forced to accept German continental domination by a U-boat blockade. Under the existing circumstances, Falkenhayn considered that a separate peace with Russia should be sought if the battles in Poland demonstrated to the Russians that they could not defeat Germany before winter. Falkenhayn recommended that moderate terms (an indemnity and slight border rectifications) be granted to encourage such an understanding.

Bethmann reluctantly accepted Falkenhayn's analysis of the situation. Bethmann foresaw mutual exhaustion as the best possible result as long as the Entente persisted. If peace could be concluded with Russia, however, Germany might decisively defeat France and Britain would be forced to surrender. Bethmann advocated renouncing most German aspirations at the expense of Russia to achieve their aims in the west. No less important Bethmann considered that the threat of future resistance to German power would be removed since the "Triple Entente would thus be destroyed."

Bethmann and Falkenhayn were thus agreed on the situation and the German strategy but they differed on tactics. Falkenhayn believed Russia might seek peace if it was stopped in Poland, whereas Bethmann thought Russia would do so only if it was expelled from Poland. Falkenhayn advocated a German initiative and moderate conditions but Bethmann rejected the first and qualified the second. Falkenhayn felt that a Russian disappointment and German moderation were sufficient to achieve German objectives, while Bethmann believed a Russian defeat and German threats were required. These two tendencies—carrot and stick—characterized German efforts to conclude a separate peace with Russia during the next three years.[1]

Zimmermann opposed Falkenhayn's analysis and response. He granted that it would be "desirable to drive a wedge between our enemies and to conclude a separate peace as soon as possible with one or another of them." A separate peace should not be sought, however, at the expense of the main objective, namely a "favorable and lasting peace." This goal required a fundamental reckoning with both England and Russia if they were not to constitute a "permanent threat" to Germany. Zimmermann felt that England was generally recognized as a "permanent threat" but he thought Russia was not, in view of the frequent suggestions of a separate peace with Russia. He felt the preservation of Austria-Hungary, of German influence in Turkey, and indeed of Germany itself required "the most thorough defeat of Russia." If the military situation made a separate peace mandatory, Zimmermann argued that it should be made with France, "the least dangerous of our main enemies." If an understanding with Russia nonetheless proved unavoidable, the initiative should be left to the Russians, since a German sounding would solidify rather than shatter the Entente. A Russian request for a separate peace might be encouraged by a Russian or Serbian defeat and should be accepted only if agreeable to Austria-Hungary and Turkey. Zimmermann accordingly advocated a perpetuation of the conflict with Russia.[2]

These exchanges precipitated a debate over policy. Falkenhayn remained adamant and assured himself of the Kaiser's support. Zimmermann's view was shared by Hindenburg, Ludendorff and Conrad. Bethmann was ambivalent. He continued to favor a separate peace with Russia and sought to de-emphasize the conflict with Russia in public statements, but his discussions with Zimmermann, Hindenburg, Ludendorff and Hoffmann confirmed his belief that a serious defeat was a precondition for a Russian request for peace. When Falkenhayn refused to alter his strategy to conform with this assumption, Bethmann unsuccessfully sought to replace him with Hindenburg. The need for a fundamental departure in policy caused divergences among the policymakers.[3]

These disagreements were provided a practical basis when the possibility of contact with Petrograd occurred during the second half of November. Even before Falkenhayn suggested that Russia might seek a separate peace, Jagow began to explore the feasibility of encouraging developments in Petrograd which might prove conducive to an understanding with Russia and thereby "shatter the Entente." He asked Friedrich von Pourtales, the former German ambassador to Russia, for his opinion on "the idea of spinning threads to a Russian personality in order to rake up the differences between the Tsar and/or his mother [on the one hand] and Grand Duke Nicholas" on the other. Pourtales replied that direct contacts would be difficult but indirect channels via Stockholm and Copenhagen might be possible since the Tsar's mother communicated with her Danish family and friends.[4]

The initial contacts were established by Ballin a few days later with Hans Andersen, the Danish statesman who encouraged an Anglo-German understanding. Bethmann was inclined to postpone an answer to Andersen until the battles in Poland were decided and then exploit the offer as a possibility of establishing contact with Petrograd. Falkenhayn insisted instead that an encouraging reply be sent immediately and he was supported by the Kaiser, who "wants a separate understanding with Russia as intensely as Mr. von Falkenhayn." Ballin was instructed by Bethmann to convert Andersen's proposal from an understanding with Britain to a separate peace with Russia. In his meeting with Andersen at the beginning of December, Ballin asserted that "an understanding with Russia was much less complicated than one with England" and that it would therefore "be more correct if the [Danish] king sounded Russia first." Andersen speculated that such an understanding would require compromises between the Tsar and Grand Duke Nicholas which would be facilitated by German moderation. Despite his obvious preference for an Anglo-German understanding, Andersen assured Ballin that Christian would get in touch with Petrograd.[5]

The Germans immediately hoped that the contact with Petrograd would produce a favorable Russian response. However, Andersen returned to Copenhagen and again directed his attention to an Anglo-German understanding. There were also noticeable differences of opinion amongst Danish leaders. Despite the Danish reaction the German envoy in Copenhagen, Ulrich von Brockdorff-Rantzau, expressed a desire that the contact could be exploited to "blow up the (enemy) coalition." Nothing further was reported and Bethmann expressed his disappointment by writing Ballin at the end of December that "the delay of an answer from Councilor Andersen leads me to conclude that either the sentiment in Petrograd is not at all ripe for peace suggestions or the Tsar does not want to answer without drawing in his allies beforehand. I would regret either equally since for us everything depends on shattering the [enemy] coalition, i.e., on a separate peace with one of our enemies—in the present military situation, with Russia." Bethmann was probably correct in his speculations about Petrograd's reaction but he was incorrect regarding the reason for the lack of response. In fact, the delay was caused in Copenhagen, not Petrograd. Christian would not write to the Tsar's mother until the beginning of January because of conflicting views among his councilors. Thus, German hopes for a Danish peace initiative were initially disappointed.[6]

The Germans meanwhile tried to establish their own channels to Petrograd. Their brightest prospect was ex-Minister President Sergei Witte, who was instrumental in negotiating the Treaty of Portsmouth in 1905 (ending the war with Japan) and was known to oppose Russian participation in the World War. The Germans had tried unsuccessfully to make contact with Witte in October and early December. Despite these failures, Bethmann told Ballin at the end of December that "it would perhaps be appropriate to make contact" with Witte, whose influence seemed to be increasing again. He therefore asked whether Ballin could dispatch "a dove with a discreet olive branch" to Witte. Ballin favored awaiting results from the Andersen sounding but did suggest a channel to Witte through Copenhagen. Bethmann and Jagow also had Witte's banker in Berlin encourage Witte to speak out in favor of peace. None of these efforts produced results by the end of 1914.[7]

The German pursuit of a separate understanding with Russia affected the achievement of German war aims at Russian expense. German leaders recognized that they would probably have to reduce their demands to induce a Russian response. The tenuous military situation on the eastern front reinforced the argument for moderation. Prussian Minister of Interior Loebell urged a separate understanding with Russia since "not sympathy but healthy [self-] interest argues for the greatest possible indulgence toward Russia at the conclusion of peace." Falkenhayn and Bethmann were relatively moderate in their demands. Falkenhayn argued for "nothing more than a sufficient war indemnity but no land except small border connections in the interest of defense." Bethmann advocated the occupation of a large part of Poland as a "pawn to force through a war indemnity" against Russia. He proposed that most of this indemnity would go to Austria-Hungary, which would also probably demand parts of Serbia for itself and Bulgaria. Russia would also have to renounce its aspirations for Constantinople. In a subsequent conversation with Stresemann and Roetger, Bethmann admitted that an indemnity might be difficult to extract even if Poland were occupied. Jagow told the Austro-Hungarian ambassador Hohenlohe that the Central Powers might not beat Russia sufficiently to demand large territorial concessions and that it might be wisest in any case to leave the Poles under Russian rule. Zimmermann probably expressed an official more than a personal view when he suggested to Hohenlohe that the Central Powers should be satisfied with Polish territory west of the Vistula and a war indemnity if Russia were willing to conclude a separate peace; he claimed that Germany would expect "only very little for itself."[8]

One corollary of this relative moderation was the persistent theme of border rectifications mentioned by Loebell, Falkenhayn and Zimmermann. German planning for a "Polish border strip" was initiated at this time and continued throughout the war as a kind of barometer for Russo-German relations. The more the Germans wanted a separate peace with Russia, the more they would reduce their other demands but fasten on the border strip as an irreducible minimum.[9]

Another result of German moderation was a de-emphasis of its efforts to revolutionize Russia. The policy was actively conducted from the outbreak of war and was consistent with Berlin's desire to seek large gains at Russian expense. Zimmermann opposed moderation and a separate understanding with Russia, so he urged continuation of these efforts. Germany pursued this objective but the unsuccessful German campaign in Poland and Turkish operations in the Caucasus caused them to fail. Berlin's shift in policy toward Russia, however, argued for subordinating revolution to a separate peace. As Jagow told his envoy in Stockholm, a Finnish revolt against Russia should not be encouraged with the promise of concessions from Russia since "we cannot immoderately encumber our program of demands should the possibility of a separate peace with Russia occur now."[10]

The relationship between German war aims and its war diplomacy now began to emerge, and the situation required that German leaders adjust ends to means. German leaders did not always adhere to this logic, but they scaled down their demands on Russia at the end of 1914 to a point which they themselves perceived as moderate. The success of their efforts ultimately depended, however, more on Russian than on German perceptions.

INVINCIBLE BUT IMMOBILIZED:
RUSSIA'S AMBIVALENT POWER

Russia's military prospects altered radically during the autumn of 1914. The withdrawal of the Central Powers from Poland in October encouraged Russian hopes for the November campaign. "Thereafter came an awful change," as Churchill observed. Instead of continued success a Russian failure became possible. The course of events was symbolized by the dismissals of Russian commanders, the evacuation of Lodz and a Russian retreat. By the end of December it was clear that Grand Duke Nicholas could not resume the offensive in the near future. The Germans were unable to force further Russian withdrawals and a stalemate ensued in the east as it had in the west. The Russian prospects thus oscillated wildly from resounding victory to serious defeat to unpromising stalemate.[11]

Russia's fluctuating power resulted in contradictory aspirations on the part of its leaders. Premier Goremykin told French Ambassador Paleologue during the Russian advance into Poland in November that Constantinople should be a free city, Russia should annex part of Armenia, and the Entente should be perpetuated during the war and after peace was restored. The Tsar told Paleologue a week later that Russia would demand part of Posen and possibly Silesia from Germany, and Galicia and part of Bukovina after Austria-Hungary dissolved into its constituent parts. The Polish question was meanwhile discussed intensively by the Russian Council of Ministers. Sharp disagreements emerged between Sazonov and Grand Duke Nicholas, both of whom advocated an autonomous Polish kingdom under Russia, on one hand, and the conservatives who opposed a Polish state in any form, on the other.[12]

The establishment of aims became a less immediate issue in December when the Russians were evacuating their own territory rather than occupying enemy territory and they became increasingly concerned about defensive rather than offensive considerations. The major Russian anxiety aside from the German threat in Poland was the Turkish campaign in the Caucasus. Unable to withdraw forces from Poland, Grand Duke Nicholas asked his allies for a diversionary action against the Dardanelles and informed Sazonov that Russia lacked the strength to take the Dardanelles by military means. The British and French acceded to Russian requests for such a diversionary action and granted Russia postwar control of the Straits in order to keep Russia in the war. The Russian demands were made and fulfilled because of Russian weakness rather than strength. Russian military failure neither diminished their aims nor encouraged their willingness to compromise. Sazonov rejected Paleologue's suggestion that

Austria-Hungary be offered moderate terms as an inducement for separate peace. Russian aspirations persisted despite military setbacks.[13]

Russian domestic conditions were also ambiguous in that great potential was qualified by severe weaknesses. The political truce continued but the radical left was increasingly in conflict with the government. Russian military failures accelerated subversive activities and government reprisals. The Germans were aware of these pressures and tried unsuccessfully to exploit them. The Russian effort to mobilize for war presented a similarly contradictory picture. Russia had an advantage in a war of attrition because of its vast human resources. But it was unable to produce the materiel—notably munitions and rifles—which were critical, particularly in offensive operations. The possibility that these shortages would be alleviated by Russia's industrialized allies was diminished by Turkey's entry into the war and the consequent closure of an access into the Mediterranean. Russian financial prospects were also mixed; taxes were insufficient and a loan from the British became necessary. Consequently, Russia neither collapsed nor prevailed. It was invincible but immobilized for the moment.[14]

CONQUEST OR CONCILIATION?
GERMAN POLICY TOWARD FRANCE

The German reappraisal of its strategy and policy at the end of 1914 implicated France. A separate peace with Russia would facilitate a German conquest of France. A separate peace with France would probably require conciliation of France. A German conquest of France seemed likely at the end of 1914 but conciliation was considered for the first time.

The general problem was raised in mid-November by Tirpitz and Falkenhayn, who initially favored an "escape more via France than Russia." Tirpitz doubted, however, that France would make peace as long as it was allied with Russia. He seemed to have persuaded Falkenhayn that a separate peace with Russia was more likely. In his subsequent discussion with Bethmann, Falkenhayn advocated a separate peace with Russia allowing Germany to defeat France and Britain so thoroughly that "we could dictate peace" to them. The conclusion of a separate understanding with Russia would, he argued, cause France "to come down a peg." The conquest of France was not the only alternative for Falkenhayn, although it was preferable. If France sought an understanding before it was defeated, Falkenhayn thought Germany should not refuse it "an honorable peace" since it was "a necessity that we reconcile ourselves with France after the peace." He felt that a separate peace with France was, however, unlikely since the French government and people were still "confident of victory and therefore firmly determined to continue the war."[15]

Bethmann accepted Falkenhayn's general analysis and advocacy of a separate peace with Russia but he did not specifically consider the possibility of a separate peace or a postwar reconciliation with France. Indeed, he was inclined to reject a French request for peace in order to defeat France and "create conditions as we pleased in the west." Bethmann concentrated more than Falkenhayn on French tenacity, but he hoped that war weariness and anglophobia would foster French defeatism. Zimmermann reversed Falkenhayn's argument by claiming that, if a separate peace were necessary, it should be with France, which he considered "the least dangerous of our enemies." France, in his view, had entered the war because of "necessity" and not preference. Since he believed the war was unpopular in France and continued only because of Anglo-Russian support, he felt the evident decline of allied help would cause the French people to demand a lasting peace with Germany. Zimmermann thought peace was possible because France was weakened and genuinely desired a reconciliation with Germany.[16]

Bethmann combined these contradictory approaches toward France. He may have reflected Zimmermann's arguments when he suggested to the Reichstag in December that the majority of Frenchmen wanted to live in peace with Germany but were misled by vindictive politicians. Zimmermann's influence was evident in Bethmann's remarks a week later to Stresemann and Roetger. Bethmann implied that German relations with France were based on considerations of power, and that peace could be restored only after France had been defeated and the conditions imposed would depend on the degree of Germany's military success. He therefore argued that a decision regarding future borders would rest with the General Staff and that "France will have to pay the whole bill" for the war (circa 30 billion marks). However, Bethmann implied that German relations with France were also affected by considerations of pity and pacification. He felt that if France had to bear the brunt of the war it would be a pity since France was Germany's least guilty and "most respectable and chivalrous opponent," which he "wished to conciliate as much as possible." Therefore, he felt he should demand little French territory and compensate France with Belgian territory. Above all, Bethmann was anxious to pacify France in order to insure against perpetuating the Entente. Thus, Bethmann regarded France as Germany's least vicious but most vulnerable opponent and he advocated a contradictory policy—to both conquer and conciliate France.[17]

These contrary objectives confronted the German leaders with a dilemma concerning their war aims vis-à-vis France. They had to choose between demanding or offering concessions. If they renounced French concessions to conciliate their enemy, Germany would have little territorial though a great political gain in shattering the Entente. If they renounced conciliation and extracted concessions from France, Germany could make territorial gains at the high political cost of perpetuating the Entente. They had to make a fundamental choice between conquest and conciliation in determining German war aims at the expense of France. This necessity was recognized by the banker Arthur Gwinner when he wrote Clemens Delbrück that "the eventual shape of peace conditions depends on whether the goal of [German] policy is to bleed France to exhaustion or to win it for reconciliation." Gwinner advocated compensating France for giving in to German demands. Bethmann seemingly agreed but Delbrück doubted, probably quite correctly, that France would respond. Bethmann characteristically avoided a choice and prepared for all eventualities instead of pursuing a consistent line. He instructed Delbrück to ascertain the "maximum desirable" and the "minimal borders which must be regarded as the least which can be achieved." Developments in the war situation and not the decisions of its leaders would consequently determine German policy.[18]

Bethmann's ambivalence may partly be explained in terms of the conflicting demands made upon him and Germany's unclear military prospects. Consistency may have been unappealing to him because it required an awkward choice between two desirable alternatives—extracting concessions from or conciliating France. More than anything else, however, the doubts of German leaders concerning the achievement of either of those contrary goals explain Bethmann's inconsistency. Both conciliation or concessions required a German conquest of France but the stalemate implied neither.

Despite the inconsistency of German policy, the leaders of both Central Powers investigated the possibility of a separate peace with France at the end of 1914. Zimmermann sought to precipitate a French request for peace negotiations by bribing Delcassé's associates. He told a reputed agent of the French government that France would receive "more advantageous" conditions if it sued for peace quickly. Berlin considered launching a "campaign against England" in the French press to encourage anglophobia in France, but a suitable intermediary could not be found. One of the more publicized and serious attempts began when the Germans were informed that pro-German former Premier Joseph Caillaux was interested in a separate peace with Germany, but Caillaux's inconvenient departure from France precluded the meeting projected by a German agent. As a substitute, the Germans tried to contact politicians reputedly close to Caillaux who were advocating a pacifist government. Despite German encouragement no results were achieved. A channel to the French politician Joseph Noulens was likewise tested without success.[19]

A separate understanding with Russia seemed less likely at the beginning of January and Bethmann then encouraged his agents to make contact with Paris via Rome. He observed to Bülow that "we have no interest in the desolation of France and could offer it an honorable peace in exchange for a commensurate war indemnity and concession of part of its 'Congo colonies.' . . . By splitting off France, we would be able to finish the war against Russia and England certain of victory. Thus we would have achieved the relative weakening of France, a dam against the Slavic danger and a shock to English world hegemony." Bethmann thus revealed the contradictions of German aspirations. Shattering the Entente was essential if Germany was to gain victory over Russia and England, but

Bethmann could not bring himself to renounce German demands, much less pay the French for a separate peace. In effect, he expected the French to bribe Germany for the privilege of destroying the Entente.[20]

Vienna meanwhile sought to establish contacts for an understanding between the Central Powers and France. Austro-Hungarian leaders seem to have acted loyally since they assumed that "Berlin was also completely prepared to talk with France and to stipulate acceptable conditions." Foreign Ministry official Alexander Hoyos consequently asked Gagern, the Austro-Hungarian envoy in Switzerland, to seek an appropriate channel of communication. Hoyos predicted that German military successes in both Flanders and Poland were necessary before France would be "sufficiently discouraged" to conclude a separate peace. Gagern ascertained that the French were interested only in a separate peace with Austria-Hungary, and Vienna did not seem to have responded to that possibility. The French response nonetheless indicated that such probes could be double-edged in that they might jeopardize the Central Powers' alliance and also strengthen the Entente by suggesting Central Power weakness. The results of these efforts demonstrated that none of the belligerents was sufficiently despondent to conclude a separate peace. Frustrations and frictions between the allies were growing but the advantages of maintaining their alliances still outweighed the disadvantages.[21]

DETERMINATION DESPITE DISCOURAGEMENT: THE RELATIVE REALISM OF FRENCH POLICY

A German success was dependent on French as well as German policy decisions. Indeed, to the extent that German success required a French decision to accept a separate peace with the Central Powers, French policy was critical.

France was as profoundly influenced by its military prospects as the other powers, and the stalemate was the major factor at the end of 1914. French soldiers and statesmen accepted it gradually and reluctantly. Joffre correctly recognized that the attack in Flanders was the last German attempt to win a quick victory. After Flanders the war of annihilation became a war of attrition in the west. But a decision still seemed possible in the east until the Russians lost the initiative. When it seemed that the Germans might win the initiative in the east, the military relationship between the Russians and their allies suddenly reversed. Instead of looking to the Russians for salvation, the French and British had to save their ally by distracting the Germans. As it turned out, the Russians discontinued their offensive but were not in serious danger. By the end of December it became clear to French leaders that a deadlock would develop on the eastern front. The stalemate in the west was confirmed by Joffre's attacks in December which demonstrated again how difficult it would be to achieve victory in the west. Worse yet, the nullification of the Russian threat again allowed the

Germans to concentrate forces in the west. The danger had become discouragement rather than defeat—although time might favor the Entente, the war would
be long.[22]

The resulting frustration fostered a search for scapegoats and alternative
strategies. Several generals argued that a decision could not be won on the
western front and should consequently be sought in the east. As Asquith and
Bethmann were also doing, Poincaré reacted favorably to this suggestion but
Joffre resisted, as did Kitchener and Falkenhayn. Joffre and Falkenhayn were
more concerned about avoiding defeat than achieving victory. Their greatest
achievements were defensive in character and their greatest failures were their
offensives on the western front. The views of Joffre, Kitchener and Falkenhayn
seemed to have prevailed at the end of 1914. The pressure for seeking an
alternative already existed, however, in French as well as German and British
councils. It erupted among French leaders in January and would alter the
subsequent course of the war. Thus, the French military prospects were mixed.
Like the other belligerents the French knew how to avoid defeat but not how to
achieve victory.[23]

French policy was constructed on the basis of these mixed prospects.
Military setbacks facilitated policy formulation in one sense by providing an
obvious immediate objective—the liberation of German-occupied territory. This
was a satisfying goal because it was both obvious and morally uplifting. But the
mere liberation of French territory would not satisfy the French desire for
revenge and security. Furthermore, that goal paled in comparison to the more
ambitious aspirations of France's allies, who were planning to divide the colonial
world between them while France was fighting for its existence. French military
failure insured that liberation would remain as their main goal, and that the goal
would be difficult to achieve. The superior defense of the French made their
self-preservation possible but national liberation required a superior offense.
Their earlier offensive failures and the practical objective of liberating national
territory thus made French leaders somewhat more realistic than the others.
They were faced with fewer choices and evidenced fewer contradictions.
Each virtue, however, seemed to contain a corresponding vice. French policy
could become narrow-minded because it was single-minded, whereas German
policy was more flexible because it was more ambiguous.[24]

Circumstances affected French domestic politics just as they did French
diplomacy and strategy. The danger that faced the nation denied the French
people the luxury of domestic dissension and prescribed the politics of unity.
The French case suggests that a limited military failure unifies a nation by
restricting its choices. The German case implies that apparent military success,
even if limited, encourages national dissension by increasing the number of
policy alternatives. Parliamentary government in France was effectively discontinued in August and the Chamber was convoked briefly in December to

approve, not to evaluate, government and army policies. Patriotism diminished partisan politics, unity was eulogized, and public criticism was renounced by politicians and the press. Less visible frictions nonetheless persisted among soldiers and statesmen. Civil-military relations were partially determined by the fluctuating military situation. The German invasion justified the exercise of greater military authority in France than elsewhere. That authority was augmented by the forced but fretful isolation of the government in Bordeaux. As long as a rapid German advance was possible, the government's isolation was reasonable, the army's domination of public affairs was justifiable, and Joffre's reputation was invulnerable. When the Germans were stopped, the balance was restored, the military situation was stabilized, the government was relocated in Paris, and Joffre criticized because he was unable to expel the Germans. Disputes consequently increased among the generals and old political problems revived to complicate the choice of political and military leaders. France was no longer in extreme danger and could afford limited dissension.[25]

The transition from a short to a long war required internal adjustments hardly less difficult than those necessitated by the change from peace to war. Emotional stresses caused personal disagreements and depression among the French leaders. Bitterness toward Germany intensified and the government sought to mobilize and maintain public enthusiasm for a long war. The French failed to alleviate munitions shortages but they managed to reestablish financial stability. Thus, France like the other powers adjusted to the prospect of a longer war and thereby made it more possible.[26]

CONSOLIDATION VERSUS DISSOLUTION:
INTRA-ENTENTE RELATIONS

The Entente was preserved by the common threat of German power which forced the allies to subordinate though not to eradicate their frictions. Just as it was essential for the Germans to shatter the Entente, it was necessary for the Entente powers to solidify their alliance. In fact, the eventual outcome of the war depended more on this issue than any other.

Russia was the least secure link in the Entente chain. Relations among the allies were a function of the strategic situation. From August to November, Russia was generally on the offensive while the western allies were on the defensive. The Russian offensive was a critical element in Anglo-French calculations, the apparent key to achieving victory and avoiding defeat. The possibility that Russia might reduce or even discontinue its offensive because of Turkey's entry therefore confronted the British and French with a fundamental choice. They could risk losing Russian aid by being unresponsive to Russian war aims or they could encourage continued Russian assistance by accepting the Russian aspirations.

The British and Russians managed to reach an accommodation over their aspirations. Sazonov was more interested in achieving Russian aims at the expense of Austria-Hungary, whereas the British tended to offer inducements at Ottoman expense. The traditional British interest in defending Ottoman integrity against Russian encroachment had lessened before the war and declined rapidly during the autumn. When the Turks entered the war, the British became willing to bribe the Russians with promises of Turkish territory. They therefore offered the Russians control over the Straits not only to compensate them for a continued campaign in Poland and concessions to Britain in Persia but also to divert Russian attention from central Europe. Sazonov tried to avoid the diversion but he eventually accepted the British offer. The prospect of gaining control over the Straits resulted in a burst of Russian confidential planning and increased public demands for annexations. Anglo-Russian agreements were reached by the end of November on the Straits, Persia, and the Russian campaign in Poland but not on Russian aspirations in Europe. The British meanwhile consolidated their control over the eastern Mediterranean (by declaring a protectorate over Egypt and Cyprus) and conquered German colonies in Africa. The British and Russians therefore fulfilled their major aspirations and relations between the two countries were better than they had been for a century.[27]

France was the least satisfied member of the alliance. The French government was not consulted before Britain offered the Straits to Russia and the French were understandably alienated. The French demanded recognition of their interests in Syria and Morocco in exchange for accepting British gains in Egypt and Cyprus. They were skeptical of Russian aspirations in central Europe and less inclined than the British to respond to Russian demands at Turkish expense. In contrast with their allies, the French were consequently dissatisfied though not sufficiently to threaten the alliance.[28]

Entente relations shifted with changes in the military situation. Russian military power collapsed rapidly at the end of November and the British and French effort to tie down enough German forces to allow the Russians to continue their offensive became the critical issue. The British and French were, however, unsuccessful. Grand Duke Nicholas informed them at the end of December that he would have to stop the offensive and conduct limited withdrawals. This news seriously concerned French and British leaders, but they gradually decided that the Russian position was not as unpromising as the Russians presented it. Russian weakness nonetheless replaced Russian strength as a major factor in Entente relations. This reversal changed the nature of the threats to the alliance. The alliance appeared to be endangered in November by reduction of the Russian offensive in Poland but in December by renunciation of a Russian offensive altogether and the possibility of a Russian reconciliation with the Central Powers. Compensating for Russian weakness rather than maintaining Russian strength therefore became the central problem for the British and French.[29]

The new military situation altered the meaning of the Anglo-Russian agreements during November. Sazonov became concerned by mid-December that control of the Straits would not be secure unless it was imposed by Russia itself, and he therefore inquired whether the military means for achieving control were available. Chief of General Staff Yanushkevich and Grand Duke Nicholas replied that the lack of prewar preparations and a precarious situation in Poland precluded allocating forces for operations against Turkey until Germany and Austria-Hungary were defeated. Indeed, Grand Duke Nicholas reinforced Russia's dependence on its allies when he asked at the end of December for an Anglo-French attack to divert the Turks from their Caucasus campaign. Despite Sazonov's reassurance the British and French feared that Russia was sufficiently discouraged by its defeats to reach a separate understanding with the Central Powers. Their anxiety caused the British and French to discontinue their own efforts to negotiate a separate peace with Austria-Hungary and to renounce their outright opposition to Russian aspirations at Austro-Hungarian expense.[30]

Their concern did not preclude mutual criticism. French bitterness declined in December because no new bargains were struck between their allies, but the French continued to be critical of Sazonov's aspirations and machinations in the Balkans. The French were concerned about the apparent British inclination to consider troop withdrawals from the continent despite British denials. The British in turn faulted the French conduct of the war and doubted the French ability to persevere. Concern nonetheless overrode criticism. The British abided by their promise not to conclude a separate peace by refusing an American suggestion of bilateral talks with the Germans; the British even implied that they would continue the war until certain of their allies' war aims were satisfied.[31]

The Entente was therefore consolidated rather than dissolved. The initial German efforts to divide the Entente failed. Indeed, those efforts had little chance for success even if they had been more cleverly conducted. Some German assumptions were accurate. Britain proved to be the most active in consolidating the alliance and most willing to offer its allies compensations to encourage their perseverance. France was least able to achieve war aims and thus was least inclined to accommodate its allies. Russia was most susceptible to inducements, first because of its apparent strength and then because of its apparent weakness. Thus, the German perception of the roles of its enemies was correct.

The military situation tended, however, to solidify rather than to shatter the Entente. The prospects for its members were neither unfavorable nor favorable enough for them to renounce each other. The alliance might have collapsed in 1914 if one of its members had been forced by a catastrophe to conclude a separate peace, as Russia finally did at the beginning of 1918. It might have dissolved in 1914 if Germany was defeated and general peace restored—as would happen at the end of 1918. Instead, the stalemate in 1914 reinforced the Entente and rendered defensive more important than offensive considerations. The Entente was consolidated because it was essential to the self-preservation of its members, whereas its dissolution was necessary only to German expansion. Like the many other factors which reinforced the stalemate, the consolidation of the Entente had paradoxical effects. It was a prerequisite for preserving the balance of power and thus the European state system. But it also increased the likelihood that war would be prolonged until the European system was either exhausted or revolutionized. The Entente could therefore prove to be a vehicle of either salvation or destruction.

THE DIAGONAL POLICY:
THE GERMAN GOVERNMENT
& PEOPLE

THE GOVERNMENT'S PROBLEM:
MAINTAINING SUPPORT WITHOUT SHARING POWER

It is only a part—and perhaps the easier part—of a government's functions to formulate policy. Leaders must also transform policy into reality. Realization of policy objectives requires that external resistance be overcome by a combination of war and diplomacy, and that a skillful domestic policy surmount internal opposition. The domestic and foreign aspects of policymaking can have contradictory implications. If the government mobilizes sufficient domestic power to overcome foreign resistance, it risks losing control over policy. If instead it refuses to mobilize domestic power, it risks failure in surmounting foreign resistance. Governments ideally seek an optimum mix, i.e., to maximize power without jeopardizing control over policy. The historian Hans Delbrück observed after a conversation with his cousin, Imperial Interior Minister Clemens Delbrück: "Public opinion!! One cannot do without it but can allow it no influence. Will Bethmann be able to manage that?"[1] This was the critical domestic problem for the German government and indeed for all war leaders.

Continuation of the war required greater mobilization. Whereas a quick victory would indicate that the government had mobilized sufficient power to overcome foreign resistance, the stalemate demonstrated that insufficient power had been mobilized. The deadlock demanded that the participants choose between a compromise peace and the continued pursuit of victory. A compromise peace would render further mobilization unnecessary, whereas victory required greater mobilization. The stalemate also implied that mobilization would have to be sustained if defeat was to be avoided. The deadlock consequently obliged all the governments to prepare their populations for both offensive and defensive reasons. To discourage pessimism, they had to look backward and explain why victory had not been won. To encourage optimism, they had to look forward and project how victory could yet be won. The stalemate necessitated the mobilization of greater popular power—but at the same time it made that mobilization more difficult. Whereas a short war implied great reward at small cost, a long war implied smaller reward at greater cost. Governments could thus produce less while asking more.

Greater mobilization was not only necessary and difficult but also dangerous. By seeking greater public support, the government risked increasing public demands to share in the formulation of policy. As governments mobilized more power, they could therefore control it less. The stalemate augmented the danger since it threatened a longer war which would increase time for public debate over policy. Public debate might reveal that the stalemate would make a compromise peace more logical than the continued pursuit of victory. Discussion might also indicate that the German government's proclaimed goal of self-preservation could be better realized through stalemate than by victory. Conversely, public debate might prove that the public was as aggressive as the government. In any case, debate might force the government to choose publicly between its proclaimed and confidential aims and thus lessen its flexibility and control over policy. But the stalemate necessitated more rather than less flexibility since it was difficult to predict outcomes and policy was dependent on military events. The deadlock also indicated that policy would have to be flexible if it was to complement strategy in breaking the stalemate, i.e., in shattering the Entente by reaching a separate peace.

Most ominously, the need for a greater mobilization created a psychological problem which was difficult for policy to resolve. The stalemate required greater flexibility in policy, but it fostered greater rigidity in public opinion. In response to pleas for a greater effort, the public demanded more definite rewards. In this way the achievement of war aims became a psychological necessity. Victory was a sufficient objective when the war was expected to be short, but even more enticing visions became necessary when the war threatened to become long. In a very important sense, visions became a substitute for victory. The stalemate made victory increasingly illusory, so the German war aims seemed increasingly real until fantasy largely replaced reality. But fantasy also complicated reality. The less possible victory proved to be, the more the nation had to be mobilized; the more the nation had to be mobilized, the more illusions had to be fostered; the more exaggerated illusions became, the greater victory had to be. The Germans accordingly expected more as the stalemate demonstrated that less could be achieved.

This situation created the need for a rationale to resolve its contradictions. The German war aims became increasingly retrospective, i.e., they sought compensation for the price already paid rather than objectives which would justify further efforts. Thus, their cost, not their feasibility, determined German objectives. As the price of war increased, the objectives became exaggerated and excessive optimism was necessary to conceal previous failure, justify further efforts, and make even more exaggerated aspirations seem realistic. Excessive optimism consequently reconciled the contradictions between illusion and reality.

Excessive optimism and exaggerated war aims involved dangers. They jeopardized the government's domestic policy by alienating the left and thus threatening national unity. Excessive expectations might threaten the government's foreign policy by unifying enemy public opinion just as the German government was hoping enemy dissension and German official moderation would encourage them to conclude a separate peace with Germany. Excessive pessimism entailed even greater risk. The stalemate suggested that a higher price would have to be paid for the expected reward or the price paid already would return less reward than expected. If the public became aware of these unsatisfying choices, general indecision or indignation might ensue. Pessimism would also endanger the government's domestic policy by alienating the right and threatening national unity. It would threaten the government's foreign policy by giving the impression that a German collapse was imminent. Excessive optimism would therefore complicate victory, while excessive pessimism would risk defeat. If they were to succeed, the Germans would have to steer a course between the Scylla of optimism and the Charybdis of pessimism.

The stalemate increased the German government's need to reconcile greater mobilization and continued control—even as it made that reconciliation more unlikely. The deadlock promised less reward at greater cost, a less flexible response to more unpredictable events, less realism and more illusion. Policy and politics were caught in a vicious cycle: the more governments mobilized national power, the less they could control it.

MOBILIZING THE NATION:
MORALE, MEN, MATERIEL & MONEY

The German government's decision to continue the war made greater mobilization of German power mandatory. It first had to persuade the German people to support a longer war rather than sue for a compromise peace. It would then be necessary to expand military forces sufficiently to break the stalemate. German industry would meanwhile have to produce the materiel which the stalemate had demonstrated was critical. Funds would have to be found to finance military expansion and war production. In short, the German government had to mobilize morale, men, materiel and money.

The most compelling necessity for the German government was the mobilization of morale. The greatest threat to morale was public discouragement which may have been Bethmann's central concern when he recognized the fact of military stalemate. If the people perceived the deadlock as proof that Germany could not win the war or conclude a favorable peace, pessimism might become widespread. It was therefore mandatory to reassure the people that victory was possible. Bethmann encouraged confidence in his December Reichstag speech which emphasized perseverance, confidence, chauvinism and arrogance. He frequently repeated these themes and claimed after the war that they were necessary to avoid a collapse of German morale. Public disinterest and despondency were less serious but nonetheless dangerous threats to morale. The war bogged down into uneventful stagnation after its initial excitement. The government responded by arguing that the war was necessary to German self-preservation and that gave the war a sense of immediacy. A sense of alienation and distaste for war also threatened public morale. The idealistic spirit of August faded by November and was replaced by disgust and indignation over its cost. The government responded by idealizing the German cause.[2]

All of the government's tactics were combined in its efforts to place responsibility for the war on Germany's enemies. The German, like all belligerent governments, sought to do so at the beginning of the war. The German campaign was less active during the autumn but it was intensified again at the end of 1914. It was partly directed toward neutral and enemy populations, but it was designed primarily for the German people. Throughout the campaign it was emphasized that the German cause was good and that the war was necessary. These claims were made on one hand in a pseudo-historical or legalistic fashion and they concentrated on the July crisis and immediate prewar period to assert that enemy governments had consciously fomented the war. The government on the other hand asserted on nationalistic-cultural grounds that the war had been caused by irreconcilable conflicts between a rising Germany and its jealous neighbors.[3]

The German assertions were contradictory. The guilt-responsibility argument accused enemy governments of causing the war and rested on the premises that war was aberrant, peace normal, and that reconciliation was possible. The national-cultural argument assumed that conflicting national interests caused the war and that war was therefore normal, peace aberrant, and reconciliation impossible. These arguments suggested contradictory German policies. If enemy governments had been responsible, Germany should pursue a limited victory, encourage changes in enemy governments, offer moderate conditions, and seek reconciliation. If instead national-cultural conflicts were inherent, the German government should seek a total victory and impose conditions sufficiently extreme to insure against future retaliation.

These arguments likewise made different appeals to the German people. By advancing the guilt-responsibility argument the German government asked the German people to condemn enemy governments but implied that all governments should be judged by the people. By contrast, the national-cultural argument suggested that the war was caused by irreconcilable conflicts and that governments were not responsible. These two arguments also implied divergent postwar aspirations. The guilt-responsibility argument suggested that prewar governments should be altered and the prewar system adjusted but not revolutionized. The national-cultural argument implied that the conflict would continue (in this or a second war) until one side was sufficiently powerful to establish a totally new system.

The German government therefore claimed that German prospects for victory were favorable to counter pessimism and discouragement. To counter disinterest and indifference, the government claimed that Germany's existence was threatened. To counter distaste and indignation, it claimed that the German cause was morally good. But these appeals were divergent. If the German people would fight because Germany was likely to be victorious, then it was untrue that Germany was in danger and irrelevant that its cause was good. If the German people would fight because Germany was threatened, it was untrue that it was likely to be victorious and irrelevant that its cause was good. If the German people would fight because Germany's cause was good, then it was irrelevant whether Germany was victorious or threatened.

The German government did not seek to resolve these inconsistencies if indeed it perceived them. German leaders were more concerned with the effects of their claims on their constituency than they were with their own consistency. They had to meet contradictory dangers and satisfy contradictory demands so they gave contradictory responses. In this sense, the inconsistencies in policy can even be interpreted as consistent with the circumstances. The government's assertions seemed to be required because of the danger that public morale might otherwise collapse. This was a possibility but in the last resort a moot question. It is possible that the government's propaganda was superfluous since the German people might have persevered without it. All of the belligerent populations had adjusted and the war was accepted by the end of 1914. To the extent that the government's propaganda was unnecessary, it did not affect public opinion. The efficacy of the government's propaganda was an academic question as long as public opinion and governmental policy ran parallel but it would become important if they diverged. As it turned out, German public opinion supported the war at the end of 1914 and thus allowed the government to mobilize the nation for a longer war.[4]

The mobilization of more manpower was necessary to win a military decision. Mobilization was easier than maintaining civilian morale because the results were measurable and the precedent of conscription already existed. The Germans actually had fewer disciplinary and recruitment problems than any of the other belligerents until the war was lost in 1918. German military and civilian leaders hoped to break the stalemate by mobilizing more men for military operations. The stalemate, however, altered the mobilization problem.

As long as the primary objective was a quick annihilation of the enemy's army, the main consideration was speed of concentration rather than total manpower. When the German objective became gradual attrition, the critical factor became total manpower and not speed of concentration. None of the belligerents, however, recognized these implications. They all tried to break the stalemate by mobilizing quickly, and thereby made a breakthrough unlikely. Their mobilization efforts reinforced the stalemate. Even if one side achieved a tactical military breakthrough, it was unlikely that the other side would surrender until its reserves had been exhausted. The more men the belligerents mobilized for military operations, the less likely a rapid military decision became.[5]

Material factors also deterred a rapid military decision but became increasingly important in the war of attrition where the critical factor was the relationship between the rate of expenditure and available supply. The rates of expenditure were more or less fixed since both sides were confronted with similar circumstances and pursued similar strategies. The available supply depended on the potential resources and efficiency of production by each side. The resources were generally finite but production varied and was therefore the critical factor. The relationship between military and nonmilitary elements was altered by the war's changing objectives. Victory in a war of attrition necessitated exhaustion of the enemy's total power so the factory and farm became as critical as the front. Exhaustion of the participants would take considerable time and would result in the de-emphasis of military operations since a rapid military victory was no longer the primary goal. But it took time before the belligerents recognized the stalemate, and it required even longer for them to perceive all the implications of the deadlock. They continued to hope for rapid victory by military means. Since they had not expected a war of attrition, none of the powers had prepared for it. The means available for disrupting enemy economics, i.e., blockade, were untried and less effective than the means available for mobilizing national economies. Thus, on balance, material factors tended to reinforce the stalemate and prolong the war.

The importance of material factors was first indicated by munitions shortages which began to concern the leaders of all belligerents soon after the Marne. By the end of October, ammunition reserves were exhausted and expenditure became dependent on current production. Despite the considerable effort to increase munitions production, it could not keep pace with demand. Shortages consequently assumed critical proportions for both sides in November and seriously affected strategy. They probably influenced Falkenhayn's decision to discontinue his Flanders campaign since he could accumulate munitions reserves sufficient to attempt a breakthrough only by reducing the rate of expenditure. Munitions shortages may have induced him to consider transferring operations to the east where such shortages might be partially overcome by greater mobility. They were perhaps a factor in his suggestion of a separate peace with Russia. The postponement of operations to accumulate munitions reserves tended to prolong the war since it left both sides with enough munitions to avoid defeat but insufficient to win. Munitions shortages consequently confirmed the stalemate.[6]

An increase in war materiel production necessitated the mobilization of industrial manpower and the shortage of labor, particularly of specialized skills, due to conscription became a problem. When the importance of material factors relative to military operations was recognized, workers with special skills were released from the army to return to industry. The residue of bad will between labor and management from the prewar period created a further difficulty. Efforts to reduce it were singularly unsuccessful, in large measure because owners preferred compulsion to cooperation. The only concessions owners were willing to make to the workers depended on the annexation of foreign industry.[7]

Prolongation of the war also produced food shortages. Prewar planning had seemed unnecessary since the harvest and reserves were sufficient to support the expected short war. When the possibility of a protracted conflict became evident in the autumn, the government reacted reluctantly and the public was lulled by optimistic press reports and the availability of luxury items. Germany was a large importer of food and thus it was vulnerable in a long war—a fact driven home by the intensification of the Entente blockade in November. Food prices mounted due to hoarding and speculation as well as actual shortages and the problem threatened to become political because of Socialist demands for price ceilings and controls. Some officials feared that food reserves would be insufficient to last until the next harvest or even beyond the spring, to which the government responded with an unsuccessful combination of veiled controls and requests for voluntary restraint. Despite the government's rejection of more energetic alternatives, the advocates of greater controls began to make their views felt in indirect ways. By the end of 1914 the government recognized the food problem and had isolated its main aspects, but the government failed to establish an effective means of control and the public's prewar resistance to government compulsion remained. The government's awareness that the war would be long was therefore canceled by its refusal to make the necessary concessions that a long war required.[8]

The mobilization of money was more feasible. The European financial structure which some feared was too delicate to withstand the shock of war actually proved to be more adaptable than morale, manpower or material factors. There were several explanations for this flexibility. The great reserve of wealth accumulated in the past could be tapped whereas reserves of munitions and food simply did not exist. The wealth expected in the future could also be tapped through the sale of war bonds but future production of munitions and food could not be consumed. Above all, the government could print money more easily than it could produce war materiel. The main problem of winning popular approval to exploit the nation's wealth was resolved when the government's budget was approved by the Reichstag in December. The secondary goal of reestablishing financial stability was achieved by the end of 1914. Germany, like the other belligerents, adapted its prewar economy to war. The government's controls were gradually extended over the following two years and compulsion replaced commerce as the operative principle in economic activities. But the very gradualism of this transition reinforced the deadlock.[9]

DREAMS OF GRANDEUR:
THE WAR AIMS OF THE GERMAN PEOPLE

The German mobilization of power was not only necessary and difficult but also dangerous. The government risked excessive popular war aims by encouraging overoptimism to maintain morale and diminish pessimism. Excessive aims from the public limited and even jeopardized the government's control over foreign policy. Those aims also threatened the government's domestic policy of maintaining national unity. War aims were linked to domestic political issues, particularly the question of reform. War aims and demands for reform conflicted since war aims implied opposition to reform, whereas reform implied opposition to war aims. Bethmann sought to avoid this conflict by procrastinating—a tactic which might have proven adequate in a short war, but which became less practicable in the longer war threatened by the stalemate.

It is difficult and perhaps meaningless to seek a precise evaluation of German public opinion toward the question of war aims at the end of 1914. A considerable number of the German people may have been discouraged, disgusted, or disinterested—as Bethmann feared—and they might have consequently renounced aggressive war aims. That question is moot, however, because those elements of the population remained silent. It is nonetheless clear that the vocal portion of the population was overwhelmingly confident and expansionist. That segment of the population comprised the ruling classes with the notable exception of Socialist politicians and some journalists. The ruling classes in all of the belligerent societies constituted a minority but enjoyed most of the power and influence on government policy. German professors, plutocrats, politicians and princes all advocated aggressive war aims. The German case indicates that the people of a state with power are as susceptible as their government to delusions of grandeur.

The military stalemate does not seem to have dampened the demands of most academics for aggressive war aims. On the contrary, they were evidently as anxious as other groups in the society to insure that the government did not lose confidence and reduce its aims as a result. Professor Schumacher produced a memorandum advocating extensive aims at the request of leading industrialists.

The Baltic Professor Theodor Schiemann demanded definite annexations in the east. The voices of moderation were as revealing as the aspirations of extremists. An awareness of the need for alternative choices began to penetrate some academics by the end of 1914 because of the military stalemate. Professor Otto Hoetzsch argued that Germany ought to seek a *modus vivendi* if not an alliance with Russia since it could not be defeated, and he therefore argued that Germany should not alter the status of Poland. He nonetheless could not resist the temptation to seek the acquisition of some Russian territory and he advocated the annexation of a Polish border strip similar to the one being considered for annexation by the government. Like other relative moderates inside and outside the government, Hoetzsch thereby sought to reconcile concessions with conciliation. Professor Friedrich Meinecke sought the same objective by simultaneously advocating a moderate peace and postwar control over Belgium.[10]

The most illustrative case in point was raised by Professor Hans Delbrück who specifically opposed the extreme aims advocated by the Pan-Germans. Delbrück wanted Belgium disarmed and controlled gradually enough by Germany to avoid European resistance. He, like Bethmann and other relative moderates, advocated what amounted to domination through deception. Instead of pursuing such a policy to its logical conclusion by publicly renouncing the annexation of Belgium, Delbrück like Bethmann wanted, however, to retain Belgium as an object for bargaining with England. The best indicator of German public opinion was Delbrück's assumption that the aims he advocated in western Europe "would certainly appear too little to the German people for the price which has been paid." Since he regarded further German expansion in western Europe as "inadvisable in every way," he concluded that "at least some indirect expansion to the east would be almost necessary as a prize of victory." Delbrück concluded after a conversation with his cousin, Clemens Delbrück, that "it will be very difficult for [Bethmann and Clemens Delbrück] to win approval for their [moderate] views [on war aims] above as well as below. Above [would be] easier since [Bethmann] assured [Hans Delbrück] that Falkenhayn is a very understanding man. But public opinion!!" Even without an open public discussion, a body of ideas and assumptions circulated among educated Germans. The publicist Victor Naumann wrote an extensive memorandum which constituted a compendium of desiderata discussed by both government and vocal members of the ruling classes. There were bitter disagreements over details and degree which could erupt into open political and personal conflict, but a general consensus nonetheless seems to have existed among educated Germans that expansive war aims in some form were desirable.[11]

An even greater area of agreement apparently existed between government and business interests. Bethmann seems to have considered the views of the industrialists Thyssen and Röchling in developing policy on Briey-Longwy and discussed the war aims of Kirdorff, Thyssen and Hugenberg with Stinnes. Krupp's war aims exceeded but resembled Bethmann's. The "War Committee of German Industry" began to take up the question of war aims in November. Bethmann agreed with Stresemann and Roetger, representatives of industry, on general points though not in detail or degree at the beginning of December. The so-called "war aims movement" and its vanguard, the Pan-German League, had heavy industry as their core. In December the leaders of the League distributed copies of an extensive war aims program which was written in September by their chairman, Class. The government prosecuted Class for violating the edict prohibiting the public discussion of war aims but the prosecution backfired when the courts decided in favor of Class. The government's prohibition may have favored the Pan-Germans since they could propagate their views through connections in high places, whereas the activities of antiannexationists were severely restricted. The aspirations of bankers Robert and Franz Mendelssohn indicated that the ideas circulating among industrialists were also current among bankers. In comparison to other elements of the German economic community, the commercial circles in Hamburg seem to have been moderate.[12]

Many politicians advocated comparable war aims but there was less unanimity among them since they represented elements of society outside the educated and economic communities. Bethmann was more anxious to pacify the politicians than the professors, press or plutocrats because he was aware that they could jeopardize his control of policy by publicly expressing their differences over war aims and launching a debate in the Reichstag. He consequently sought to deter their opposition by repeating his theme of cautious confidence to members of the Reichstag before his December speech. He assured them that Germany's military situation was secure and promising, but he warned that war aims would be dependent on military events, that enemy strength was underestimated, that Germany would probably not win a complete victory over all its enemies, and that restoring peace could be complicated. These confidential statements were generally more qualified and realistic than his demogogic Reichstag speech.[13]

The politicians of the center and right were in general agreement with each other but differed over details. When the Progressive Party leader, Conrad Haussmann, proposed that the nonsocialist parties designate their vote for war credits as an indication of confidence in the government's relatively moderate official aims, the National Liberal and Conservative leaders refused. National Liberal aims were represented most notably by Stresemann's extreme annexationism. Conservative leader Kuno Westarp was more moderate than some in advocating a rapprochement with Russia but contradictory in demanding annexations at Russian expense. Another parliamentarian, Winckler, meanwhile urged moderation toward Russia and France but incorporation of the "old German lands," Belgium and Luxemburg.[14]

The greatest gulf existed between the Socialists and the other parties. The Conservatives and National Liberals criticized the government's official moderation and the Progressives applauded it, but the Socialists demanded it. The government's request for war credits in December caused a crisis in the Socialist Party. Karl Liebknecht, who had resisted the war increasingly since September, sought to mobilize opposition among his party colleagues in the Reichstag. When this failed, he courageously decided to register his lone vote in the Reichstag against credits and thereby embarked on the path which led to his assassination in 1919. Hugo Haase, the Socialist spokesman, reiterated the party's contentions that the war was caused by economic conflicts (i.e., not Entente governments), that it was defensive, that annexations should not be demanded, and that peace should be concluded as soon as possible. Haase's speech was sufficiently confident and vague on war aims to be given prior approval by the government, and all members of the Socialist Reichstag delegation except Liebknecht voted for war credits. More revealing, Liebknecht's vote was immediately repudiated by his Socialist colleagues in the Reichstag. The Socialists thus proved to be a useful tool with which the government might restrain the extremists, justify its prohibition of a war aims discussion, retain support of the workers, and maintain the myth of national unity. The actual differences between Socialist and government aims were therefore disregarded for the moment.[15]

The princes and statesmen of the German Bundesstaaten entertained war aims similar to the rest of the ruling classes. In contrast to the political and economic motives of the politicians and interest groups, the aspirations of Bundesstaaten leaders were particularistic and constitutional. They were anxious that Germany gain by the war and that these gains be acquired so as to reinforce rather than threaten the dynastic and federal character of the Empire. Duke Albert and Prime Minister Karl von Weizsäcker of Württemberg raised the question of Belgium's future at the beginning of November. The Bavarian demands were especially awkward to parry because they were persistent and particularistic. Bavarian Minister President Georg von Hertling earlier made it clear that Bavaria did not want annexations to threaten the federal balance of power. Bavarian King Ludwig intensified his demands for annexations, perhaps because extreme war aims were suggested by Grand Duke August II of Oldenburg. Bethmann's response was vague and he sought Hertling's assistance in dampening Ludwig's enthusiasm by arguing that such schemes were "utopian" until a military decision was achieved and Germany's enemies collapsed. Bethmann opposed outright annexation of Belgium as undesirable for domestic political reasons and advocated instead German domination over the North Sea coast and the establishment of German military and economic control over Belgium. Hertling attempted unsuccessfully to restrain Ludwig, who refused to renounce Belgium and ordered Hertling to take a stronger line in pursuit of Bavarian interests. Bethmann again refused Hertling's attempt to secure a guarantee of annexations for Bavaria. Bethmann's main concern was apparently to conceal or squelch such discussions. Ludwig may have advocated annexations in fear of being swept aside otherwise by Bavarian public opinion—effectively a choice between radically reduced personal power because he exercised restraint or greater power through demagoguery. This interpretation suggests that the gap between the German leaders and their public was not great and that the distinction between conservatism and mass radicalism was becoming blurred.[16]

It is therefore fairly clear that educated and powerful Germans were generally more annexationist than the government. The extreme annexationists were less realistic than the government in the sense of being more ambitious. But they were at least consistent since they based their unrealistic aims on the unrealistic prospects presented by the government, whereas the government pursued war aims which were not justified by the military situation. Bethmann's refusal to permit public discussions of German war aims was likewise based on a contradiction. If the achievement of war aims depended on the final military situation, then confidential government discussions were as unjustified as public debates. But the military stalemate demonstrated that diplomacy had to complement strategy. Since diplomacy involved war aims, a decision concerning them could not be postponed pending a German victory. Consequently, a public debate was no less justified than official discussion. A public debate was, however, less convenient since it might jeopardize the government's control over policy. The government therefore opposed a debate on political, not logical, grounds. This gulf between logical consistency and political necessity increased. The clearer the military stalemate became, the more diplomacy was needed to assist strategy; the more important diplomacy became, the more war aims were implicated; the more war aims were involved, the more difficult it became for the government to prevent public debate. Ever greater government control and prevarication were required to conceal this contradiction.

POLICY VERSUS POLITICS:
RESTRAINT, REFORM, REACTION

The government's central concern in regard to the German people was to maintain its control over policymaking, and popular demands for participation in the establishment of war aims constituted one serious threat. Domestic political conflicts created another problem for the government. The critical domestic political issue was reform of the government structure, and the questions of reform and war aims became increasingly involved as the war continued. Germans who favored extensive war aims generally opposed reform, whereas those who favored reform generally opposed extensive war aims. Alfred Hugenberg, Director of the Krupp works, expressed the relationship most candidly: "it would be useful in order to avoid domestic difficulties [i.e., demands for reform] to distract the attention of the people by giving them room for fantasies of expanding German territory."[17]

In the last resort, these two positions reflected conflicting evaluations of the character and aspirations of average Germans. The annexationists assumed that the German masses would continue to accept political domination at home in order to make Germany dominant abroad, but the reformers assumed that the German people preferred democracy for both themselves and others. The annexationists furthermore assumed there was a fundamental conflict between nations, while the reformers advocated harmony between peoples. Since success for one group insured failure for the other, a dangerous impasse resulted. The conflict could jeopardize the national unity which was a precondition for achieving victory and avoiding defeat. The government's control over policy therefore necessitated its avoidance of domestic conflict.

The politics of reform reversed the roles of war aims politics. Politicians on the right and in the center were activists and the left were resisters over the war aims question. Politicians on the left were activists and on the right the resisters over the reform question. The primary prewar goal of the Socialists was reform of the German and particularly the Prussian political constitution which would give the Socialists power in proportion to the size of their constituency and thus control over the state. As long as the initial enthusiasm for war lasted and a short war seemed possible, the question of reform was obscured. The government's fear of resistance to the war had proven groundless when the workers responded with patriotism. Mass patriotism and national unity nonetheless endangered government control since they implied egalitarianism. When it soon became clear that the ruling classes would not grant the people genuine equality, the Socialists warned that working class soldiers would demand it. The arguments of the reformers and annexationists were consequently analogous but antithetical. Both sides expected the German people would have to be paid for their war effort, but one side advocated reforms and the other annexations as the payment.[18]

The reformers claimed that German soldiers and workers would become disenchanted, resist further mobilization, and jeopardize the war effort if reforms were not forthcoming. Haase reflected the reformer's sense of alienation in his December Reichstag speech in which he generally played down the military and diplomatic aspects of the war and thereby minimized the importance of war aims. His main concern was the domestic repercussions of the war—relief for military dependents, unemployment, food shortages, and the government's policy toward the unions. Beyond these specific problems he expressed a concern for inequality: "considering the cooperation of all members of society" in supporting the war, he regretted the "limitations of the constitutional rights" of some citizens. He argued that press censorship was unjustified and contradicted the government's claims about the "maturity and determination of the German people." In short, Haase argued that, if the German people participated equally in the war, they should share power equitably and be allowed to express their views freely.[19]

The parties of the center played a relatively passive role in the question of reform. They supported the government's policy of postponing reform. The Progressive Friedrich Naumann felt that Bethmann and Delbrück could not promise anything definite under existing conditions. "If one wants to maintain the *Burgfrieden* between the parties during the war, it is completely necessary to throw no material for domestic conflict into the debate. For those of us who belong to the party leadership, it is impossible during the war to enter into a movement [for the reform of] the Prussian suffrage."[20]

The parties of the right were opposed to reform more actively than the left advocated it. The opposition to reform among big industrialists and extreme conservatives began to crystallize by the end of October even before the government had begun to consider it seriously. A "sub-committee for the Preparation of National and Economic-Political Goals for the Present War" was established by the "War Committee of German Industry" and tried to formulate war aims for German industry in its first meeting at the beginning of November. Hugenberg, typically forthright, argued that they should encourage exaggerated war aims among the workers to prevent their demands for domestic political and economic concessions. The representative of the "Union of Industrialists in Rhineland and Westphalia" agreed. Stresemann's tactics involved a combination rather than a choice when he suggested that the workers be won over to extensive annexations by offers of moderate social reforms. Government officials were disagreed: the conservative Prussian Minister of Culture thought that the Socialists' postwar policies were unpredictable; Prussian Minister of Interior Loebell predicted they would be radical; and Prussian Minister of Commerce Sydow expected them to be moderate. The conservative point of view was best expressed by Westarp: "the idea that one should strengthen the right wing of the SPD [vis-à-vis the left wing] by concessions to its demands was as false as the optimistic belief in the evolution of the [Socialist] party" toward moderation.[21]

The government's response was a typical compromise designed to conceal the problems it could not resolve. Bethmann hinted at a postwar "new orientation" in a meeting with Reichstag party leaders at the beginning of November. He attempted to negate the issue in his December Reichstag speech by asserting that the war had swept away all the old social and political dissensions and thereby created a "sacred" spirit of national unity. In short, he implied that an egalitarian society already existed. The achievement of victory would depend on preservation of national unity and politics would have to be subordinated to it until the German victory permitted the luxury of dissension. Bethmann tried to reinforce a spirit of unity by proclaiming that there was a common commitment to national defense and a general belief in national superiority. Kaempf, the president of the Reichstag, repeated these themes in his speech. Bethmann's felicitous phrases expressed both his hopes and concerns. He had long been anxious about the potential Socialist threat to the war effort. Prussian Minister of Interior Loebell suggested in November that the Socialists had not renounced their prewar internationalism and opposition to German expansion, but Bethmann disagreed on the grounds that the Socialists wanted to serve Germany and should therefore not be treated as enemies of the state in the manner advocated by conservatives. Although Loebell remained unconvinced, Bethmann ordered him to investigate the central question for reform, the Prussian suffrage.[22]

Bethmann's attempt at pacification and his procrastination aroused opposition which threatened his tenure. His apparent weakness was widely criticized by many including the Crown Prince and King Ludwig of Bavaria, who was concerned that Bethmann would not have sufficient perseverance and might conclude a premature peace. Lerchenfeld was sympathetic toward Bethmann, who he felt suffered from comparison with his more flamboyant predecessor, Bülow. Hertling was unimpressed by Bethmann, and Tirpitz condemned his conduct of the war. Bethmann was continually excoriated by Pan-Germans and other annexationists because of his war aims policy and by conservatives for his apparent sympathy toward reform.[23]

Bethmann was aware of this criticism and survived in part by responding to it. The arrogance of his December Reichstag speech was a conscious and fairly successful response to the prevailing desire for a strong man. He seemed to have satisfied some important elements, including Hoffmann, Hindenburg, and Ludendorff. At the same time, he gave the impression of sympathizing with the demands of contending factions. He appeared ambitious to annexationists but moderate to antiannexationists, responsive to reformers but cautious to antireformers. Consequently, the criticism was at least partly misdirected. His critics mistook reticence for weakness, whereas he probably resorted to it as a substitute for specificity. The annexationists thought Bethmann's official moderation reflected his opposition to their war aims; in fact, he favored their extensive war aims but he could not say so without risking his control over policy. The conservatives interpreted his vague hints of postwar reform as sympathy but be probably intended those remarks to put off the reformers with promises. Bethmann may ultimately have survived precisely because criticism came from both sides. He could refuse to commit himself on war aims because the reformers opposed it and on reform because the annexationists opposed it. The reform and war aims issues effectively canceled each other.[24]

Bethmann's vulnerability may therefore have been the key to his viability. His vulnerability was largely due to the political impasse. If the demands for annexations and reform were mutually exclusive, annexationists and reformers could not be satisfied. If either side was appeased, the other would be alienated. If neither was appeased, both would be alienated. Reconciliation was impossible and alienation undesirable, so obfuscation became necessary. The conduct of war therefore required Bethmann's "policy of the diagonal," i.e., a policy which would steer a course between the extremes and avoid the issues. But the reverse was also true. Bethmann's policy was one of nonpolitics and feasible only in wartime. The policy of the diagonal was likewise the most natural policy for Bethmann, who was basically apolitical in the sense of being unsympathetic toward partisan aspirations and conflicts. More important for German diplomatic and strategic policy, the policy of the diagonal permitted Bethmann to exercise maximum control over foreign policy. As long as partisan politics was suspended, the influence of domestic political forces on foreign policy would be limited.[25]

Bethmann's control over foreign policy depended on the domestic political impasse, and the impasse affected his foreign policy. He could not allow his foreign policy to threaten the domestic political truce. He was therefore able to formulate foreign policy as long as it remained secret. Government policy which remains secret is, however, tentative since policy is fixed only when the government is publicly committed. Consequently, Bethmann and his associates consciously postponed their final decisions. They conducted extensive policy discussions on war aims and advocated extensive aspirations but their projections were always recognized as conditional on the military situation when peace was restored. Likewise, although the military stalemate made decisive war diplomacy more necessary, the diplomatic policies advocated by Bethmann and his associates (e.g., separate peace with Russia) were dependent on military events. Thus, their final decisions on domestic politics, war aims and war diplomacy were all postponed.[26]

Whatever pragmatic advantages it may have had, Bethmann's procrastination had ominous implications since it essentially negated policy. The conduct of war without a policy can become war without foreseeable end or purpose. Unless opponents envisage what they want in war, they have no standard for concluding peace, and only exhaustion or convulsion can end such a conflict. The impasse in German domestic politics therefore both complicated the formulation of German foreign policy and reinforced the stalemate in European international politics.

CONCLUSION:
A CATALOGUE
OF CONTRADICTIONS

Most European leaders assumed a short war. This assumption may have been essential to their decision for war. Few of them would have opted for war if they had foreseen a protracted, revolutionary or unsuccessful conflict. They assumed that a short war would be decisive, limited and productive. The assumption was therefore made because it was desirable and not because any evidence made it likely.

The short-war assumption implied the corollary that power was equivalent to military force. A government would presumably conclude peace immediately after defeat because it would prefer the disadvantages of a limited setback to the uncertainty of a long war. It would neither draw in the masses nor declare a revolutionary struggle. A short war consequently implied a limited war.

The short-war assumption implied a limited and nonrevolutionary war, but all the participants had far-reaching and revolutionary aspirations. The Germans wanted to adapt the state system to their recently increased power and thereby to dominate it. The Austro-Hungarians were anxious to reassert their great power status by ruling eastern Europe and the Balkans, a goal which would have threatened Russia's role as a European great power. Russia strove to dominate these same areas and demote Austria-Hungary from the ranks of the great powers. France wanted to undo the results of the Franco-Prussian War by retrieving Alsace-Lorraine and by reducing German power. Britain projected the demise of "Prussian militarism" and the establishment of a league of nations which would maintain the *status quo*, preclude war and include the United States. All belligerent governments pursued these revolutionary aspirations with revolutionary means. The Germans sought to revolutionize the Russian and British Empires; the Austro-Hungarians to destroy the Russian Empire; the Russians to revolutionize the Hapsburg and Ottoman Empires; the British to dissolve the Ottoman Empire; and the French to shatter the German, Hapsburg and Ottoman Empires. None of these efforts was very successful, but they demonstrated that even the most conservative governments were willing to use all available means to defend and extend their power. In other words, their behavior was consistent with the traditional assumptions of great power status. It was, however, inconsistent with the assumption of a short and limited war.

The domestic policies of the participants involved analogous contradictions. A short war would have to remain limited through the maintenance of tight governmental control over policy and the achievement of a rapid victory. Such governmental control required the exclusion of the masses from influence over policy. All governments tried, however, to win a rapid victory by national mobilization which implied threats to governmental control of policy and the possibility of total war. Governments, in effect, wanted to win a limited war with unlimited means.

All governments hoped that a short war would extricate them from these contradictions. To exclude the masses from policy formulation, governments claimed that victory required national unity, unity necessitated a political truce, a truce implied the end of criticism and thus popular influence on policy. All governments accordingly sought to mobilize maximum power while maintaining maximum control over policy at the same time and the precedent established by previous short wars seemed to justify their efforts. As in the Austro-Prussian and Franco-Prussian wars, a short war might allow successful governments both to buy off the masses with war booty and to reinforce domestic control. A war could, however, be short only if it was limited, i.e., if the masses were not drawn in. The domestic means used by all the governments therefore jeopardized the objectives they sought.

The widely expected short war proved to be an illusion by the end of 1914. The basic military explanation was the relatively equal power of the two alliances. Strategists on both sides made similar and simultaneous moves which tended to cancel each other. Despite the mystique of the offensive, commanders took basically conservative decisions after the initial offensive thrusts. In particular, the French decision to preserve their forces virtually precluded the encirclement essential to a rapid German victory. Furthermore, the German west wing on the western front lacked the superiority in manpower and mobility necessary to encircle the French. Material factors favored the defense more than the offense. Therefore, the military preconditions for a short war did not exist.

Even if a military decision had been achieved, the diplomatic policies of the belligerents made a short war dubious. All the governments had revolutionary aspirations and used revolutionary political means but gave priority to conservative considerations. Above all, the consolidation of the opposing alliances made the rapid surrender of a defeated power unlikely. Those who assumed the war would be short mistakenly interpreted the Franco-Prussian War as proof of the efficacy of military means. In fact, the French surrendered in 1871 largely because their diplomatic isolation made perpetuating the war unpromising. In this sense the short war became impossible not at the Marne but at Tannenberg and Mons, i.e., when the Russians and British demonstrated that they intended to fulfill their alliance commitments to the French. Therefore, the diplomatic requirements for a short war did not exist.

Domestic political considerations might have prevented a short war if military and diplomatic policies had not. Mobilization of the masses meant mass involvement in the outcome of the war. Mass involvement implied the risk of revolt if a government surrendered. Governments were more likely to refuse surrender and to continue the war than they were to surrender and risk rebellion. They would have been likely to surrender only if that would avoid revolt. But mass involvement made revolt more likely after surrender. Thus, the domestic political preconditions for a short war also did not exist.

When the short-war assumption proved fallacious, a new situation was created. Since the assumption was the basis of all strategies and policies, fundamental decisions became necessary. Because victory was impossible under existing conditions, victory had to be renounced or the conditions had to be changed. If victory was renounced, a compromise peace or general exhaustion were the only options. If the conditions were changed, new strategies and policies were required.

All governments rejected a compromise peace and the possibility of general exhaustion. A compromise peace meant a return to the *status quo ante bellum* and that implied either another war or permanent peace. But, since the prospect of another war was unappealing and since a permanent peace seemed impractical, a compromise peace was dismissed. The prospect of general exhaustion was also unattractive, but all the governments made decisions which reinforced the stalemate and consequently made general exhaustion a more likely outcome.

All the governments consequently elected to pursue victory by changing the conditions. They tried to shatter the military stalemate by adopting a new strategy of breakthrough which was essentially an attempt to adapt a mobile war to immobile conditions. Concentration therefore replaced encirclement as the means and enemy confusion was substituted for annihilation as the objective. Nonetheless, the assumption which had been made during the early months of the war remained—as it must for all military operations—that strategy would determine the outcome of the war, in particular, that a defeated power would surrender. But the national mobilization which was necessary to continue military operations made this assumption increasingly questionable since mobilization involved the masses in the war and threatened to raise political questions. The new strategy therefore jeopardized the primacy of strategy as the critical element. As long as a short war seemed possible, diplomacy merely sought to preserve the chances for a military victory and project the shape of peace which would follow. When strategy failed to produce victory, diplomacy was called upon to create the preconditions of military success. If the stalemate was to be broken, the relative strength of the two alliances would have to be altered. All the powers therefore intensified their efforts to preserve and extend their alliances and to shatter the enemy alliance.

Shattering the Entente became the primary objective of German policy. German leaders regarded Britain as the main enemy and decided that a separate peace with either Russia or France was necessary. Because they were more committed to the conflict with France and apparently less able to defeat Russia decisively, they regarded peace with Russia more likely and desirable. A German victory therefore seemed to depend above all on the restoration of peace with Russia.

German policy and strategy were, however, caught in a vicious cycle. Military victory seemed to depend on the ability of German diplomacy to shatter the Entente. But, if diplomacy could have achieved that goal, the war would probably not have started. A dissolution of the Entente during the July crisis would probably have caused its members to accept diplomatic defeat rather than fight alone against Germany. The war occurred because German diplomacy failed to divide the Entente powers, which were more dependent on one another in war than in peace and therefore less likely to leave the alliance after the war began. Yet a German victory depended on the wartime dissolution of the Entente. The war was therefore necessary when it was unlikely to be successful for Germany but might have been successful only when it would have been unnecessary. German leaders never escaped that dilemma.

The end of the short-war illusion in military stalemate marked a turning point in the World War. The belligerents went to war in pursuit of the prewar objectives which had escaped them in the July crisis. As long as a short war seemed possible, they could look back to prewar problems and precedents. When a short war turned out to be impossible, breaking the stalemate became the central problem. The more difficult it proved to break the stalemate, the more leaders looked forward to victory rather than backward to prewar considerations. Breaking the deadlock required new military, diplomatic and domestic means which would have far-reaching implications for the war's outcome. Thus, whereas prewar goals had precipitated the decisions to go to war, the war once begun would produce its own goal of victory and would shape the postwar world in ways unforeseen by the participants.

In a broader sense, stalemate became the fundamental fact of European international relations for the next thirty years. The Entente had enough power to restrain Germany but not enough to remove the German threat. Germany had sufficient strength to destroy the system but not to dominate it. As the German academic, Otto Hintze, observed during World War I, "if worst comes to worst, we shall let ourselves be buried beneath the ruins of European civilization."[1] Hitler echoed this sentiment at the end of World War II. The stalemate of 1914 prefigured the demise of the traditional European state system in 1945.

Reference Matter

NOTES

CHAPTER 1

1 The question of continuity is raised among others by: K.D. Bracher, NPL, 1962, pp. 471-82; Ludwig Dehio, *Germany and World Politics in the Twentieth Century*, London, 1959, pp. 11-38 (hereafter Dehio, *Germany*); Klaus Epstein, "German War Aims in the First World War," WP, XV, 1, 1962, pp. 163-85 (hereafter Epstein, "Aims"); Fritz Fischer, *Griff nach der Weltmacht*, Düsseldorf, 1964, p. 12 (hereafter Fischer, *Griff*); Michael Freund, "Bethmann Hollweg, der Hitler des Jahres 1914?" FAZ, 28 March 1964 (hereafter Freund, "Bethmann Hollweg"); Golo Mann, "Der Griff nach der Weltmacht," NZZ, 28 April 1962 (hereafter Mann, "Griff"); Rudolf Neck, "Kriegszielpolitik im ersten Weltkrieg," MOS, XV, pp. 565-76 (hereafter Neck, "Kriegszielpolitik"); Gerhard Ritter, "Eine neue Kriegsschuldthese? Zu Fritz Fischers Buch 'Griff nach der Weltmacht,' " HZ, 191, p. 646 (hereafter Ritter, "Kriegsschuldthese"). For the continuity argument, see: Fischer, *Griff*, pp. 39, 108; Fritz Fischer, *Weltmacht oder Niedergang: Deutschland im ersten Weltkrieg*, Frankfurt am Main, 1965, pp. 37-9 (hereafter Fischer, *Weltmacht*); Imanuel Geiss, *Julikrise und Kriegsausbruch 1914*, Hanover, 1963-4, II, pp. 721-3 (hereafter Geiss, *Julikrise*). For the discontinuity argument, see: Ritter, "Kriegsschuldthese," pp. 646-8. For examples of these views of the July crisis, see: Fischer, *Weltmacht*, p. 51; Fischer, *Griff*, pp. 59-108; Fischer, in *Die Zeit*, 3 September 1965; Ritter, "Kriegsschuldthese," pp. 646-68.
2 For a more detailed presentation of the author's interpretation of the July crisis, see: "The Limits of Choice: July 1914 Reconsidered," JCR, XVI, 1, pp. 1-23.
3 The limits of space make possible only a general survey of the literature on this question. For the view that a short war was expected by most Europeans, see: B.H. Liddell Hart, *The Real War, 1914-1918*, Boston and Toronto, 1930, p. 43 (hereafter Liddell Hart, *War*); J.P.T. Bury, *France, 1814-1940*, New York, 1962, p. 238 (hereafter Bury, *France*); A.J.P. Taylor, *The Struggle for Mastery in Europe, 1848-1918*, Oxford, 1954, pp. 529-30 (hereafter Taylor,

Struggle); A.J.P. Taylor, *A History of the First World War*, New York, 1963, p. 16 (hereafter Taylor, *History*); Fritz Klein (editor), *Deutschland im ersten Weltkrieg*, Berlin, 1970, p. 309 (hereafter Klein, *Deutschland*); Peter Kielmansegg, *Deutschland und der Erste Weltkrieg*, Frankfurt, 1968.

4 Gerhard Ritter, *Staatskunst und Kriegshandwerk*, Munich, 1960, II, pp. 243-4, 282-304, 1964, III, p. 23 (hereafter Ritter *Staatskunst*); Gordon A. Craig, *The Politics of the Prussian Army, 1640-1945*, Oxford, 1955, pp. 274-7, 281 (hereafter Craig, *Politics*); Klein, *Deutschland*, pp. 133, 144-5; Franz Conrad von Hötzendorf, *Aus meiner Dienstzeit*, Vienna/Leipzig/ Munich, 1922-5, I, pp. 381-2, III, pp. 144-5, IV, p. 194 (hereafter Conrad, *Dienstzeit*); *Der Weltkrieg 1914-1918, Kriegsrüstung und Kriegswirtschaft*, Berlin, 1930, I, p. 287 (hereafter *Weltkrieg, Kriegsrüstung*); Helmuth von Moltke, *Erinnerungen-Briefe-Dokumente, 1877-1916*, Stuttgart, 1922, p. 10 (hereafter Moltke, *Erinnerungen*); Winston S. Churchill, *The World Crisis, 1911-1914*, London, 1923, p. 262 (hereafter Churchill, *Crisis*); Richard Grelling, *J'Accuse*, New York, 1915, p. 30; C.R.M.F. Cruttwell, *A History of the Great War, 1914-1918*, Oxford, 1934, p. 5 (hereafter Cruttwell, *History*); Wilhelm Foerster, *Mein Kampf gegen das militaristische und nationalistische Deutschland*, Stuttgart, 1920, p. 121; Fritz Fischer, *Krieg der Illusionen*, Düsseldorf, 1969, pp. 663-82, 777 (hereafter Fischer, *Krieg*); Wilhelm Groener, *Lebenserinnerungen*, Göttingen, 1957, p. 160 (hereafter Groener, *Lebenserinnerungen*); *Der Weltkrieg 1914-1918*, Berlin, 1925, I, p. 440, V, pp. 295-350 (hereafter *Weltkrieg*).

5 B.H.M.K. Bülow, *Denkwürdigkeiten*, Berlin, 1931, III, p. 173 (hereafter Bülow, *Denkwürdigkeiten*); Egmont Zechlin, "Deutschland zwischen Kabinettskrieg und Wirtschaftskrieg," HZ, 199, pp. 369-70 (hereafter Zechlin, "Deutschland"); Baron Beyens, *L'Allemagne avant la guerre*, Brussels/Paris, 1915, p. 24; Princess Evelyn Blücher, *An English Wife in Berlin*, London, 1920, pp. 12, 16, 137 (hereafter Blücher, *Wife*); Lerchenfeld Documents, in typescript, edited by Ernst Deuerlein, p. 188 (hereafter Lerchenfeld); Brand Whitlock, *Belgium*, New York, 1920, I, p. 64; Karl Kautsky (editor), *Outbreak of the World War*, New York, 1924, p. 736 (hereafter Kautsky, *Outbreak*); For war aims discussions, see: Fischer, *Krieg*, pp. 739-774; Fischer, *Griff*, pp. 109-37; Klein, *Deutschland*, pp. 351-436.

6 Craig, *Politics*, pp. 280-1; Barbara Tuchman, *The Guns of August*, New York, 1962, p. 335 (hereafter Tuchman, *Guns*); *Weltkrieg, Kriegsrüstung*, I, pp. 197-244, 271-84, 331-78, 400-12, 476; Fischer, *Griff*, pp. 134-7; Fischer, *Krieg*, pp. 283, 640, 747-9; *Weltkrieg*, I, p. 46; Klein, *Deutschland*, pp. 122-7; Zechlin, "Deutschland," pp. 394-5.

7 Pius Dirr (editor), *Bayerische Dokumente zum Kriegsausbruch und zum Versailler Schuldspruch*, Munich/Berlin, 1925, 1 (hereafter Dirr, *Dokumente*); Eduard David, *Das Kriegstagebuch des Reichstagsabgeordneten Eduard David, 1914-1918*, Düsseldorf, 1966, p. 15 (hereafter David, *Kriegstagebuch*); H.P. Hanssen, *Diary of a Dying Empire*, Bloomington, Indiana, 1955, p. 32 (hereafter Hanssen, *Diary*); Conrad Haussmann, *Schlaglichter: Reichstagsbriefe und Aufzeichnungen*, Frankfurt am Main,

1924, pp. 25-7 (hereafter Haussmann, *Schlaglichter*); Carl E. Schorske, *German Social Democracy, 1905-1917,* Cambridge, 1955, p. 292 (hereafter Schorske, *Democracy*); Arthur Rosenberg, *The Birth of the German Republic, 1871-1918,* New York, 1931, pp. 73-7 (hereafter Rosenberg, *Birth*); Blücher, *Wife,* p. 137; Willibald Gutsche, "Bethmann Hollweg und die Politik der 'Neuorientierung,'" ZfG, 1965, pp. 216-7 (hereafter Gutsche, "Bethmann"); Zechlin, "Deutschland," p. 431; Egmont Zechlin, "Friedensbestrebungen und Revolutionierungsversuche," PAPZ, 15 May 1963, pp. 44-7 (hereafter Zechlin, "Friedensbestrebungen"); K.H. Janssen, *Macht und Verblendung: Kriegszielpolitik der deutschen Bundesstaaten, 1914-1918,* Göttingen, 1963, pp. 22, 30, 33-4 (hereafter Janssen, *Macht*); Moltke, *Erinnerungen,* pp. 380, 385; Alfred Tirpitz, *Erinnerungen,* Leipzig, 1919, pp. 399-408 (hereafter Tirpitz, *Erinnerungen*); Groener, *Lebenserinnerungen,* p. 193; *Weltkrieg,* V, pp. 14-5.

8 Ritter, *Staatskunst,* II, pp. 282-97; Craig, *Politics,* p. 290; Kautsky, *Outbreak,* 13; *Diplomatische Aktenstücke zur Vorgeschichte des Krieges, 1914,* Vienna, 1919, I, 1, 2, 8, 12 (hereafter *Aktenstücke*); Roderich Gooss, *Das Wiener Kabinette und die Entstehung des Weltkrieges,* Vienna, 1919, pp. 26-9, 50-62 (hereafter Gooss, *Kabinette*).

9 Paul Guinn, *British Strategy and Politics, 1914 to 1918,* Oxford, 1965, pp. 1-32 (hereafter Guinn, *Strategy*); A.J.P. Taylor, *English History, 1914-1945,* Oxford, 1965, p. 4 (hereafter Taylor, *English History*); Tuchman, *Guns,* pp. 118-9; Philip Magnus, *Kitchener,* New York, 1959, p. 279; *British Documents on the Origins of the War, 1898-1914,* London, 1926, XI, 487 (hereafter *British Documents*); Edward Grey, *Twenty-Five Years,* London, 1925, II, p. 20 (hereafter Grey, *Years*); David Lloyd George, *War Memoirs,* London, 1938, I, pp. 61-74 (hereafter Lloyd George, *Memoirs*); Churchill, *Crisis,* pp. 235, 281.

10 Tuchman, *Guns,* pp. 28-43; Jere King, *Generals and Politicians,* Berkeley/Los Angeles, 1951, p. 18 (hereafter King, *Generals*); Joseph J.-C. Joffre, *Memoirs,* New York, 1932, I, p. 53 (hereafter Joffre, *Memoirs*); Raymond Poincaré, *Au Service de la France,* Paris, 1928, IV, p. 458, V, pp. 168, 282, 513 (hereafter Poincaré, *Service*); Georges Clemenceau, *Grandeur and Misery of Victory,* London, 1930, p. 15 (hereafter Clemenceau, *Grandeur*).

11 Gleb Botkin, *The Real Romanovs,* New York, Revell, 1931, p. 112; Vasili Gourko, *War and Revolution in Russia, 1914-1917,* New York, 1919, p. 542; Joffre, *Memoirs,* I, p. 23; *Weltkrieg,* V. p. 14; Antonio Salandra, *Italy and the Great War: From Neutrality to Intervention,* London, 1932, p. 96 (hereafter Salandra, *Italy*); André Scherer and Jacques Grunewald (editors), *L'Allemagne et les problemes de la paix pendant la première guerre mondiale,* Paris, 1962, I, p. 4 (hereafter Scherer, *L'Allemagne*); Edward House, *The Intimate Papers of Colonel House,* London, 1926, I, pp. 340-1 (hereafter House, *Papers*).

12 Gerhard Ritter, *Der Schlieffenplan: Kritik eines Mythos,* Munich, 1956; Ritter, *Staatskunst,* II, pp. 239-81; Craig, *Politics,* pp. 277-80; Tuchman, *Guns,* pp. 17-25; *Weltkrieg,* I, pp. 49-76; Cruttwell, *History,* pp. 7-9; Luigi

Albertini, *The Origins of the War of 1914,* London, 1957, III, pp. 236-42 (hereafter Albertini, *Origins).*

13 Schlieffen modeled his strategy on the battle of Cannae, in which the precipitous Roman advance at the Carthaginian center was critical to Hannibal's success.

14 *Weltkrieg,* I, pp. 84-90; Tuchman, *Guns,* pp. 28-43; Cruttwell, *History,* pp. 9-10; Joffre, *Memoirs,* I, pp. 36-112.

15 *Weltkrieg,* I-IV; Cruttwell, *History;* Joffre, *Memoirs,* I; Tuchman, *Guns;* Liddell Hart, *War.*

16 *Weltkrieg,* IV, pp. 255-67, 508-43; Tuchman, *Guns,* pp. 435-8; Craig, *Politics,* pp. 300-1; Cruttwell, *History,* pp. 31-5; Liddell Hart, *War,* pp. 82-102; Groener, *Lebenserinnerungen,* pp. 150-77. On the critical west wing of both armies, the Anglo-French forces were superior to the Germans (*Weltkrieg,* IV, p. 524). The numerical relationship of total German to Anglo-French-Belgian forces was 73:92 (divisions) or 1.8:2.38 (millions of men). Even if the Belgians are subtracted, the Anglo-French forces still totaled 2.28 million (*Weltkrieg,* I, p. 22).

17 Liddell Hart, *War,* pp. 47-9, 85; Hajo Holborn, in E.M. Earle (editor), *Makers of Modern Strategy,* New York, 1970, pp. 195-9; Ritter, *Staatskunst,* II, p. 272; Craig, *Politics,* pp. 300-1; Tuchman, *Guns,* pp. 309, 436-7.

18 *Weltkrieg,* V; Tirpitz, *Erinnerungen;* Cruttwell, *History;* Joffre, *Memoirs,* I; Poincaré, *Service,* V; Liddell Hart, *War;* Churchill, *Crisis;* French, Field Marshal Sir John French, *1914,* London, 1919 (hereafter French, *1914);* Thoumin, Richard, *The First World War,* New York, 1964 (hereafter Thoumin, *War);* Lloyd George, *Memoirs,* I; Tuchman, *Guns.*

19 *Weltkrieg,* V, pp. 8-11, 19-22, 417-8; Ritter, *Staatskunst,* III, pp. 55-6; Craig, *Politics,* p. 301; Bernhard Poll, *Deutsches Schicksal,* Berlin, 1937, p. 100 (hereafter Poll, *Schicksal);* Groener, *Lebenserinnerungen,* p. 179; Ludwig Reiners, *In Europa gehen die Lichter aus. Der Untergang des wilhelminischen Reiches,* Munich, 1955, p. 232 (hereafter Reiners, *Europa).*

20 *Weltkrieg,* V; Cruttwell, *History;* Liddell Hart, *War.*

CHAPTER 2

1 Craig, *Politics,* pp. 307, 310; Ritter, *Staatskunst,* III, pp. 33-5; A. Tirpitz, *Politische Dokumente,* Berlin, 1926, II, pp. 21, 58 (hereafter Tirpitz, *Dokumente);* Groener, *Lebenserinnerungen,* p. 160; Kautsky, *Outbreak,* 662.

2 Zechlin, "Deutschland," p. 369.

3 Kautsky, *Outbreak,* Supplement IV, p. 35; Lerchenfeld, p. 188; Egmont Zechlin, "Die Illusion vom begrenzten Krieg: Berlins Fehlkalkulation im Sommer 1914," *Die Zeit,* 17 September 1965 (hereafter Zechlin, "Illusion"); Zechlin, "Deutschland," pp. 369-70; K.D. Erdmann, "Zur Beurteilung Bethmann Hollwegs," GWU, September 1964, pp. 527, 538-9 (hereafter Erdmann, "Beurteilung"); Schulthess' *Europäischer Geschichtskalender, 1914,* Munich, 1917, p. 391 (hereafter Schulthess, *Geschichtskalender, 1914);* G.A. Müller, *Regierte der Kaiser?* Göttingen, 1959, p. 50 (hereafter

Müller, *Kaiser*); Tuchman, *Guns*, pp. 280-5; Ritter, *Staatskunst*, III, p. 23; Groener, *Lebenserinnerungen*, p. 160; *Weltkrieg*, I, p. 440.

4 Schulthess, *Geschichtskalender, 1914*, pp. 381-5; Bülow, *Denkwürdigkeiten*, III, p. 173; Zechlin, "Illusion," p. 9; Tirpitz, *Dokumente*, II, pp. 58, 65.

5 Schulthess, *Geschichtskalender, 1914*, pp. 381-5; Zechlin, "Friedensbestrebungen," 17 May 1961, 14 June 1961, 21 June 1961, 15 May 1963; Fritz Fischer, "Deutsche Kriegsziele: Revolutionierung und Separatfrieden im Osten, 1914-1918," HZ, 188, pp. 249-310 (hereafter Fischer, "Kriegsziele"); Fischer, *Griff*, pp. 62, 156-7, 161-2, 169, 174; Werner Conze, *Polnische Nation und deutsche Politik*, Cologne, 1958, pp. 46-7, 62 (hereafter Conze, *Nation*); Tirpitz, *Dokumente*, II, p. 62,

6 Kautsky, *Outbreak*, 401, 736; Schulthess, *Geschichtskalender, 1914*, pp. 382-5, 390-4; Ritter, *Staatskunst*, II, p. 339, III, pp. 28-9; Zechlin, "Deutschland," pp. 375-82; Zechlin, "Friedensbestrebungen," 15 May 1963, p. 14; Zechlin, "Illusion," p. 9; Tuchman, *Guns*, p. 216; Tirpitz, *Dokumente*, II, pp. 58, 62, 65, 209; Fischer, *Weltmacht*, pp. 66-7; Fischer, "Kriegsziele," p. 260; Fischer, *Griff*, pp. 139-41, 146; Bülow, *Denkwürdigkeiten*, III, p. 197.

7 Schulthess, *Geschichtskalender, 1914*, pp. 380-5, 390, 760; Tirpitz, *Dokumente*, II, pp. 58, 65; Lerchenfeld, p. 186; Fischer, *Griff*, p. 217; Erdmann, "Beurteilung," p. 538; Janssen, *Macht*, pp. 21-2.

8 *Weltkrieg*, I, p. 440; Tirpitz, *Erinnerungen*, p. 395; Groener, *Lebenserinnerungen*, pp. 160-1; Müller, *Kaiser*, p. 51.

9 Tirpitz, *Erinnerungen*, pp. 396-9; Tirpitz, *Dokumente*, II, p. 63; Groener, *Lebenserinnerungen*, p. 160; Müller, *Kaiser*, pp. 52-4; Zechlin, "Illusion," pp. 9-10; Zechlin, "Deutschland," p. 377; *Weltkrieg*, III, pp. 3, 188, 315-8; *Weltkrieg 16: Haltung Rumäniens*, Box 394, document 554; Helfferich, *Weltkrieg*, II, pp. 279, 413; Conrad, *Dienstzeit*, IV, pp. 655-6; Hugo Pohl, *Aus Aufzeichnungen und Briefen während der Kriegszeit*, Berlin, 1920, p. 39 (hereafter Pohl, *Aufzeichnungen*).

10 Tuchman, *Guns*, pp. 415, 419-20; Liddell Hart, *War*, pp. 87, 94-5, 97-8; *Weltkrieg*, IV, pp. 3-6, 135-9, 143-4, 220-3, 232-43, 256-66, 314-24, 400-1; Dorothea Groener-Geyer, *General Groener: Soldat und Staatsmann*, Frankfurt am Main, 1953, pp. 41-2 (hereafter Groener-Geyer, *Groener*); Tirpitz, *Erinnerungen*, pp. 399-401; Pohl, *Aufzeichnungen*, p. 49; Moltke, *Erinnerungen*, pp. 384-6.

11 *Weltkrieg*, IV, pp. 324-9; 481-4; Tirpitz, *Erinnerungen*, pp. 401-4; Müller, *Kaiser*, pp. 57, 59; Zechlin, "Deutschland," p. 377; Erdmann, "Beurteilung," p. 527; Moltke, *Erinnerungen*, p. 385.

12 German Foreign Ministry Archives, document number AA 1886, File number WK 15 Adh (hereafter listed by document and file numbers); AH 741, WK 21; Hans W. Gatzke, *Germany's Drive to the West: A Study of Germany's Western War Aims during the First World War*, Baltimore, 1950, pp. 9-11 (hereafter Gatzke, *Drive*); Fischer, *Griff*, pp. 115-7, 124, 133; Ritter, *Staatskunst*, III, pp. 15, 39, 592 (footnote 31), 594 (footnote 42); Janssen, *Macht*, pp. 30, 240; Erich O. Volkmann (editor), *Das Werk des Unter-*

suchungsausschusses . . . , Berlin, 1929, Fourth Series, Volume XII, I, pp. 35-6 (hereafter UA, 4, Series XII, 1, pp. . . .); Tirpitz, *Dokumente*, II, p. 65; Zechlin, "Deutschland," pp. 366-8, 395-7; Erdmann, "Beurteilung," p. 538.

13 Schulthess, *Geschichtskalender, 1914*, pp. 395-6, 686; Tuchman, *Guns*, pp. 318-22, 362, 385; Zechlin, "Deutschland," pp. 378-9; *Weltkrieg*, III, p. 307.

14 Zechlin, "Deutschland," pp. 379-81, 408; Pohl, *Aufzeichnungen*, p. 39; *Weltkrieg*, III, p. 317.

15 Werner Basler, *Deutschlands Annexionspolitik in Polen und in Baltikum*, Berlin, 1962, pp. 381-5 (hereafter Basler, *Annexionspolitik*); Zechlin, "Friedensbestrebungen," 15 May 1963, pp. 41-4; Zechlin, "Deutschland," pp. 405-6; Fischer, *Griff*, pp. 116-8; Ritter, *Staatskunst*, III, pp. 41-2; Scherer, *L'Allemagne*, I, p. 5; zu AH 741, zu AH 1057, WK 21.

16 See footnote 12; Henry Cord Meyer, *Mitteleuropa in German Thought and Action, 1815-1945*, The Hague, 1955 (hereafter Meyer, *Mitteleuropa*); Zechlin, "Deutschland," pp. 395-400, 421-30, 434; Zechlin, "Friedensbestrebungen," 15 May 1963, pp. 14-6, 41, 44-7; Fischer, *Griff*, pp. 113-7, 122-3; Tirpitz, *Dokumente*, II, p. 68; Tirpitz, *Erinnerungen*, pp. 400-3; M. Eynern (editor), *Walther Rathenau–ein preussischer Europäer*, Berlin, 1955, p. 120 (hereafter Eynern, *Rathenau*); Hans Zwehl, *Erich von Falkenhayn, General der Infanterie: eine biographische Studie*, Berlin, 1926, pp. 61, 65 (hereafter Zwehl, *Falkenhayn*); Groener, *Lebenserinnerungen*, p. 182; Erdmann, "Beurteilung," p. 538.

17 See footnote 15; Tirpitz, *Erinnerungen*, pp. 396-404; Tirpitz, *Dokumente*, II, pp. 62-3, 67, 79, 93; Zechlin, "Illusion," pp. 9-10; Pohl, *Aufzeichnungen*, pp. 46-50, 56; Müller, *Kaiser*, pp. 55, 59; Scherer, *L'Allemagne*, I, p. 5; Tuchman, *Guns*, pp. 356-7; *Weltkrieg*, III, p. 307; Groener, *Lebenserinnerungen*, pp. 143-4; Walther Hubatsch, *Der Weltkrieg, 1914-1918*, Constance, 1955, p. 18 (hereafter Hubatsch, *Weltkrieg*); Schulthess, *Geschichtskalender, 1914*, pp. 395-8, 581, 959; Theobald von Bethmann Hollweg, *Betrachtungen zum Weltkriege*, Berlin, 1919, I, p. 180 (hereafter Bethmann, *Betrachtungen*); James W. Gerard, *My Four Years in Germany*, New York, 1917, p. 210 (hereafter Gerard, *Years*).

18 AA 1886, WK 15 Adh; Fischer, "Kriegsziele," p. 284; Fischer, *Griff*, pp. 113, 117, 149; Zechlin, "Friedensbestrebungen," 15 May 1963, pp. 13-5; Zechlin, "Deutschland," pp. 392-7, 428; Müller, *Kaiser*, pp. 54-9; Tirpitz, *Dokumente*, II, pp. 65-7, 79, 95; Tirpitz, *Erinnerungen*, pp. 398-402; Pohl, *Aufzeichnungen*, pp. 37-9, 46-50, 56; Schulthess, *Geschichtskalender, 1914*, pp. 397-8; Eynern, *Rathenau*, p. 120; Walther Rathenau, *Briefe*, Dresden, 1926, I, p. 158 (hereafter Rathenau, *Briefe*).

19 See footnotes 15 and 18; Zechlin, "Deutschland," pp. 395-8, 425-8, 434; Zechlin, "Friedensbestrebungen," 15 May 1963, pp. 14-5; Egmont Zechlin, "Probleme des Kriegskalküls und der Kriegsbeendigung im Ersten Weltkrieg," GWU, February 1965, p. 75 (hereafter Zechlin, "Probleme"); Fischer, *Griff*, pp. 117, 126; AA 1886, WK 15 Adh; Tschirschky to Foreign Ministry, 9 September, WK 2; Janssen, *Macht*, pp. 30, 235; Erdmann, "Beurteilung," p.

538; Schulthess, *Geschichtskalender, 1914*, p. 395; *Weltkrieg*, III, pp. 7-8; Gatzke, *Drive*, pp. 86, 94; Müller, *Kaiser*, p. 53.

20 See footnote 15; Scherer, *L'Allemagne*, I, pp. 4-5; Zechlin, "Probleme," p. 75; Zechlin, "Deutschland," pp. 395-7, 428; Zechlin, "Friedensbestrebungen," 15 May 1963, pp. 14-5; Eynern, *Rathenau*, p. 120; Imanuel Geiss, *Der polnische Grenzstreifen, 1914-1918*, Lübeck/Hamburg, 1960, p. 71 (hereafter Geiss, *Grenzstreifen*); Fischer, *Griff*, pp. 117, 129; Fischer, "Kriegsziele," pp. 298, 302; Harold Shukman, *Lenin and the Russian Revolution*, New York, 1967, p. 161 (hereafter Shukman, *Lenin*).

21 Tirpitz, *Erinnerungen*, pp. 403-11, 415-25; Müller, *Kaiser*, pp. 57-67; Groener, *Lebenserinnerungen*, pp. 182, 193-4; 197-8; Groener-Geyer, *Groener*, pp. 42-3; Erich von Falkenhayn, *Die Oberste Heeresleitung 1914-16 in ihren wichtigsten Entschliessungen*, Berlin, 1920, p. 20 (hereafter Falkenhayn, *Heeresleitung*); *Weltkrieg*, V, pp. 12, 48, 147-8, 179-80, 187, 556-60; Erdmann, "Beurteilung," p. 527; Lerchenfeld, p. 193; Eberhard von Vietsch, *Arnold Rechberg und das Problem der politischen West-Orientierung Deutschlands nach dem 1. Weltkrieg*, Koblenz, 1958, p. 25 (hereafter Vietsch, *Rechberg*); Max Hoffmann, *Die Aufzeichnungen des Generalmajors Max Hoffmann*, Berlin, 1929, I, p. 59 (hereafter Hoffmann, *Aufzeichnungen*).

22 Tirpitz, *Erinnerungen*, pp. 404-25; Groener, *Lebenserinnerungen*, pp. 182-3; Groener-Geyer, *Groener*, p. 42; Paul Herre, *Kronprinz Wilhelm: Seine Rolle in der Politik*, Munich, 1954, p. 54 (hereafter Herre, *Wilhelm*); Müller, *Kaiser*, pp. 57, 67; Erdmann, "Beurteilung," pp. 527, 539-40.

23 Müller, *Kaiser*, p. 57; Falkenhayn, *Heeresleitung*, p. 20; *Weltkrieg*, V, p. 12; Clemens von Delbrück, *Die wirtschaftliche Mobilmachung in Deutschland 1914*, Munich, 1924, pp. 127-8, 150-1 (hereafter Delbrück, *Mobilmachung*); Zechlin, "Friedensbestrebungen," 17 May 1961, p. 272 and 15 May 1963, p. 47; Zechlin, "Deutschland," pp. 377, 420, 438; Fischer, *Griff*, pp. 124-6, 134; Fischer, *Weltmacht*, p. 64; Janssen, *Macht*, pp. 30, 235 (footnote 88), 237 (footnote 121); Erdmann, "Beurteilung," pp. 527, 538; Ritter, *Staatskunst*, III, pp. 44, 49; UA, 4, Series XII, 1, p. 37.

24 Groener, *Lebenserinnerungen*, pp. 193-4; Groener-Geyer, *Groener*, p. 42; *Weltkrieg*, V, pp. 48, 147-8; Tirpitz, *Erinnerungen*, pp. 408-12; Erdmann, "Beurteilung," p. 527; zu AH 1057, WK 21; Loebell's memorandum, 29 October, WK 15 Adh; RK 1507/14, WK 15 Adh; 23 October, WK 15, I; Ritter, *Staatskunst*, III, pp. 44, 49, 593 (footnote 36); Fischer, *Griff*, pp. 124-6, 134; Fischer, *Weltmacht*, p. 32; Zechlin, "Deutschland," pp. 377-8, 425-7, 434-8; Zechlin, "Friedensbestrebungen," 17 May 1961, p. 283, and 15 May 1963, p. 16; UA, 4, Series XII, 1, pp. 37, 187-93; Janssen, *Macht*, p. 237 (footnote 121); Gatzke, *Drive*, p. 12; Eynern, *Rathenau*, pp. 125-7; Schulthess, *Geschichtskalender, 1914*, pp. 401-2; Vietsch, *Rechberg*, pp. 27-8.

25 Tirpitz, *Erinnerungen*, pp. 424-5; Zechlin, "Deutschland," pp. 378, 425, 434-7; Schulthess, *Geschichtskalender, 1914*, pp. 406-8; Gatzke, *Drive*, pp. 10, 17, 86, 99.

26 Schulthess, *Geschichtskalender, 1914*, pp. 401-2, 406-12, 422-5; Vietsch, *Rechberg*, pp. 27-8; RK 1507/14, WK 15 Adh; 23 October, WK 15, I; Loebell's memorandum, 29 October, WK 15 Adh; Tirpitz, *Erinnerungen*, pp. 311-7, 404-19, 425; Müller, *Kaiser*, p. 59; Bernhard Huldermann, *Albert Ballin*, Oldenburg/Berlin, 1922, pp. 326-9 (hereafter Huldermann, *Ballin*); Cruttwell, *History*, p. 103; *Weltkrieg*, V, pp. 10, 414; Hubatsch, *Weltkrieg*, p. 21; Taylor, *History*, pp. 27-8; Ritter, *Staatskunst*, II, p. 28; Marion C. Siney, *The Allied Blockade of Germany, 1914-1916*, Ann Arbor, 1957, p. 62 (hereafter Siney, *Blockade*); Arno Spindler, *Der Handelskrieg mit U-booten*, Berlin, 1932-4, I, pp. 40-58 (hereafter Spindler, *Handelskrieg*).

27 Tirpitz, *Erinnerungen*, p. 406; *Weltkrieg*, V, pp. 419-28; Fischer, "Kriegsziele," pp. 259, 288, 292, 296, 300; Fischer, *Griff*, pp. 169-71, 178; Zechlin, "Friedensbestrebungen," 21 June 1961, pp. 345-7, 358; Heinz Lemke, "Georg Cleinow und die deutsche Polenpolitik 1914-1916," in *Politik im Krieg*, Berlin, 1964, pp. 135-8 (hereafter Lemke, *Politik*); RK 1507/14, Loebell's memorandum, 29 October, WK 15 Adh; 23 October, AS 2739, WK 15, I; A 26681, WK 2; A 27791, A 28166, WK 2 geh; Lerchenfeld, pp. 196-201.

28 Conze, *Nation*, pp. 62-6; Fischer, *Griff* pp. 129-30; Zechlin, "Deutschland," pp. 374, 404; Lemke, *Politik*, p. 137; *Weltkrieg*, IV, pp. 328-9 and V, pp. 181, 220, 405, 409-10, 415; Tirpitz, *Dokumente*, II, p. 58; Tirpitz, *Erinnerungen*, pp. 403-5, 413, 419, 423; Robert Hopwood, "Interalliance Diplomacy: Count Czernin and Germany, 1916-1918," unpublished Ph.D. dissertation, Stanford University, pp. 4-6 (hereafter Hopwood, "Diplomacy"); Conrad, *Dienstzeit*, V, p. 986.

29 *Weltkrieg*, V, pp. 402-7; Ritter, *Staatskunst*, III, p. 76; Groener, *Lebenserinnerungen*, p. 200; Fischer, *Griff*, pp. 104, 137, 157; Gordon A. Craig, "The World War I Alliance of the Central Powers in Retrospect: The Military Cohesion of the Alliance," JMH, XXXVII, 1965, pp. 336-44; AS 2079, WK 2; Hopwood, "Diplomacy," pp. 5-7; Schulthess, *Geschichtskalender, 1914*, pp. 487-93; Müller, *Kaiser*, pp. 60-1; AS 2079, WK 2; A.F. Pribram, *Austrian Foreign Policy, 1908-1918*, London, 1923, pp. 73-4 (hereafter Pribram, *Policy*); Hartmut Lehmann, "Österreich-Ungarns Belgienpolitik im ersten Weltkrieg. Ein Beitrag zum deutsch-österreichischen Bündnis," HZ, 192, p. 68 (hereafter Lehmann, "Belgienpolitik"); House, *Papers*, I, p. 336.

30 Zechlin, "Deutschland," pp. 378, 395-6, 421-37; Zechlin, "Friedensbestrebungen," 15 May 1963, pp. 16-7, 47; Fischer, *Griff*, p. 117.

31 Fischer, "Kriegsziele," pp. 249-310; Fritz Fischer, "Kontinuität des Irrtums: Zum Problem der deutschen Kriegszielpolitik im ersten Weltkrieg," HZ, 191, pp. 83-100 (hereafter Fischer, "Kontinuität"); Fischer, *Griff*, pp. 113-9; Fischer, *Weltmacht*, pp. 7-34, 61-70; Hans Herzfeld, "Zur deutschen Politik im Ersten Weltkrieg: Kontinuität oder permanente Krise?" HZ, 191, pp. 67-82 (hereafter Herzfeld, "Politik"); Hans Herzfeld, "Die deutsche Kriegspolitik im Ersten Weltkrieg," VfZ, July, 1963, pp. 224-45 (hereafter Herzfeld, "Kriegspolitik"); Ritter, *Staatskunst*, III, pp. 41-54; Zechlin, "Friedensbestrebungen," 15 May 1963, pp. 10-23; Zechlin, "Deutschland," pp. 347-458. For further contributions and a bibliography of the debate, see:

Ernst W. Graf Lynar, *Deutsche Kiregsziele, 1914-1918,* Frankfurt/Berlin, 1964 (hereafter Lynar, *Kriegsziele*) and James J. Sheehan, "Germany, 1890-1918: A Survey of Recent Research," CEH, December, 1968, pp. 359-60; Kielmansegg, *Deutschland.*

32 Fischer, "Kriegsziele," pp. 251, 255; Fischer, "Kontinuität," pp. 83, 86; Fischer, *Griff,* p. 119; Fischer, *Weltmacht,* pp. 25, 63-9; Herzfeld, "Politik," pp. 69, 73-6; Herzfeld, "Kriegspolitik," pp. 236-7; Ritter, *Staatskunst,* III, pp. 44-7, 52; Zechlin, "Friedensbestrebungen," 15 May 1963, pp. 10, 23.

33 Fischer, "Kontinuität," p. 83; Fischer, *Griff,* p. 119; Fischer, *Weltmacht,* pp. 25, 63-5; Herzfeld, "Politik," p. 69; Ritter, *Staatskunst,* III, p. 46; Zechlin, "Friedensbestrebungen," 15 May 1963, pp. 10, 23.

34 Herzfeld, "Politik," pp. 73-6, 82; Fischer, "Kontinuität," p. 86; Fischer, *Weltmacht,* pp. 65-9; Ritter, *Staatskunst,* III, pp. 41-7, 51-3; Zechlin, "Friedensbestrebungen," 15 May 1963, pp. 11-2.

35 Fischer, "Kriegsziele," p. 251; Fischer, *Griff,* p. 119; Fischer, *Weltmacht,* pp. 65-9; Herzfeld, "Kriegspolitik," pp. 236-7; Ritter, *Staatskunst,* III, p. 44; Zechlin, "Friedensbestrebungen," 15 May 1963, pp. 11-2, 16.

36 Fischer, *Weltmacht,* pp. 69-70; Zechlin, "Friedensbestrebungen," 15 May 1963, pp. 14-6, 19-22, 14 June 1961, pp. 316-7.

37 Müller, *Kaiser,* p. 57; Zechlin, "Friedensbestrebungen," 15 May 1963, pp. 14-6, 19-22.

38 Herzfeld, "Politik," p. 82; Ritter, *Staatskunst,* III, pp. 15-54; Erwin Hölzle, "Das Experiment des Friedens im Ersten Weltkrieg, 1914-1917," GWU, August, 1962, pp. 465-522 (hereafter Hölzle, "Experiment").

CHAPTER 3

1 Egmont Zechlin, "Bethmann Hollweg, Kriegsrisiko und SPD 1914," *Monat,* January 1966, pp. 17-32 (hereafter Zechlin, "Bethmann"); Jürgen Kuczynski, *Der Ausbruch des Ersten Weltkrieges und die deutsche Sozialdemokratie,* Berlin, 1957, pp. 53-5 (hereafter Kuczynski, *Ausbruch*); Schorske, *Democracy,* pp. 288-90; Schulthess, *Geschichtskalender, 1914,* pp. 381-8; Gutsche, "Bethmann," p. 213; House, *Papers,* I, p. 341; Klaus Schwabe, "Zur politischen Haltung der deutschen Professoren im ersten Weltkrieg," HZ, 193, p. 605 (hereafter Schwabe, "Haltung"); Klaus Schwabe, "Ursprung und Verbreitung des alldeutschen Annexionismus in der deutschen Professorenschaft im ersten Weltkrieg," VfZ, April 1966, p. 110 (hereafter Schwabe, "Ursprung"); Gerald D. Feldman, *Army, Industry and Labor in Germany, 1914-1918,* Princeton, 1966, p. 27 (hereafter Feldman, *Army*); Fischer, *Griff,* p. 110; Philipp Scheidemann, *Memoiren eines Sozialdemokraten,* Dresden, 1928, I, p. 235 (hereafter Scheidemann, *Memoiren*); Zechlin, "Bethmann," pp. 29-30.

2 Schulthess, *Geschichtskalender, 1914,* pp. 381-6; Schorske, *Democracy,* p. 292; Rosenberg, *Birth,* pp. 73-7; Bethmann, *Betrachtungen,* II, pp. 31-7.

3 Schulthess, *Geschichtskalender, 1914,* pp. 386, 397-8c; Zechlin, "Friedensbestrebungen," 14 June 1961, p. 332; A21248, WK 2; Ritter, *Staatskunst,* III, p. 591 (footnote 24); Kuno Westarp, *Konservative Politik im letzten*

Jahrzehnt des Kaiserreiches, Berlin, 1936, II, p. 1 (hereafter Westarp, *Politik*); Erich O. Volkmann, *Der Marxismus und das deutsche Heer im Weltkriege,* Berlin, 1925, pp. 101, 273-5 (hereafter Volkmann, *Marxismus*); Gutsche, "Bethmann," pp. 213, 218; *Dokumente und Materielien zur Geschichte der deutschen Arbeiterbewegung,* Series II: 1914-1945, I, Berlin, 1958, p. 28 (hereafter DMGA); Johanna Schellenberg, "Die Herausbildung der Militärdiktatur in den ersten Jahren des Krieges," in *Politik im Kreig,* Berlin, 1964, p. 42 (hereafter Schellenberg, *Politik*); Ernest R. May, *The World War and American Isolation, 1914-1917,* Cambridge, Mass., 1959, p. 98 (hereafter, May, *War*).

4 Kuczynski, *Ausbruch,* pp. 208-9; Rosenberg, *Birth,* p. 88; Zechlin, "Friedensbestrebungen," 15 May 1963, pp. 44-7; Klein, *Deutschland,* p. 292; Fischer, *Weltmacht,* p. 93; Schellenberg, *Politik,* p. 45.

5 See footnote 4; Zechlin, "Friedensbestrebungen," 15 May 1963, pp. 44-7; Schorske, *Democracy,* pp. 295-8; Willibald Gutsche, "Erst Europa–und dann die Welt," ZfG, 1964, p. 757 (hereafter Gutsche, "Europa"); Heinz Lemke, "Konferenz über den ersten Weltkrieg," p. 1431 (hereafter Lemke, "Konferenz"); Rosenberg, *Birth,* p. 77; Arno J. Mayer, *Political Origins of the New Diplomacy, 1917-1918,* New Haven, 1959, pp. 11, 23 (hereafter Mayer, *Origins*).

6 Zechlin, "Friedensbestrebungen," 15 May 1963, pp. 44-7; Rosenberg, *Birth,* pp. 111-2; Westarp, *Politik,* II, p. 307; Gutsche, "Bethmann," p. 218.

7 Zechlin, "Friedensbestrebungen," 15 May 1963, pp. 44-7; Gutsche, "Bethmann," pp. 216-7; Werner Richter, *Gewerkschaften, Monopolkapitalisten und Staat im ersten Weltkrieg und in der November Revolution, 1914-1919,* Berlin, 1959, p. 50 (hereafter Richter, *Gewerkschaften*).

8 Gutsche, "Bethmann," p. 216; Zechlin, "Deutschland," p. 431.

9 Rosenberg, *Birth,* pp. 111-2; Tirpitz, *Erinnerungen,* pp. 405-11, 423-4; Müller, *Kaiser,* pp. 60-2; Lerchenfeld, p. 203; Schwabe, "Ursprung," p. 110; Bülow, *Denkwürdigkeiten,* III, p. 42.

10 See footnote 4; Ritter, *Staatskunst,* III, pp. 32-3; Schulthess, *Geschichtskalender, 1914,* pp. 414-22; Gutsche, "Bethmann," p. 217; Lerchenfeld, pp. 199-201.

11 Rosenberg, *Birth,* p. 58; Bethmann, *Betrachtungen,* II, pp. 31-7; Craig, *Politics,* p. 311; Gatzke, *Drive,* pp. 27, 130-1; Heinrich Class, *Wider den Strom: Vom Werden und Wachsen der nationalen Opposition im alten Reich,* Leipzig, 1932, pp. 307, 321 (hereafter Class, *Strom*); R.H. Lutz, *The Fall of the German Empire, 1914-1918,* Stanford, 1932, I, p. 359 (hereafter Lutz, *Fall*); Schulthess, *Geschichtskalender, 1914,* p. 386; Ritter, *Staatskunst,* III, p. 591 (footnote 24); Westarp, *Politik,* II, p. 1; Fischer, *Griff,* p. 120; Schwabe, "Ursprung," pp. 116-7; A 20291, WK 15 Adh; Janssen, *Macht,* pp. 31-2; Lerchenfeld, pp. 198-203.

12 Schulthess, *Geschichtskalender, 1914,* p. 386; Ritter, *Staatskunst,* III, pp. 36, 591 (footnote 24), 592 (footnote 31); Westarp, *Politik,* II, pp. 1, 40-4; Fischer, *Griff,* pp. 121-2, 158, 188-9, 215; Marvin L. Edwards, *Stresemann and the Greater Germany, 1914-1918,* New York, 1963, pp. 30, 55 (hereafter

Edwards, *Stresemann*); Zechlin, "Deutschland," pp. 367, 419; Zechlin, "Friedensbestrebungen," 14 June 1961, p. 332; Klaus Epstein, *Matthias Erzberger and the Dilemma of German Democracy*, Princeton, 1959, p. 106 (hereafter Epstein, *Erzberger*); Gatzke, *Drive*, pp. 18, 21; Tirpitz, *Dokumente*, II, p. 69; Tirpitz, *Erinnerungen*, pp. 258, 411; Matthias Erzberger, *Erlebnisse im Weltkrieg*, Stuttgart, 1920, p. 228 (hereafter Erzberger, *Erlebnisse*); W. Patin, *Beiträge zur Geschichte der deutsch-vatikanischen Beziehungen in den letzten Jahrzehnten*, Berlin, 1942, pp. 107, 266 (hereafter Patin, *Beiträge*); Frida Wacker, *Die Haltung der Deutschen Zentrumspartei zur Frage der Kriegsziele im Weltkrieg, 1914-1918*, Lohr am Main, 1937, p. 4 (hereafter Wacker, *Haltung*); Schwabe, "Haltung," p. 296; Gutsche, "Europa," p. 763; Scheidemann, *Memoiren*, I, pp. 261, 279; Schorske, *Democracy*, p. 297; Klein, *Deutschland*, p. 290.

13 Janssen, *Macht*, pp. 22, 30, 33-4; Lerchenfeld, pp. 202-3; Zechlin, "Deutschland," p. 367; Gatzke, *Drive*, pp. 10, 27, 30, 64; Fischer, *Griff*, pp. 113, 120-4; AH 741, WK 21; A 30825, WK 2; A20291, WK 15 Adh; Scherer, *L'Allemagne*, I, p. 6; Class, *Strom*, p. 321; Schwabe, "Ursprung," pp. 116-7; W.R. Thayer (editor), *Out of Their Own Mouths: Utterances of German Rulers, Statesmen,...*, New York, 1917, pp. 129-31 (hereafter Thayer, *Mouths*).

14 Gutsche, *Politik*, p. 66; Schwabe, "Ursprung," pp. 110-2, 117-9; Schwabe, "Haltung," pp. 610-1; Thoumin, *War*, p. 105; Thayer, *Mouths*, pp. 49-51; Gerhard Pretsch, "Dietrich Schäfer, der Alldeutsche," WZKMU, 1959/60, p. 732 (hereafter Pretsch, "Schäfer"); Max Weber, *Gesammelte politische Schriften*, Munich, 1921, p. 458 (hereafter Weber, *Schriften*); Fischer, *Griff*, p. 186; Fischer, *Weltmacht*, p. 49; Schulthess, *Geschichtskalender, 1914*, pp. 402-3; Salomon Grumbach, *Das annexationistische Deutschland*, Lausanne, 1917, pp. 239-41 (hereafter Grumbach, *Deutschland*).

15 Tirpitz, *Dokumente*, II, p. 94; Tirpitz, *Erinnerungen*, p. 401; Gatzke, *Drive*, pp. 10, 64.

16 Ritter, *Staatskunst*, III, p. 592 (footnote 31); Lerchenfeld, pp. 185-6, 199-203; Janssen, *Macht*, pp. 21-2; Schwabe, "Ursprung," p. 112; Fischer, *Griff*, p. 158; Schulthess, *Geschichtskalender, 1914*, pp. 386, 414-21; Basler, *Annexionspolitik*, pp. 381-3; Zechlin, "Friedensbestrebungen," 15 May 1963, pp. 41-4.

17 Fischer, *Griff*, p. 119; Ritter, *Staatskunst*, III, pp. 46, 53; AA 1886, WK 15 Adh.

18 Mayer, *Origins*, pp. 7-8, 14-22, 34-7.

19 Schwabe, "Ursprung," pp. 117-8; Schwabe, "Haltung," p. 611.

20 Schulthess, *Geschichtskalender, 1914*, pp. 397-8, 959; Gerard, *Years*, p. 210; Zechlin, "Friedensbestrebungen," 15 May 1963, pp. 44-7; Tirpitz, *Erinnerungen*, p. 403; House, *Papers*, I, p. 342; Delbrück, *Mobilmachung*, p. 144; Janssen, *Macht*, pp. 37, 237 (footnote 112); Tuchman, *Guns*, p. 419.

21 Tirpitz, *Erinnerungen*, pp. 399-404, 408; Huldermann, *Ballin*, pp. 326-9; Groener, *Lebenserinnerungen*, p. 193; Moltke, *Erinnerungen*, p. 385; Janssen, *Macht*, pp. 37, 237 (footnote 112).

22 Tirpitz, *Erinnerungen,* pp. 405-6; Müller, *Kaiser,* p. 60; Schulthess, *Geschichtskalender, 1914,* pp. 414-21; *Weltkrieg,* V, pp. 14-5; Bethmann, *Betrachtungen,* II, pp. 25-6; Fischer, *Weltmacht,* p. 82; Fischer, *Griff,* p. 137; Delbrück, *Mobilmachung,* pp. 144-8; Volkmann, *Marxismus,* pp. 33, 88; Tuchman, *Guns,* p. 103; Groener, *Lebenserinnerungen,* p. 193.

23 Schulthess, *Geschichtskalender, 1914,* pp. 398h-401, 414-22; Feldman, *Army,* pp. 31, 45-7, 51, 99; *Weltkrieg,* V, pp. 6-7; Müller, *Kaiser,* p. 66; Schorske, *Democracy,* p. 289; Poll, *Schicksal,* p. 266; Hubatsch, *Weltkrieg,* pp. 8, 52; Delbrück, *Mobilmachung,* pp. 120-3.

24 Feldman, *Army,* pp. 7-8, 33, 41, 52-3, 64, 82-3, 99; Delbrück, *Mobilmachung,* pp. 117, 122-3, 144, 318-9; Müller, *Kaiser,* p. 66; Hubatsch, *Weltkrieg,* pp. 8, 42; *Weltkrieg, Kriegsrüstung,* I, pp. 329-33; *Weltkrieg,* V, pp. 6-8, 187, 560-1; Tirpitz, *Erinnerungen,* p. 406; G.P. Gooch, *Germany,* London, 1926, p. 115 (hereafter Gooch, *Germany*); Schulthess, *Geschichtskalender, 1914,* pp. 414-7; Zechlin, "Deutschland," p. 439; Zechlin, "Friedensbestrebungen," 15 May 1963, p. 45.

25 Feldman, *Army,* pp. 7-8, 33, 52, 64, 99.

26 Schulthess, *Geschichtskalender, 1914,* pp. 399-401, 425; A 30825, WK 2; Scherer, *L'Allemagne,* p. 6.

CHAPTER 4

1 Poincaré, *Service,* V, pp. 68-72, 89, 99, 102-3, 159-68, 263, 269-70, 273, 281-3, 292-3, 311, 333, 382, 386; Eubank, *Cambon,* pp. 180-1; S.B. Fay, *The Origins of the World War,* New York, 1928-30, II, p. 531 (hereafter Fay, *Origins*); Joffre, *Memoirs,* I, pp. 140, 156-7, 177, 277, 280, 294; Albert Pingaud, *Histoire diplomatique de la France pendant la grand guerre,* Paris, 1940, III, pp. 100, 110 (hereafter Pingaud, *Histoire*); Guinn, *Strategy,* p. 25; French, *1914,* pp. 33, 55; Lloyd George, *Memoirs,* I, pp. 93-4.

2 Schulthess, *Geschichtskalender, 1914,* pp. 478-85, 688, 690; Poincaré, *Service,* V, pp. 19-22, 33, 67-8, 91-3, 95-6, 102-3, 125-6, 169-83, 186, 192-4, 196-7, 208-9, 212, 228-30, 236, 238-9; Tabouis, *Cambon,* pp. 276-8; Cambon, *Correspondance,* III, p. 73; Tuchman, *Guns,* pp. 262, 373-5, 383-9, 403-11; Georges Bonnefous, *Histoire politique de la troisième république,* Paris, 1957, II, pp. 40-7 (hereafter Bonnefous, *Histoire*); Mayer, *Origins,* pp. 11, 46, 143-4; Liddell Hart, *War,* p. 75; Churchill, *Crisis,* pp. 268, 275-6.

3 Schulthess, *Geschichtskalender, 1914,* pp. 478-85, 690-95, 698; Poincaré, *Service,* V, pp. 19-22, 67-8, 91-3, 95-6, 102-3, 125-6, 185-91, 282-3, 292-3, 331-5, 340, 346-56, 378, 394, 398; Joffre, *Memoirs,* I, pp. 280, 283-4; *Weltkrieg,* V, pp. 142-3, 366; King, *Generals,* p. 34.

4 Tuchman, *Guns,* pp. 286, 296, 309; Paleologue, *Russie,* I, p. 104.

5 Poincaré, *Service,* V, pp. 100-1, 111, 240-1; Schulthess, *Geschichtskalender, 1914,* pp. 839-41, 843-7, 850; Paleologue, *Russie,* I, pp. 92-3; 128, 135-6; Edmond Taylor, *The Fall of the Dynasties,* Garden City, 1963, p. 243 (hereafter Taylor, *Fall*); Alexander Dallin, *Russian Diplomacy and Eastern Europe, 1914-1919,* New York, 1963, pp. 5, 8-13, 79-80, 82-3, 86, 90

(hereafter Dallin, *Diplomacy*); C.J. Smith, *The Russian Struggle for Power, 1914-1917*, New York, 1956, pp. 9-12, 17-9 (hereafter Smith, *Struggle*); Zechlin, "Friedensbestrebungen," 21 June 1961, p. 349; Conze, *Nation*, pp. 74-5; Buchanan, *Mission*, I, p. 218; Tuchman, *Guns*, p. 308; Meyer, *Mitteleuropa*, p. 261; Siney, *Blockade*, pp. 21-2.

6 Paleologue, *Russie*, I, pp. 46-8; Schulthess, *Geschichtskalender, 1914*, pp. 839-42, 845-51; Poincaré, *Service*, V, pp. 102, 240-1; Dallin, *Diplomacy*, pp. 11-3; Conze, *Nation*, p. 74; Siney, *Blockade*, pp. 21-2; Buchanan, *Mission*, I, p. 217; Churchill, *Crisis, 1915*, p. 12; Shukman, *Lenin*, pp. 141-2; A 26412, A 26618, A 27090, WK 2.

7 Tuchman, *Guns*, p. 262; May, *War*, p. 13; Asquith, *Memories*, II, pp. 34-6, 39-40, 49-51, 54-7; Churchill, *Crisis*, pp. 267-71, 278-80, 367-8, 376, 386, 388, 397; Lloyd George, *Memoirs*, I, pp. 51-2; Cruttwell, *History*, p. 37; Schulthess, *Geschichtskalender, 1914*, pp. 401-2, 578-80, 592-3; Martin, *Peace*, pp. 49-51, 61; Taylor, *English History*, p. 20; House, *Papers*, I, pp. 339-40, 345; Scherer, *L'Allemagne*, I, p. 5; Riddell, *Diary*, pp. 34, 36; Higgins, *Churchill*, pp. 79-81; French, *1914*, pp. 142, 155-7; Tirpitz, *Erinnerungen*, p. 411; W.M. Jordan, *Great Britain, France and the German Problem, 1918-1939*, London, 1943, pp. 3-4 (hereafter Jordan, *Great Britain*); James Joll, *Britain and Europe: Pitt to Churchill, 1793-1940*, London, 1950, pp. 232-3 (hereafter Joll, *Britain*); A 23893, WK 2.

8 Schulthess, *Geschichtskalender, 1914*, pp. 401-2, 551-9, 563-6, 574-5, 580, 593-4, 695-6, 962; Eubank, *Cambon*, pp. 180-3; Asquith, *Memories*, II, pp. 31, 36-8, 54-5, 70; May, *War*, pp. 11, 17-77; Taylor, *English History*, pp. 13, 20; Taylor, *History*, p. 27; Riddell, *Diary*, p. 12; Cruttwell, *History*, pp. 65, 191; Churchill, *Crisis*, pp. 229, 306-9, 384, 524-5; Tuchman, *Guns*, pp. 137-63, 340; Pingaud, *Histoire*, I, p. 134; G.M. Trevelyan, *Grey of Fallodon*, London, 1940, p. 317 (hereafter Trevelyan, *Grey*); Higgins, *Churchill*, pp. 61, 68-70; Siney, *Blockade*, pp. 21-30, 56, 149; Poincaré, *Service*, V, pp. 221-2, 229-30; Guinn, *Strategy*, pp. 4, 36-7; Hubatsch, *Weltkrieg*, p. 20; House, *Papers*, I, pp. 309-16, 339-40, 345; Scherer, *L'Allemagne*, I, p. 5; Bethmann, *Betrachtungen*, II, p. 146.

9 Schulthess, *Geschichtskalender, 1914*, pp. 551-80, 592, 595-8; Riddell, *Diary*, pp. 9-10, 14; May, *War*, p. 81; Poincaré, *Service*, V, pp. 128, 136; Trevelyan, *Grey*, pp. 35-6, 353; Feldman, *Army*, p. 27; Jordan, *Great Britain*, pp. 3-4; Lloyd George, *Memoirs*, I, pp. 51-2, 61, 88-90; Beaverbrook, *Politicians*, pp. 47-50; Asquith, *Memories*, II, pp. 13-4, 24, 31-41, 56; Fay, *Origins*, II, p. 538; Joll, *Britain*, pp. 232-3; Martin, *Peace*, pp. 49-51, 61, 63; Churchill, *Crisis*, pp. 37, 273-5, 278, 402, 440-1; House, *Papers*, I, pp. 339-40, 345; Taylor, *English History*, pp. 3-7, 20; Higgins, *Churchill*, p. 70; Tuchman, *Guns*, p. 387; A 23893, WK 2.

10 Schulthess, *Geschichtskalender, 1914*, pp. 678-9, 684; Paleologue, *Russie*, I, pp. 45ff.; Poincaré, *Service*, V, pp. 100-3, 111, 115-7, 128; Buchanan, *Mission*, I, p. 211; Erwin Hölzle, "Das Experiment des Friedens im Ersten Weltkrieg, 1914-1917," GWU, August, 1962, p. 467 (hereafter Hölzle, "Experiment"); *Die Internationalen Beziehungen im Zeitalter des Imperialismus*, Series II,

Volume 6, I, pp. 14, 154, 161 (hereafter IB); Ritter, *Staatskunst*, III, p. 54.
11 Poincaré, *Service*, V, pp. 181, 193-6, 211, 220-3, 232; Hölzle, "Experiment,"
p. 467; Taylor, *Struggle*, p. 539; Tabouis, *Life*, p. 280; Tuchman, *Guns*, pp.
309, 373-6, 383-6; Paleologue, *Russie*, I, p. 106; Dallin, *Diplomacy*, p. 16;
Mowat, *History*, p. 7; Grey, *Years*, II, p. 164; FYB, p. 175; Schulthess,
Geschichtskalender, 1914, p. 571.
12 Poincaré, *Service*, V, pp. 286-7, 294, 301, 314-6, 369-70, 379-80, 385-6;
Weltkrieg, V, pp. 125-30, 375-6; Paleologue, *Russie*, I, p. 128; Taylor,
Struggle, p. 539; IB, VI, p. 203; Asquith, *Memories*, II, p. 56.
13 IB, VI, pp. 195, 203, 213, 253, 304; Smith, *Struggle*, pp. 50-1, 55-7; Hölzle,
"Experiment," pp. 467-8; Potiemkine, *Histoire*, II, p. 297, Ritter, *Staats-
kunst*, III, pp. 601-2 (footnote 58); Zechlin, "Friedensbestrebungen," 17
May 1961, pp. 272-3; Paleologue, *Russie*, I, pp. 119-20; Sazonov, *Years*, p.
22; Poincaré, *Service*, V, pp. 314-6; Link, *Wilson*, III, p. 206.

CHAPTER 5

1 Salandra, *Italy*, p. 96.
2 Kautsky, *Outbreak*, 45, 71, 102, 117, 141, 144, 147, 149, 256, 285, 320,
411, 508, 517, 662, 726, 733, 743, 795, 836, 854; Schulthess, *Geschichtskalender, 1914*, pp. 872-5; Poincaré, *Service*, V, pp. 24, 81, 86-7; Tuchman,
Guns, pp. 137-62; Trumpener, "Entry," pp. 369-71; Trumpener, *Germany*,
pp. 21-38; Gottlieb, *Studies*, pp. 34, 57-8; Albertini, *Origins*, III, pp. 610-23;
Taylor, *Struggle*, p. 533; Mowat, *History*, p. 11; *Weltkrieg*, II, p. 262, III, pp.
317-8, V, pp. 13-4; Zechlin, "Deutschland," p. 393; Fischer, *Griff*, p. 149;
Fischer, "Kriegsziele," p. 287; Müller, *Kaiser*, pp. 56-7; Tirpitz, *Erinnerungen*, p. 401; Tirpitz, *Dokumente*, II, p. 95.
3 Poincaré, *Service*, V, pp. 7, 51, 71, 81-2, 86-7, 97, 112, 115-7, 142, 163, 185,
210; Schulthess, *Geschichtskalender, 1914*, pp. 557, 874; Asquith, *Memories*,
II, pp. 32-3, 37, 55; Mowat, *History*, pp. 12, 14, 27; Albertini, *Origins*, III,
pp. 617-20; Taylor, *Struggle*, p. 534; Stieve, *Iswolski*, pp. 87, 107-8, 165;
Higgins, *Churchill*, pp. 56-7; Churchill, *Crisis*, pp. 487-90.
4 Schulthess, *Geschichtskalender, 1914*, pp. 872-5; Trumpener, "Entry," pp.
370-1; Trumpener, *Germany*, p. 36.
5 *Weltkrieg*, V, p. 14.
6 Trumpener, *Germany*, pp. 39-60; Trumpener, "Entry," pp. 371-80; Fischer,
Griff, pp. 148-50; Taylor, *Struggle*, p. 534; Stieve, *Iswolski*, p. 118; Tirpitz,
Erinnerungen, p. 419; Zechlin, "Friedensbestrebungen," 21 June 1961, p.
354.
7 Mowat, *History*, p. 14; Churchill, *Crisis*, pp. 492-4, 496; Higgins, *Churchill*,
pp. 57, 89, 91; Pingaud, *Histoire*, I, pp. 187-9; Potiemkine, *Histoire*, II, p.
297; Trumpener, "Entry," pp. 373, 377; Trumpener, *Germany*, pp. 51, 58,
62; Taylor, *Struggle*, p. 534; Hubatsch, *Weltkrieg*, p. 25; Guinn, *Strategy*, p.
43; Zechlin, "Friedensbestrebungen," 14 June 1961, p. 358; Schulthess,
Geschichtskalender, 1914, pp. 599-601, 604-8, 697-8, 851, 877-9.
8 Taylor, *Struggle*, pp. 534-5.

9 Asquith, *Memories*, II, p. 34; Albertini, *Origins*, III, pp. 296-337; Gottlieb, *Studies*, pp. 166-74, 191-5, 201, 204, 208-9, 212, 218, 228, 240, 392; Taylor, *Struggle*, p. 532; Schulthess, *Geschichtskalender, 1914*, pp. 560, 721-2; Zechlin, "Angebot," pp. 533-4; Lehmann, "Belgienpolitik," p. 70; Poincaré, *Service*, V, pp. 15, 41, 49-50, 72, 76-80, 113-4, 127, 194-5, 223, 233-4; Riddell, *Diary*, pp. 10-11; Pingaud, *Histoire*, I, pp. 22-4; Trevelyan, *Grey*, pp. 331-2; Potiemkine, *Histoire*, II, p. 290; Mayer, *Origins*, p. 263; Stieve, *Iswolski*, pp. 77, 86, 110; A 21248, WK 2.

10 Poincaré, *Service*, V, pp. 275, 285-6; Tirpitz, *Erinnerungen*, p. 400; Renzi, "Neutrality," pp. 1414-8, 1423-8; Mayer, *Origins*, pp. 263-5; Tabouis, *Life*, pp. 282-4; Stieve, *Iswolski*, pp. 114, 117-8; Tirpitz, *Erinnerungen*, pp. 405, 411; Müller, *Kaiser*, p. 60; Renouvin, *Crise*, I, p. 27; Gottlieb, *Studies*, pp. 177, 183-4, 189, 196, 221-2, 228-9, 233-4, 237; Schulthess, *Geschichtskalender, 1914*, pp. 726-8; Potiemkine, *Histoire*, II, p. 290; Epstein, *Erzberger*, p. 119; Conrad, *Dienstzeit*, V, pp. 156-7, 206; A 25726, WK 2.

11 Albertini, *Origins*, III, pp. 266-76, 579-80; Poincaré, *Service*, V, pp. 33, 71-2, 96-7, 111-2, 209-10, 224; Asquith, *Memories*, II, p. 39; *Weltkrieg*, II, p. 262; Gottlieb, *Studies*, p. 309; Stieve, *Iswolski*, pp. 82-3, 86; Document 554, WK 16, *Haltung Rumäniens*, Box 394.

12 Albertini, *Origins*, III, pp. 597, 601-3; Silberstein, "Campaign," p. 54; Stieve, *Iswolski*, pp. 82-3; Poincaré, *Service*, V, pp. 88, 223-232; Schulthess, *Geschichtskalender, 1914*, pp. 902-4; Smith, *Struggle*, pp. 37, 39-40.

13 Stieve, *Iswolski*, pp. 108-17; Hopwood, "Diplomacy," p. 7; Tirpitz, *Erinnerungen*, pp. 405-7; Müller, *Kaiser*, pp. 60-1, 64; *Weltkrieg*, V, pp. 13, 554, 557; Poincaré, *Service*, V, pp. 301-2, 309, 322, 372, 379-80; Pribram, *Policy*, p. 74; Renzi, "Neutrality," p. 1428; Albertini, *Origins*, III, p. 580; Taylor, *Struggle*, p. 533; Churchill, *Crisis*, pp. 492-4; Schulthess, *Geschichtskalender, 1914*, pp. 917, 919; Trumpener, *Germany*, p. 50; Higgins, *Churchill*, p. 89.

14 Valentin, *Aussenpolitik*, pp. 277-8; Schulthess, *Geschichtskalender, 1914*, pp. 850, 876, 903-5; Stieve, *Iswolski*, p. 109; Churchill, *Crisis*, pp. 493-4; Higgins, *Churchill*, pp. 58, 89; Pingaud, *Histoire*, pp. 192-3; Trumpener, *Germany*, p. 50; *Weltkrieg*, V, p. 554.

15 Poincaré, *Service*, V, pp. 96, 101-2; Asquith, *Memories*, II, p. 34; Smith, *Struggle*, p. 37; Albertini, *Origins*, III, p. 579; Schulthess, *Geschichtskalender, 1914*, p. 903; Churchill, *Crisis*, pp. 486-7, 489; Grey, *Years*, II, p. 179; Higgins, *Churchill*, pp. 57-8; Trevelyan, *Grey*, pp. 321-2; Lloyd George, *Memoirs*, I, p. 390; Tirpitz, *Erinnerungen*, p. 401.

16 Poincaré, *Service*, V, pp. 192-3; Schulthess, *Geschichtskalender, 1914*, p. 779. Neutrality was announced by Holland on 6 August, Denmark on the 5th and 7th, Switzerland on the 7th, Norway and Sweden jointly on the 8th, Portugal on the 8th, and Spain on the 17th (Schulthess, *Geschichtskalender, 1914*, pp. 508, 512d, 747-8, 772, 779, 795).

17 Pingaud, *Histoire*, I, p. 74; Schulthess, *Geschichtskalender, 1914*, pp. 563, 959, 1006-8; Poincaré, *Service*, V, pp. 52, 91, 232-45, 249; Hubatsch, *Weltkrieg*, pp. 18-9; Tirpitz, *Erinnerungen*, p. 393; *Weltkrieg*, V, p. 2; Potiemkine, *Histoire*, II, p. 285; Morley, *Thrust*, p. 12; Asquith, *Memories*, II,

p. 37; Grey, *Years,* II, p. 103; Scherer, *L'Allemagne,* I, pp. 4-5; Zechlin, "Probleme," p. 75.

18 Schulthess, *Geschichtskalender, 1914,* pp. 258-9, 571; House, *Papers,* I, pp. 290-2, 298-9; Tirpitz, *Dokumente,* II, pp. 59, 65; Martin, *Peace,* pp. 88, 90; Seymour, *Diplomacy,* p. 7; Trevelyan, *Grey,* pp. 355-6; May, *War,* pp. 19, 44, 55, 69, 118; Grey, *Years,* II, p. 160; Churchill, *Crisis,* p. 526; Dennis, *Alliance,* p. 61.

19 Poincaré, *Service,* V, pp. 26-8; House, *Papers,* I, pp. 282; Scherer, *L'Allemagne,* I, p. 1; Link, *Wilson,* III, pp. 191-200; *Papers, 1914,* pp. 48-50, 60, 78; Gerard, *Years,* pp. 200-2; A 16470, A 16746, A 16954, WK 2.

20 *Papers, 1914,* pp. 98, 105; Page, *Life,* III, pp. 401-2; Scherer, *L'Allemagne,* I, pp. 2, 4-5; House, *Papers,* I, pp. 327-9; Link, *Wilson,* III, p. 196; May, *War,* pp. 73; Straus, *Administrations,* pp. 379-86; Bernstorff, *Years,* pp. 7-8, 57-60; Forster, *Failures,* pp. 62-4; Gatzke, *Drive,* pp. 16-7; Stadelmann, "Friedensversuche," pp. 498-502; Spring-Rice, *Letters,* II, p. 222; Jusserand, *Sentiment,* pp. 27-8.

21 Scherer, *L'Allemagne,* I, pp. 2-5; Schulthess, *Geschichtskalender, 1914,* pp. 398b, 398e-f, 576-7, 960; Fischer, *Weltmacht,* p. 82; A 19228, A 23255, WK 2.

22 *Papers, 1914,* pp. 98-100; Spring-Rice, *Letters,* II, p. 222; Page, *Letters,* III, pp. 408-11; House, *Papers,* I, p. 332; Poincaré, *Service,* V, pp. 272-3, 277; Stieve, *Iswolski,* pp. 110-1.

23 House, *Papers,* I, pp. 330-40; *Papers, 1914,* p. 104; Link, *Wilson,* III, pp. 196, 200, 203-5; Forster, *Failures,* p. 63; May, *War,* p. 74; Spring-Rice, *Letters,* II, pp. 224-7; A 24225, WK geh.

24 Fischer, *Weltmacht,* p. 83; AS 27267, zu AS 27267, A 27497, WK 2.

CHAPTER 6

1 *Weltkrieg,* V, pp. 555-9; VI, pp. 36-7.

2 *Ibid.,* V, pp. 557-64; VI, pp. 1-2, 19, 35-7, 92; Groener, *Lebenserinnerungen,* pp. 198-203.

3 *Weltkrieg,* VI, pp. 1, 4-9; Groener, *Lebenserinnerungen,* p. 202.

4 *Weltkrieg,* VI, pp. 10-2, 15-24, 29-33; Groener, *Lebenserinnerungen,* pp. 199, 425; Cruttwell, *History,* pp. 105-6; Thoumin, *War,* pp. 113-6; Joffre, *Memoirs,* I, p. 316; Callwell, *Wilson,* I, p. 186.

5 *Weltkrieg,* VI, pp. 34-5.

6 *Ibid.,* pp. 195-6.

7 *Ibid.,* pp. 38-57; Groener, *Lebenserinnerungen,* p. 202; 2172, WK 1, II.

8 *Weltkrieg,* VI, pp. 58-103, 188-9, 197-205; Hoffmann, *Aufzeichnungen,* I, p. 61.

9 Tirpitz, *Erinnerungen,* pp. 426-7; Müller, *Kaiser,* p. 72; *Weltkrieg,* VI, p. 93; Groener, *Lebenserinnerungen,* pp. 201-3; zu AH 2344, WK 21.

10 Tirpitz, *Dokumente,* II, pp. 160-1, 166-8.

11 AS 2769, WK 2 geh; Sweet, "Leaders," pp. 229-31; Scherer, *L'Allemagne,* I, pp. 15-9.

12 *Weltkrieg*, VI, pp. 95, 101-2, 189, 246-7; Conrad, *Dienstzeit*, V, p. 542; Tirpitz, *Erinnerungen*, pp. 428-9; Groener, *Lebenserinnerungen*, pp. 203-4.

13 *Weltkrieg*, VI, pp. 95-6.

14 *Ibid.*, pp. 104-263; Hoffmann, *Aufzeichnungen*, I, p. 61; Ludendorff, *Kriegserinnerungen*, p. 84; Paleologue, *Russie*, I, p. 208.

15 *Weltkrieg*, VI, pp. 249-56.

16 *Ibid.*, pp. 95-6, 255, 371-80, 480-1.

17 Groener, *Lebenserinnerungen*, pp. 204-6; Janssen, "Wechsel," p. 341.

18 AS 2769, WK 2 geh; Sweet, "Leaders," pp. 233-4; Scherer, *L'Allemagne*, I, pp. 26-9; Janssen, "Wechsel," p. 341; Bethmann, *Betrachtungen*, II, p. 46.

19 Ritter, *Staatskunst*, III, p. 63; Hoffmann, *Aufzeichnungen*, I, p. 62; *Weltkrieg*, VI, p. 415; Zechlin, "Friedensbestrebungen," 14 June 1961, p. 335.

20 *Weltkrieg*, VI, pp. 415-6; Bethmann, *Betrachtungen*, II, p. 44; Ritter, *Staatskunst*, III, pp. 63-4; Schulthess, *Geschichtskalender, 1914*, p. 443.

21 *Weltkrieg*, VI, pp. 253-322; Conrad, *Dienstzeit*, V, pp. 650-1.

22 *Weltkrieg*, VI, pp. 373-87.

23 *Ibid.*, pp. 391-2.

24 *Ibid.*, pp. 354-64, 417-23; Conrad, *Dienstzeit*, V, p. 851.

25 Falkenhayn, *Heeresleitung*, p. 37; Groener, *Lebenserinnerungen*, pp. 209-11; *Weltkrieg*, VI, pp. 421-30.

26 Ritter, *Staatskunst*, III, pp. 64-72; Groener, *Lebenserinnerungen*, pp. 209, 529.

CHAPTER 7

1 Scherer, *L'Allemagne*, I, pp. 26-9.

2 Tirpitz, *Erinnerungen*, p. 426; Groener, *Lebenserinnerungen*, pp. 205-6; *Weltkrieg*, VI, pp. 41, 44, 49-56, 363-4, 417; Müller, *Kaiser*, pp. 73-4.

3 *Weltkrieg*, VI, pp. 38-9; Conrad, *Dienstzeit*, V, pp. 374, 542-3, 817-20, 918.

4 Gottlieb, *Studies*, pp. 296-8; Schulthess, *Geschichtskalender, 1914*, p. 493; Pingaud, *Histoire*, I, p. 269; Conrad, *Dienstzeit*, V, pp. 910-1; Redlich, *Tagebuch*, II, pp. 7, 22; *Weltkrieg*, VI, p. 56; AS 2585, AS 2588, AS 2597, AS 2676, WK 2 geh.

5 AS 2743, AS 2758, AS 2769, zu AS 2769, AS 2783, AS 2834, A 36675, A 36801, AS 3035, WK 2 geh; AS 3114, WK 15 geh; Scherer, *L'Allemagne*, I, pp. 15-9, 25-9, 41-2; Conrad, *Dienstzeit*, V, pp. 754, 848, 898, 915.

6 AS 2769, zu AS 2769, WK 2 geh; Scherer, *L'Allemagne*, I, pp. 15-9, 26-9; Conrad, *Dienstzeit*, IV, p. 256, V, pp. 754, 811, 822-3, 849, 900; Conze, *Nation*, p. 70; Lehmann, "Belgienpolitik," pp. 67-90; IB, II, p. 644; Meyer, *Mitteleuropa*, pp. 152, 183; Schulthess, *Geschichtskalender, 1914*, p. 503; Tirpitz, *Erinnerungen*, p. 429.

7 Zu AH 2369, WK 21; AS 2724, AS 2758, WK 2 geh; Scherer, *L'Allemagne*, I, pp. 7-9, 23-4, 29.

8 Schulthess, *Geschichtskalender, 1914*, pp. 428d, 433, 440-2, 497-8.

9 Cruttwell, *History*, pp. 88-92, Schulthess, *Geschichtskalender, 1914*, pp. xxvii-xxxii, 493-501; *Weltkrieg*, VI, pp. 304-5; Ritter, *Staatskunst*, III, pp.

78, 601 (footnote 50); Conrad, *Dienstzeit*, V, pp. 226, 618, 690, 715, 849-51, 957.

10 Gottlieb, *Studies*, p. 282; Fischer, *Griff*, p. 105; Ritter, *Staatskunst*, pp. 78-9; Lehmann, "Belgienpolitik," p. 70; Hoyos, *Gegensatz*, p. 92; Conrad, *Dienstzeit*, V, pp. 542-3.

11 Meyer, *Mitteleuropa*, pp. 127-8; Ritter, *Staatskunst*, III, pp. 79-84.

12 Trumpener, *Germany*, pp. 65, 104-5, 271; Mühlmann, *Deutschland*, pp. 81-5.

13 Trumpener, *Germany*, pp. 68-79, 113-22, 317-8, 370; zu AS 2769, AS 2769, WK 2 geh; Scherer, *L'Allemagne*, I, pp. 15-9, 26-9; *Weltkrieg*, VI, pp. 419-20; Churchill, *Crisis, 1915*, p. 13; Zechlin, "Friedensbestrebungen," 21 June 1961, p. 355.

14 Trumpener, *Germany*, pp. 62-7, 82, 271-5; AS 2769, WK 2 geh; Scherer, *L'Allemagne*, I, pp. 26-9.

15 Trumpener, *Germany*, pp. 108-13; Gottlieb, *Studies*, p. 395.

16 AS 2724, AS 2744, AS 2769, zu AS 2769, WK 2 geh; Scherer, *L'Allemagne*, I, pp. 15-9, 23, 25-9; Tirpitz, *Dokumente*, II, pp. 160-1, 166-8; *Weltkrieg*, VI, pp. 409-12.

17 *Weltkrieg*, VI, pp. 409-12; Trumpener, *Germany*, pp. 79, 121-2, 140; Guinn, *Strategy*, pp. 43, 53; Gottlieb, *Studies*, p. 77; Smith, "Great Britain," p. 1032.

18 Gottlieb, *Studies*, pp. 51, 67, 73-4; Smith, "Great Britain," p. 1023; Paleologue, *Russie*, I, p. 194.

19 Zechlin, "Friedensbestrebungen," 15 May 1963, p. 24; Gottlieb, *Studies*, pp. 277-8, 284; AS 2685, WK 2; Schulthess, *Geschichtskalender, 1914*, pp. 428c, 441; Lerchenfeld, pp. 201, 212; Tirpitz, *Erinnerungen*, pp. 425-6; Deuerlein, *Bundesratsausschuss*, p. 323; Bülow, *Denkwürdigkeiten*, III, p. 188.

20 Schulthess, *Geschichtskalender, 1914*, pp. 728-40; Renzi, "Neutrality," p. 1428; Gottlieb, *Studies*, pp. 233, 239-42; Mowat, *History*, p. 24.

21 Schulthess, *Geschichtskalender, 1914*, pp. 734-7; Mowat, *History*, p. 19; Gottlieb, *Studies*, pp. 238-46, 282-4, 300-1; Conrad, *Dienstzeit*, V, pp. 854, 910-11, 957; Hopwood, "Diplomacy," p. 9; Zechlin, "Angebot," p. 536; Zechlin, "Friedensbestrebungen," 15 May 1963, p. 48.

22 Gottlieb, *Studies*, pp. 233-4, 239, 279-80, 296-7, 320; Poincaré, *Service*, V, pp. 490, 511-2; House, *Papers*, I, p. 306; Smith, *Struggle*, pp. 119-20; Smith, "Great Britain," p. 1032.

23 Pingaud, *Histoire*, I, pp. 192-3; Poincaré, *Service*, V, pp. 426, 429.

24 *Weltkrieg*, VI, pp. 417-8; Trumpener, *Germany*, pp. 72-5; Pingaud, *Histoire*, I, pp. 194-5, 203; Poincaré, *Service*, V, pp. 444, 470, 507-8; Asquith, *Memories*, II, p. 58; Smith, "Great Britain," pp. 1031-2.

25 Silberstein, "Campaign," pp. 51, 55.

26 Poincaré, *Service*, V, pp. 434, 448, 531; Pingaud, *Histoire*, I, pp. 8, 203; II, pp. 7-8; Gottlieb, *Studies*, p. 309.

27 *Weltkrieg*, V, p. 563; VI, pp. 56, 101-2; AS 2769, WK 2 geh; Scherer, *L'Allemagne*, I, pp. 26-9; Poincaré, *Service*, V, p. 515.

28 Tirpitz, *Erinnerungen*, p. 426; *Weltkrieg*, VI, p. 409; Trumpener, *Germany*, p. 140.

29 Tirpitz, *Erinnerungen*, pp. 433-4; *Weltkrieg*, VI, pp. 409-12, 417-20; AS 2769, WK 2 geh; Scherer, *L'Allemagne*, I, pp. 28-9.

30 Conrad, *Dienstzeit*, V, pp. 814-20, 849; Gottlieb, *Studies*, p. 275; AS 2916, WK 2 geh.

CHAPTER 8

1 Tirpitz, *Erinnerungen*, p. 427; zu AS 2769, WK 2 geh; Scherer, *L'Allemagne*, I, pp. 15-9; *Weltkrieg*, VI, p. 96.

2 AS 2724, zu AS 2769, WK 2 geh; Scherer, *L'Allemagne*, I, pp. 15-9, 23; Trumpener, *Germany*, p. 109.

3 AS 2769, WK 2 geh; Scherer, *L'Allemagne*, I, pp. 26-9; Tirpitz, *Erinnerungen*, pp. 428-9; Cruttwell, *History*, p. 103; Groener, *Lebenserinnerungen*, p. 528.

4 Zu AS 2769, WK 2 geh; Scherer, *L'Allemagne*, I, pp. 15-9; Bethmann, *Betrachtungen*, II, p. 27; Groener, *Lebenserinnerungen*, p. 528; Schulthess, *Geschichtskalender, 1914*, p. 443; House, *Papers*, I, p. 343.

5 Cruttwell, *History*, p. 103; Gooch, *Germany*, p. 118; Schulthess, *Geschichtskalender, 1914*, pp. 428c, 433-8; GP, XXXIX, p. 640; zu A 35964, WK 2.

6 Groener, *Lebenserinnerungen*, p. 528; AS 2744, WK 2 geh; Scherer, *L'Allemagne*, I, p. 25; Fischer, *Griff*, pp. 138-9, 143, 151-2.

7 Hoffmann, *Aufzeichnungen*, II, p. 83; Janssen, *Macht*, pp. 35, 237; Schulthess, *Geschichtskalender, 1914*, pp. 428d-g, 435, 444-5; AS 2724, WK 2 geh; Scherer, *L'Allemagne*, I, pp. 23, 35-6; Zechlin, "Friedensbestrebungen," 14 June 1961, pp. 335-7.

8 Volkmann, *Annexionsfragen*, pp. 193-9; Fischer, *Griff*, pp. 126, 327-9; Ritter, *Staatskunst*, III, p. 49; Gatzke, *Drive*, p. 13; zu AS 2769, WK 2 geh; Scherer, *L'Allemagne*, I, pp. 15-9; *Weltkrieg*, VI, pp. 5, 96; Tirpitz, *Erinnerungen*, p. 431; Zechlin, "Friedensbestrebungen," 15 May 1963, p. 37; Groener, *Lebenserinnerungen*, p. 529.

9 Mowat, *History*, p. 65; A 34519, A 30381, A 34775, WK 2; A 36687, WK 15; Janssen, *Macht*, p. 36.

10 Scherer, *L'Allemagne*, I, pp. 7-10.

11 AS 2708, WK 2; AS 2724; zu AS 2793, AS 2796, WK 2 geh; Scherer, *L'Allemagne*, I, pp. 7-9, 23-4, 31, 34-5; House, *Papers*, I, pp. 345-6; Deuerlein, *Bundesratsausschuss*, p. 323.

12 AS 2735, AS 2744, AS 2793, zu AS 2793, AS 2818, A 31432, WK 2 geh; Scherer, *L'Allemagne*, I, pp. 19-22, 31-4; Zechlin, "Friedensbestrebungen," 17 May 1961, pp. 286, 295.

13 House, *Papers*, I, pp. 302, 304-6, 340-6; Lloyd George, *Memoirs*, I, pp. 405-6; Martin, *Peace*, p. 89; Page, *Life*, I, pp. 416-7; Scherer, *L'Allemagne*, I, pp. 34-7; A 35331, A 35689, WK 2 geh.

14 House, *Papers*, I, pp. 347-9; Trevelyan, *Grey*, pp. 356-8; Asquith, *Memories*, II, p. 61.

15 House, *Papers*, I, pp. 345-6, 350-1; Scherer, *L'Allemagne*, I, pp. 34-7, 42-3; A 34380, WK 2; zu A 35684, A 35688, WK 2 geh.

16 French, *1914*, pp. 303-7, 320-43; Asquith, *Memories*, II, pp. 60-1.
17 Lloyd George, *Memoirs*, I, pp. 212-9; Higgins, *Churchill*, pp. 93-101; Churchill, *Crisis, 1915*, pp. 2-5, 14-6, 44-5; Asquith, *Memories*, II, pp. 60-2.
18 Schulthess, *Geschichtskalender, 1914*, pp. 608-11, 618-21; Beaverbrook, *Politicians*, pp. 55-6; Taylor, *English History*, pp. 14-5, 20-7, 43-4; Lloyd George, *Memoirs*, I, pp. 97, 106, 155, 211-2; Higgins, *Churchill*, pp. 91-4; Guinn, *Strategy*, p. 42; Martin, *Peace*, pp. 57-8; Riddell, *Diary*, pp. 41-3.
19 Martin, *Peace*, p. 63; Taylor, *English History*, pp. 20-2, 28-9, 52; Schulthess, *Geschichtskalender, 1914*, pp. 610, 613; Asquith, *Memories*, II, p. 60; Higgins, *Churchill*, p. 70; Liddell Hart, *War*, p. 83; Pitt, *Act*, pp. 19-20; Lloyd George, *Memoirs*, I, pp. 67, 70-3, 86-7, 97-8, 113; French, *1914*, pp. 348-50; Riddell, *Diary*, p. 42.
20 French, *1914*, p. 337; Asquith, *Memories*, II, p. 61.
21 Taylor, *English History*, pp. 13-4; Schulthess, *Geschichtskalender, 1914*, p. xxvii; Churchill, *Crisis*, pp. 411-39, 464-78; Müller, *Kaiser*, pp. 68-72, 75-6, 98; Tirpitz, *Erinnerungen*, pp. 425, 430-1; Riddell, *Diary*, p. 45.
22 Churchill, *Crisis*, pp. 426-39, 501; Asquith, *Memories*, II, p. 56; Higgins, *Churchill*, p. 193; Schulthess, *Geschichtskalender, 1914*, pp. xxvii, xxx; Müller, *Kaiser*, pp. 72-3; Tirpitz, *Erinnerungen*, p. 425; Taylor, *English History*, p. 13.
23 Higgins, *Churchill*, p. 89; Churchill, *Crisis*, pp. 442-51, 464-77, 503-4, *Crisis 1915*, pp. 20-2.
24 Cruttwell, *History*, p. 195; Hubatsch, *Weltkrieg*, p. 18; Seymour, *Diplomacy*, p. 86; Siney, *Blockade*, pp. 29-30, 34-5, 56, 86-7; Bell, *Blockade*, p. 63; Schulthess, *Geschichtskalender, 1914*, pp. 598-9, 611-4, 619, 623; *1915*, p. 724; Taylor, *English History*, p. 14; Trevelyan, *Grey*, pp. 346-9; May, *War*, pp. 27-8, 64.
25 Carlgren, *Neutralität*, pp. 63-74.
26 Spindler, *Handelskrieg*, I, pp. 40-77; Tirpitz, *Erinnerungen*, pp. 342-3, 430-3; Müller, *Kaiser*, pp. 76-7; zu AS 2969, WK 2 geh; Scherer, *L'Allemagne*, I, pp. 15-8; Ritter, *Staatskunst*, III, p. 152; Valentin, *Aussenpolitik*, p. 283.
27 Spindler, *Handelskrieg*, I, pp. 78-81; Tirpitz, *Erinnerungen*, p. 421.

CHAPTER 9

1 Zu AS 2769, WK 2 geh; Scherer, *L'Allemagne*, I, pp. 15-9.
2 AS 2769, WK 2 geh; Scherer, *L'Allemagne*, I, pp. 26-9.
3 AS 2744, AS 3042, WK 2 geh; Scherer, *L'Allemagne*, I, pp. 25, 37; *Weltkrieg*, VI, p. 415; Ritter, *Staatskunst*, III, p. 63; Zechlin, "Friedensbestrebungen," 14 June 1961, p. 335; Schulthess, *Geschichtskalender, 1914*, pp. 433-8.
4 Scherer, *L'Allemagne*, I, pp. 10-5.
5 A 31432, AS 2735, AS 2793, zu AS 2793, AS 2818, AS 2877, WK 2 geh; Scherer, *L'Allemagne*, I, pp. 19-22, 31-4.
6 AS 2927, AS 2977, AS 3042, AS 3093, zu AS 15, AS 20, AS 24, AS 71, AS 85, WK 2 geh; AS 2780, WK 21, I, Box 394; Scherer, *L'Allemagne*, I, pp. 37, 43-4.

7 A 27791, A 28166, A 28234, AS 2853, AS 2870, AS 3042, AS 3061, AS 3082, AS 3115, AS 3116, zu AS 3116, zu AS 15, AS 80, WK 2 geh; A 34780, WK 2; Scherer, *L'Allemagne*, I, pp. 37-41; Paleologue, *Russie*, I, pp. 117-24; Stadelmann, "Friedensversuche," p. 493; Bülow, *Denkwürdigkeiten*, II, p. 44; Huldermann, *Ballin*, p. 217; Buchanan, *Mission*, I, p. 222.

8 Volkmann, *Annexionsfragen*, p. 19; Zechlin, "Friedensbestrebungen," 17 May 1961, p. 283; 14 June 1961, p. 335; Fischer, *Griff*, pp. 131-2; Ritter, *Staatskunst*, III, pp. 89, 593 (footnote 38); zu AS 2769, WK 2 geh; Scherer, *L'Allemagne*, I, pp. 15-9; Geiss, *Grenzstreifen*, pp. 72-8.

9 See footnote 8; Fischer, "Kriegsziele," p. 291.

10 AS 2769, WK 2 geh; Scherer, *L'Allemagne*, I, pp. 26-9; Fischer, *Griff*, pp. 160-1; Fischer, "Kriegsziele," p. 288; Zechlin, "Friedensbestrebungen," 14 June 1961, pp. 332, 336, 348, 354, 360; Schulthess, *Geschichtskalender, 1914*, pp. 852-5.

11 Joffre, *Memoirs*, I, p. 321; Churchill, *Crisis, 1915*, p. 11; Schulthess, *Geschichtskalender, 1914*, pp. 851, 854; *Weltkrieg*, VI, pp. 318-9; Poincaré, *Service*, V, pp. 484, 512-3; Taylor, *Struggle*, p. 535.

12 Smith, *Struggle*, pp. 97-9; Poincaré, *Service*, V, p. 436; Paleologue, *Russie*, I, pp. 195-205; Dallin, *Diplomacy*, pp. 10, 88-9; Stadelmann, "Friedensversuche," p. 489; Gottlieb, *Studies*, p. 299.

13 Dallin, *Diplomacy*, pp. 13-5, 18; Conze, *Nation*, p. 74; Taylor, *Struggle*, p. 540; Gottlieb, *Studies*, pp. 75-7, 298.

14 Schulthess, *Geschichtskalender, 1914*, pp. 852-4; Mayer, *Origins*, p. 61; A 35083, zu AS 2769, WK 2 geh; Scherer, *L'Allemagne*, I, pp. 15-9; Fischer, "Kriegsziele," pp. 259, 300; Fischer, *Griff*, p. 178; Churchill, *Crisis, 1915*, pp. 11-2; Lloyd George, *Memoirs*, I, pp. 262-3; Riddell, *Diary*, p. 45; *Weltkrieg*, VI, pp. 3-4.

15 Tirpitz, *Erinnerungen*, p. 427.

16 AS 2769, zu AS 2769, WK 2 geh; Scherer, *L'Allemagne*, I, pp. 15-9, 26-9.

17 Schulthess, *Geschichtskalender, 1914*, p. 436; Zechlin, "Friedensbestrebungen," 14 June 1961, p. 335.

18 Zechlin, "Deutschland," pp. 378, 424; Volkmann, *Annexionsfragen*, p. 36; Fischer, *Griff*, p. 124; Ritter, *Staatskunst*, III, pp. 592 (footnote 31).

19 AS 2618, AS 2656, AS 2687, AS 2743, AS 2866, AS 2866 I, A 34554, AS 2923, AS 2934, AS 2949, AS 2980, AS 1423, A 10062, WK 2 geh; 2413, I, WK 1; AS 2489, AS 2762, AS 2846, AS 2911, zu AS 2911, AS 2917, zu AS 2917, AS 2938, WK 2 geh Spez Blitz; Adam, *Treason*, pp. 147-55; Tirpitz, *Dokumente*, II, p. 167; Lancken, *Dienstjahre*, pp. 102-7; Poincaré, *Service*, V, pp. 213-6, 523; Vietsch, *Rechberg*, pp. 28-31.

20 AS 48, WK 2 geh; Zechlin, "Friedensbestrebungen," 20 May 1963, pp. 24-6, 48.

21 Zechlin, "Friedensbestrebungen," 20 May 1963, p. 24; Gottlieb, *Studies*, p. 298; A 36807, A 326, A 838, A 1292, WK 2.

22 Poincaré, *Service*, V, pp. 433, 444-6, 454, 483-504, 510-13, 522-7, 534-8; Joffre, *Memoirs*, I, pp. 320-1; *Weltkrieg*, VI, p. 381; AS 2769, WK 2 geh; Scherer, *L'Allemagne*, I, pp. 15-9.

23 Poincaré, *Service*, V, pp. 530-2; VI, pp. 2-3; Joffre, *Memoirs*, I, pp. 320-2; Lloyd George, *Memoirs*, I, pp. 228-9; Higgins, *Churchill*, p. 119.

24 Poincaré, *Service*, V, pp. 436, 482; Schulthess, *Geschichtskalender, 1914*, pp. 703-6.

25 Poincaré, *Service*, V, pp. 429, 450-1, 485, 494, 501, 517-22, 532; Schulthess, *Geschichtskalender, 1914*, pp. 703-7; Mayer, *Origins*, p. 146; Thoumin, *War*, pp. 127-8; Lloyd George, *Memoirs*, I, p. 228.

26 Poincaré, *Service*, V, pp. 428, 437-9, 450-1, 455, 491, 502, 509, 514-6; Schulthess, *Geschichtskalender, 1914*, pp. 699, 703: Albertini, *Origins*, III, p. 141; Joffre, *Memoirs*, I, p. 321; *Weltkrieg*, VI, p. 380; King, *Generals*, pp. 38-9; French, *1914*, pp. 341-2; Riddell, *Diary*, p. 44.

27 Smith, "Great Britain," pp. 1016-7, 1021-33; Smith, *Struggle*, pp. 86-7; Pingaud, *Histoire*, I, pp. 128, 242-4; Taylor, *Struggle*, pp. 359-71, 445-6, 462-89, 504-19, 540-1; Gottlieb, *Studies*, pp. 63-74; Trevelyan, *Grey* pp. 34, 342; Poincaré, *Service*, V, pp. 425-8; Adamov, *Konstantinopel*, 25; Buchanan, *Mission*, I, pp. 224-5; Schulthess, *Geschichtskalender, 1914*, p. 851; Trumpener, *Germany*, pp. 58, 145; Paleologue, *Russie*, I, p. 194; Guinn, *Strategy*, p. 40.

28 Poincaré, *Service*, V, pp. 424-36, 440, 443-4, 470, 512; Smith, "Great Britain," p. 1032; Paleologue, *Russie*, I, pp. 194-205; Taylor, *Struggle*, p. 541; Pingaud, *Histoire*, I, pp. 242-3; Gottlieb, *Studies*, pp. 67, 72.

29 Poincaré, *Service*, V, pp. 456, 470-1, 484-92, 500, 510-13; Riddell, *Diary*, p. 42; Schulthess, *Geschichtskalender, 1914*, p. 622; Churchill, *Crisis, 1915*, pp. 12-3; *Weltkrieg*, VI, pp. 318, 380-92; French, *1914*, pp. 305, 335-7, 341-2; Pingaud, *Histoire*, I, p. 124; Asquith, *Memories*, II, p. 60.

30 Poincaré, *Service*, V, p. 430; Buchanan, *Mission*, I, pp. 220-2; Stieve, *Iswolski*, pp. 126-7; Taylor, *Struggle*, p. 540; Gottlieb, *Studies*, pp. 68-9, 75-7, 298-9.

31 Poincaré, *Service*, V, pp. 473-4, 481, 497-8, 514; Paleologue, *Russie*, I, pp. 223-4; Riddell, *Diary*, p. 44.

CHAPTER 10

1 Schwabe, "Ursprung," p. 119.

2 Lerchenfeld, p. 208; zu AH 2344, WK 21; Janssen, *Macht*, p. 35; Schulthess, *Geschichtskalender, 1914*, pp. 433-8; Ritter, *Staatskunst*, III, p. 53; Poincaré, *Service*, V, p. 497.

3 Schulthess, *Geschichtskalender, 1914*, pp. 428d-45e.

4 House, *Papers*, I, p. 343.

5 Schulthess, *Geschichtskalender, 1914*, pp. 441-2.

6 *Weltkrieg*, V, pp. 560-1; VI, pp. 12-4, 20, 93; Tirpitz, *Erinnerungen*, p. 434; Groener, *Lebenserinnerungen*, p. 528.

7 *Weltkrieg*, V, pp. 560-1; Feldman, *Army*, pp. 82-3; Gutsche, "Bethmann," pp. 218-9.

8 *Weltkrieg*, VI, pp. 430-2; Groener, *Lebenserinnerungen*, pp. 527-9; House, *Papers*, I, p. 343; Feldman, *Army*, pp. 99-101; Schulthess, *Geschichtskalender, 1914*, p. 442.

9 Schulthess, *Geschichtskalender, 1914*, pp. 428d-30, 439, 445e.

10 Gutsche, "Bethmann," pp. 218-9; Schwabe, "Ursprung," pp. 112, 121-2; Friedrich Meinecke, *Strassburg, Freiburg, Berlin, 1901-1919: Erinnerungen*, Stuttgart, 1949, p. 201.

11 Fischer, *Griff*, p. 198; Schwabe, "Ursprung," pp. 119-20; Naumann's memorandum, 23 October, WK 21; Zechlin, "Friedensbestrebungen," 15 May 1963, p. 36; Hoffmann, *Aufzeichnungen*, II, p. 83.

12 AS 2631, zu AS 2769, WK 2 geh; Schumancher memorandum, 4 December, WK 15 Adh; Mendelssohn memorandum, 3 December, WK 15; Fischer, *Griff*, pp. 121-4, 197-9, 203-4; Scherer, *L'Allemagne*, I, pp. 15-9; Zechlin, "Friedensbestrebungen," 14 June 1961, pp. 335, 341-2; Ritter, *Staatskunst*, III, pp. 50-1.

13 Zechlin, "Friedensbestrebungen," 17 May 1961, p. 280; Hanssen, *Diary*, pp. 83-4.

14 Winckler memorandum, 5 December, WK 15 Adh; Schulthess, *Geschichtskalender, 1914*, pp. 430-3, 439-40; Haussmann, *Schlaglichter*, p. 18; Zechlin, "Friedensbestrebungen," 14 June 1961, p. 335; Edwards, *Stresemann*, pp. 21, 26-8, 52-4, 178, 188; Fischer, *Griff*, p. 189; Schwabe, "Haltung," p. 613.

15 Schorske, *Democracy*, p. 301; Schulthess, *Geschichtskalender, 1914*, pp. 439-41; Deuerlein, *Bundesratsausschuss*, p. 323.

16 AH 2344, zu AH 2344, AH 2534, WK 21; AS 18, WK 15; Volkmann, *Annexionsfragen*, p. 36; Janssen, *Macht*, pp. 34-41, 236-8 (footnotes 125 and 129); Fischer, *Griff*, pp. 218-9; Zechlin, "Friedensbestrebungen," 17 May 1961, p. 280; Scherer, *L'Allemagne*, I, pp. 41-2; Lerchenfeld, p. 223.

17 Gutsche, "Bethmann," pp. 218-9; Schulthess, *Geschichtskalender, 1914*, pp. 430-3, 438-9.

18 Rosenberg, *Birth*, pp. 88-90.

19 Schulthess, *Geschichtskalender, 1914*, pp. 438-9.

20 Haussmann, *Schlaglichter*, p. 18; Gutsche, "Bethmann," p. 217.

21 Gutsche, "Bethmann," pp. 208, 218-9; Feldman, *Army*, p. 136; Westarp, *Politik*, II, pp. 24-7, 290, 307; Rosenberg, *Birth*, pp. 88, 112.

22 Gutsche, "Bethmann," pp. 217-9; Schulthess, *Geschichtskalender, 1914*, pp. 430-40.

23 Herre, *Wilhelm*, p. 54; Janssen, *Macht*, p. 36; Zechlin, "Friedensbestrebungen," 17 May 1961, pp. 280-2 and 15 May 1963, p. 25; Fischer, *Griff*, p. 218; Lerchenfeld, p. 212; Deuerlein, *Bundesratsausschuss*, pp. 323-4; Westarp, *Politik*, II, p. 307; Tirpitz, *Erinnerungen*, pp. 426-9.

24 Westarp, *Politik*, II, p. 307; Deuerlein, *Bundesratsausschuss*, pp. 323-4; Hanssen, *Diary*, pp. 83-4; *Staatskunst*, III, p. 47.

25 Bethmann, *Betrachtungen*, II, pp. 34-5.

26 *Ibid.*, p. 35.

CONCLUSION

1 Dehio, *Germany*, p. 20.

BIBLIOGRAPHY

ABBREVIATIONS FOR PERIODICALS & NEWSPAPERS

AHR *American Historical Review*
BMH *Berliner Monatshefte*
CEH *Central European History*
CH *Current History*
CJH *Canadian Journal of History*
DOB *Deutsche Offizier Bund*
DR *Deutsche Revue*
FAZ *Frankfurter Allgemeine Zeitung*
GWU *Geschichte in Wissenschaft und Unterricht*
HZ *Historische Zeitschrift*
JCEA *Journal of Central European Affairs*
JCH *Journal of Contemporary History*
JCR *Journal of Conflict Resolution*
JfG *Jahrbuch für Geschichte*
JGO *Jahrbücher für die Geschichte Osteuropas*
JGUdS SRVLE *Jahrbuch für Geschichte der UdSSR und der Volksdemokratischen Länder Europas*
JMH *Journal of Modern History*
KSF *Kriegsschuldfrage*
MOS *Mitteilungen des Österreichischen Staatsarchivs*
Der Monat
NPL *Neue Politische Literatur*
NYRB *New York Review of Books*
Neue Welt
NZZ *Neue Züricher Zeitung*
PAPZ *Das Parlament, Aus Politik und Zeitgeschichte*
PP *Past and Present*
QFAB *Quellen und Forschungen aus italienischen Archiven und Bibliotheken*
RP *Review of Politics*
SM *Süddeutsche Monatshefte*
SMH *Schweizer Monatshefte*
SR *Slavic Review*
VfSWG *Vierteljahrsschrift für Sozial–und Wirtschaftsgeschichte*
VfZ *Vierteljahreshefte für Zeitgeschichte*
WG *Welt als Geschichte*
WP *World Politics*
WW *Wissen und Wehr*
WZKMU *Wissenschaftliche Zeitschrift der Karl-Marx-Universität* (Leipzig)
ZfG *Zeitschrift für Geschichtswissenschaft*

PUBLISHED & UNPUBLISHED DOCUMENTS,
OFFICIAL HISTORIES, & CHRONOLOGIES
Arranged Alphabetically by Title

L'Allemagne et les problèmes de la paix pendant la première guerre mondiale, Volume I. André Scherer and Jacques Grunewald, eds. Paris, 1962.

Les Armées francaises dans la grande guerre, Tome I, Volumes I-II–Tome X, Volumes I-II. Ministère de la Guerre, État-Major de l'Armée, Service Historique. Paris, 1922-5.

Bayerische Dokumente zum Kriegsausbruch und zum Versailler Schuldspruch. Pius Dirr, ed. Munich/Berlin, 1925.

British Documents on the Origins of the War, 1898-1914, Volume XI. G.P. Gooch and H.W.V. Temperley, eds. London, 1926.

Die Deutsche Nationalversammlung 1919/1920, Volumes I-II. Stenographische Berichte über die öffentlichen Verhandlungen des 15. Untersuchungs-ausschusses der Verfassunggebenden Nationalversammlung. Berlin, 1920.

Diplomatische Aktenstücke zur Vorgeschichte des Krieges 1914, Volume I. Vienna, 1919.

Diplomatischer Schriftwechsel Alexander Graf von Benckendorff. B. Siebert, ed. Berlin/Leipzig, 1928.

Dokumente und Materielien zur Geschichte der deutschen Arbeiterbewegung, Series II (1914-1945), Volume I. Berlin, 1958.

Die Europäischen Mächte und die Türkei während des Weltkrieges: Konstantinopel und die Meerengen, Volume I. Nach den Geheimdokumenten des ehemaligen Ministeriums für Auswärtige Angelegenheiten, E.A. Adamov, ed. Dresden, 1930.

Europäischer Geschichtskalender, 1912-1914. Schulthess. Munich, 1915-7.

The Fall of the German Empire, 1914-1918, Volume I. Ralph Haswell Lutz, ed. Stanford, 1932.

German Foreign Ministry Archives. File Numbers: WK 1, WK 2, WK 2 geh, WK 2 geh Spez Blitz, WK 15, WK 15 geh, WK 15 Adh, WK 16, WK 21.

History of the Great War, Volumes I-II, Historical Section of the Committee of Imperial Defence. J.E. Edmonds, ed. London, 1922-7.

Die Internationalen Beziehungen im Zeitalter des Imperialismus. Dokumente aus den Archiven der Zarischen und Provisorischen Regierung, ed. Kommission beim Zentralexekutivkomitee der Sowjetregierung unter dem Vorsitz von M.N. Prokowski. Otto Hoetzsch, ed., German edition, Series III, 1, 2. Berlin, 1933-43.

Iswolski im Weltkriege. Der diplomatische Schriftwechsel Iswolskis aus den Jahren 1914-1917, Volume I. Friedrich Stieve, ed. Berlin, 1925.

Kriegsreden Bethmann Hollwegs. Friedrich Thimme, ed. Berlin, 1919.

Lerchenfeld Documents (unpublished). Collected and edited by Ernst Deuerlein. Munich.

Österreich-Ungarns letzter Krieg 1914-1918, Volumes I-II. E. von Glaise-Horstenau, ed. Österreiches Bundesministerium für Heerwesen und von Kriegsarchiv. Vienna, 1931-8.
Out of Their Own Mouths: Utterances of German Rulers, Statesmen, ... W.R. Thayer, ed. New York, 1917.
Outbreak of the World War. German Documents collected by Karl Kautsky. Max Montgelas and Walther Schüking, eds. New York, 1924.

Papers Relating to the Foreign Relations of the United States, Supplement 1914. Washington, D.C., 1927.
Politische Dokumente, Volumes I-II. A. Tirpitz, ed. Berlin; Volume I, 1924; Volume II, 1926.

Der Weltkrieg 1914-1918, Volumes I-VI. Reichsarchiv, Berlin, 1925-9.
Der Weltkrieg 1914-1918, Kriegsrüstung und Kriegswirtschaft, Volume I. Reichsarchiv, Berlin, 1930.
Das Werk des Untersuchungsausschusses der Verfassunggebenden Nationalversammlung und des Deutschen Reichstags 1919 bis 1928, Third Series, Völkerrecht im Weltkrieg, 1914-1918, Volume I, Fourth Series, Die Ursachen des Deutschen Zusammenbruchs im Jahre 1918, Volume XII, Part I, Die Annexionsfragen des Weltkrieges. Erich O. Volkmann, ed. Berlin, 1929.
Das Wiener Kabinette und die Entstehung des Weltkrieges. Roderich Gooss, ed. Vienna, 1919.

OTHER WORKS

Adams, G. *Treason and Tragedy: An Account of French War Trials,* London, 1929.
Ahlswede, Dieter, "Friedensbemühungen zwischen dem Deutschen Reich und Grossbritannien, 1914-1918," University of Bonn PhD dissertation, 1959.
Albertini, Luigi. *The Origins of the War of 1914,* London/New York/Toronto, 1952-7, Volumes I-III.
Andrassy, J. *Diplomacy and the World War,* London, 1921.
Asquith, Herbert Henry. *Memories and Reflections, 1852-1927,* Boston, 1928, Volumes I-II.
Auerbach, Bertrand. *L'Autriche et la hongrie pendant la guerre,* Paris, 1925.

Barthels, Walter. *Die Linken in der Sozialdemokratie im Kampf gegen Militarismus und Krieg,* Berlin, 1958.
Basler, Werner. "Die Politik des deutschen Imperialismus gegenüber Litauen, 1914-1918," JGUdSSRVLE, IV, Berlin, 1960.
—— *Deutschlands Annexionspolitik in Polen im Baltikum,* Berlin, 1962.

Bauer, Hermann. *Reichsleitung und U-Booteinsatz 1914-1918,* Lippoldsberg, 1956.

Bauer, Max. *Der grosse Krieg in Feld und Heimat. Erinnerungen und Betrachtungen aus der Zeit des Weltkrieges,* Tübingen, 1921.

Beaverbrook, Lord. *Politicians and the War, 1914-1916,* London, 1928.

Beck, Ludwig. *Studien,* Stuttgart, 1955.

Bell, Archibald C. *A History of the Blockade of Germany and of the Countries Associated with her in the Great War, 1914-1918,* London, 1961.

Berlau, Joseph. *The German Social Democratic Party, 1914-1921,* New York, 1949.

Bernstorff, Johann H. *My Three Years in America,* London, 1920.

——. *Erinnerungen und Briefe,* Zurich, 1936.

Bertie, Lord. *Diary of Lord Bertie of Thame, 1914-1918,* ed. Lady Algernon Gordon Lennox, London, 1924.

Bethmann Hollweg, Theobald. *Betrachtungen zum Weltkriege,* Berlin, Volume I, 1919, Volume II, 1922.

Beyens, Baron. *L'Allemagne avant la guerre,* Brussels/Paris, 1915.

Beyer, Hans. *Die Mittelmächte und die Ukraine,* Munich, 1956.

Birnbaum, Karl E. *Peace Moves and U-boat Warfare: A Study of Imperial Germany's Policy towards the United States, April 18, 1916-January 9, 1917,* Stockholm, 1958.

Blücher, Princess Evelyn. *An English Wife in Berlin,* London, 1920.

Bonnefous, Georges. *Histoire politique de la troisième république,* Paris, 1957, Volume II.

Botkin, Gleb. *The Real Romanovs,* New York, 1931.

Bracher, K.D. NPL, 1962, pp. 471-82.

Buchanan, George. *My Mission to Russia and Other Diplomatic Memories,* Boston, 1923, Volume I.

Bülow, B.H.M.K. *Denkwürdigkeiten,* Berlin, 1931, Volume III.

Bülter, Horst. "Zur Geschichte Deutschlands im ersten Weltkrieg (1914-1915)," ZfGW, III, 1955, pp. 835-55.

Bury, J.P.T. *France, 1814-1940,* New York, 1962.

Callwell, C.E. *Field Marshal Sir Henry Wilson: His Life and Diaries,* London, 1927, Volume I.

Cambon, Paul. *Correspondance, 1870-1924,* Paris, 1946, Volume III.

Carlgren, W.M. *Neutralität oder Allianz: Deutschlands Beziehungen zu Schweden in den Anfangsjahren des ersten Weltkrieges,* Stockholm/Göteborg/Uppsala, 1962.

Carroll, E.M. *Germany and the Great Powers. A Study in Public Opinion and Foreign Policy,* New York, 1938.

Carsten, F.L. "Living with the Past: What German Historians are Saying," *Encounter,* 127, April, 1964, pp. 100-10.

Cassar, George H. *The French and the Dardanelles: A Study of Failure in the Conduct of War,* London, 1971.

Caukin, E. "Peace Proposals of Germany and Austria-Hungary, 1914-1918," Unpublished PhD dissertation, Stanford University, 1927.

Cecil, Lamar. *Albert Ballin: Business and Politics in Imperial Germany, 1888-1918*, Princeton, 1967.

Churchill, W.S. *The World Crisis*, Volume I: *1911-1914*, London, 1923; Volume II: *1915*, London, 1925.

Class, Heinrich. *Wenn ich der Kaiser wäre*, Berlin, 1912.

———. *Wider den Strom: Vom Werden und Wachsen der nationalen Opposition im alten Reich*, Leipzig, 1932.

Clemenceau, Georges. *Grandeur and Misery of Victory*, London, 1930.

Conrad von Hötzendorf, Franz. *Aus meiner Dienstzeit*, Vienna/Leipzig/Munich, 1922-5, Volumes III-V.

Conze, Werner. *Polnische Nation und deutsche Politik*, Cologne, 1958.

———. "Nationalstaat oder Mitteleuropa: Die Deutschen des Reiches und die Nationalitätenfragen Ostmitteleuropas im ersten Weltkrieges," *Deutschland und Europa: Historische Studien zur Völker–und Staatenordnung des Abendlandes*, Düsseldorf, 1951, pp. 201-32.

Craig, Gordon A. *The Politics of the Prussian Army 1640-1945*, Oxford, 1955.

———. "The World War I Alliance of the Central Powers in Retrospect: The Military Cohesion of the Alliance," JMH, September, 1965, pp. 336-45.

Cramon, A. *Unser österreichisch-ungarischer Bundesgenosse im Weltkriege*, Berlin, 1920.

———, and Fleck, P. *Deutschlands Schicksalsbund mit Österreich-Ungarn. Von Conrad von Hötzendorf zu Kaiser Karl*, Berlin, 1932.

Cruttwell, C.R.M.F. *A History of the Great War 1914-1918*, Oxford, 1934.

Czernin, Ottokar. *Im Weltkriege*, Berlin/Vienna, 1919.

Dallin, Alexander. *Russian Diplomacy and Eastern Europe, 1914-1919*, New York, 1963.

Danilov, Youri. *La Russie dans la guerre mondiale (1914-1917)*, Paris, 1927.

David, Eduard. *Das Kriegstagebuch des Reichstagsabgeordneten Eduard David, 1914-1918*, Düsseldorf, 1966.

Dehio, Ludwig. *The Precarious Balance*, New York, 1962.

———. *Germany and World Politics in the Twentieth Century*, London, 1959.

Deist, Wilhelm. *Militär und Innenpolitik im Weltkrieg 1914-1918*, Düsseldorf, 1970, Volume I.

Delbrück, Clemens. *Die wirtschaftliche Mobilmachung in Deutschland 1914*, Munich, 1924.

Dennis, Alfred L.P. *The Anglo-Japanese Alliance*, Berkeley, 1923.

Deuerlein, Ernst. *Der Bundesratsausschuss für auswärtige Angelegenheiten 1870 bis 1918*, Regensburg, 1955.

Dix, Arthur. *Wirtschaftskrieg und Kriegswirtschaft: zur Geschichte des deutschen Zusammenbruchs*, Berlin, 1920.

Droz, Jacques. "Die politische Kräfte in Frankreich während des Ersten Weltkrieges," GWU, 1966, pp. 159-79.

Ebert, Friedrich. *Schriften, Aufzeichnungen, Reden*, Dresden, 1926.

Edwards, Marvin L. *Stresemann and the Greater Germany, 1914-1918*, New York, 1963.

Eggert, S. "Die deutschen Eroberungspläne im ersten Weltkrieg," *Neue Welt*, II (1947), pp. 45-7.

Epstein, Fritz T. "Ost-Mitteleuropa als Spannungsfeld zwischen Ost und West um die Jahrhundertwende bis Ende des ersten Weltkrieges," WG, 1956, pp. 64-123.

———. "Die deutsche Ostpolitik im Ersten Weltkreig," JGO, 1962, pp. 381-94.

Epstein, Klaus. *Matthias Erzberger and the Dilemma of German Democracy*, Princeton, 1959.

———. "German War Aims in the First World War," WP, October, 1962, pp. 163-85.

Erdmann, Karl Dietrich. "Zur Beurteilung Bethmann Hollwegs," GWU, September, 1964, pp. 525-40.

Ernst, Fritz. *The Germans and their Modern History*, New York, 1966.

Erzberger, Matthias. *Erlebnisse im Weltkrieg*, Stuttgart, 1920.

Esher, Reginald Viscount. *Journals and Letters*, ed. M.V. Brett, London, 1934-8, Volume III.

Eubank, Keith. *Paul Cambon: Master Diplomatist*, Norman, Oklahoma, 1960.

Evans, Geoffrey. *Tannenberg. 1410:1914*, London, 1970.

Eyck, Erich. *Das persönliche Regiment Wilhelms II*, Zurich, 1948.

Eynern, M., ed. *Walther Rathenau—ein preussischer Europäer*, Berlin, 1955.

Fainsod, Merle. *International Socialism and the World War*, Cambridge, 1935.

Falkenhayn, Erich. *Die Oberste Heeresleitung 1914-16 in ihren wichtigsten Entschliessungen*, Berlin, 1920.

Farrar, L.L., Jr. "The Limits of Choice: July 1914 Reconsidered," JCR, March, 1972, pp. 1-23.

Fay, Sidney Bradshaw. *The Origins of the World War*, New York, 1928-30, Volumes I-II.

Feldman, Gerald D. *Army, Industry and Labor in Germany, 1914-1918*, Princeton, 1966.

———, ed. *German Imperialism, 1914-1918: The Development of a Historical Debate*, New York, 1972.

Fellner, F. Comment on statements by Ritter and Fischer, in *Comité International des Sciences Historiques*, XII Congrès International des Sciences Historiques, Vienna, 29 août-5 septembre 1965, Vienna, 1965, V, Actes, pp. 746-8.

Fischer, Fritz. *Griff nach der Weltmacht. Die Kriegszielpolitik des kaiserlichen Deutschland 1914-18*, Düsseldorf, 1964.

———. "Deutsche Kriegsziele, Revolutionierung und Separatfrieden im Osten, 1914-1918," HZ, 188, pp. 249-310.

———. "Kontinuität des Irrtums: Zum Problem der deutschen Kriegszielpolitik im ersten Weltkrieg," HZ, 191, pp. 83-100.

———. "Weltpolitik, Weltmachtstreben und deutsche Kriegsziele," HZ, 199, pp. 265-346.

———. *Weltmacht oder Niedergang: Deutschland im ersten Weltkrieg*, Frankfurt am Main, 1965.

——. Reply to Ritter, in *Comité International des Sciences Historiques,* XII Congrès International des Sciences Historiques, Vienna, 29 août-5 septembre, Vienna, 1965, V, Actes, pp. 721-5.

——. *Die Zeit,* 3 September 1965.

——. *Krieg der Illusionen,* Düsseldorf, 1969.

Foch, Ferdinand. *Mémoires pour servir à l'histoire de la guerre de 1914/1918,* Paris, 1931, Volume I.

Foerster, Wilhelm. *Mein Kampf gegen das militaristische und nationalistische Deutschland,* Stuttgart, 1920.

Foerster, Wolfgang. *Graf Schlieffen und der Weltkrieg,* Berlin, 1925.

Forster, Kent. *The Failures of Peace,* Washington D.C., 1941.

Frantz, G. "Friedensfühler bis Ende 1915: ein Beitrag nach russischen Quellen," BMH, XI, 1933, pp. 581-601.

French, Field Marshal. *1914,* London, 1919.

Freund, Michael. "Bethmann Hollweg, der Hitler des Jahres 1914?", FAZ, 28 March 1964.

Freytag-Loringhoven, Freiherr von. *Menschen und Dinge wie ich sie in meinem Leben sah,* Berlin, 1923.

Gallieni, Joseph S. *Mémoires du Général Gallieni: défense de Paris 25 août-11 septembre 1914,* Paris, 1920.

Gatzke, Hans W. *Germany's Drive to the West: A Study of Germany's Western War Aims during the First World War,* Baltimore, 1950.

Gehrke, U. "Persien in der deutschen Orientpolitik während des ersten Weltkrieges," Hamburg University PhD dissertation, 1960.

Geiss, Imanuel. *Der polnische Grenzstreifen 1914-1918,* Lübeck/Hamburg, 1960.

——. *Die Erforderlichkeit des Unmöglichen: Deutschland am Vorabend des ersten Weltkrieges,* Frankfurt am Main, 1965.

——. "The Outbreak of the First World War and German War Aims," JCH, July, 1966, pp. 75-90.

——. *Julikrise und Kriegsausbruch 1914,* Hanover, 1963-4, Volumes I-II.

Gerard, James W. *My Four Years in Germany,* New York, 1917.

Gilbert, Martin. *Winston S. Churchill,* Volume III: 1914-1916, London, 1971.

Gooch, G.P. *Germany,* London, 1926.

Gottlieb, W.W. *Studies in Secret Diplomacy during the First World War,* London, 1957.

Gourko, Vasili. *War and Revolution in Russia, 1914-1917,* New York, 1919.

Gratz, G., and Schüller, R. *The Economic Policy of Austria-Hungary during the War,* New Haven, 1929.

Grelling, Richard. *J'accuse,* New York, 1915.

Grey, Edward. *Twenty-Five Years, 1892-1916,* New York, 1925, Volumes I-II.

Groener, Wilhelm. *Lebenserinnerungen,* Göttingen, 1957.

Groener-Geyer, Dorothea. *General Groener: Soldat und Staatsmann,* Frankfurt am Main, 1953.

Grumbach, Salomon. *Das annexionistische Deutschland,* Lausanne, 1917.

Grünberg, Carl. *Die Internationale und der Weltkrieg,* Leipzig, 1916, Volume I.

Guinn, Paul. *British Strategy and Politics, 1914-1918,* Oxford, 1965.

Gutsche, Willibald. "Erst Europa—und dann die Welt," ZfG, 1964, pp. 745-67.
———. "Bethmann Hollweg und die Politik der 'Neurorientierung': Zur innenpolitischen Strategie und Taktik der deutschen Reichsregierung während des ersten Weltkrieges," ZfG, 1965, pp. 209-34.
———. "Zu einigen Fragen der staatsmonopolistischen Verflechtung in den ersten Kriegsjahren am Beispiel der Ausplünderung der belgischen Industrie und der Zwangsdeportation von Belgiern," *Politik im Krieg*, Berlin, 1964, pp. 66-89.
———, F. Klein, H. Kral, and J. Petzold, "Neue Forschungen zur Geschichte Deutschlands im ersten Weltkrieg," JfG, Berlin, 1967, I, pp. 282-306.
———. "Die Beziehungen zwischen der Regierung Bethmann Hollweg und dem Monopolkapital in den ersten Monaten des ersten Weltkrieges," Unpublished Habilitationsschrift, University of Berlin, 1967.

Hallays, André. *L'Opinion allemande pendant la guerre 1914-1918*, Paris, 1919.
Hammann, Otto. *Bilder aus der letzten Kaiserzeit*, Berlin, 1922.
Hanak, Harry. *Great Britain and Austria-Hungary during the First World War—A Study in the Formation of Public Opinion*, Oxford, 1962.
Hanssen, H.P. *Diary of a Dying Empire*, ed. R.H. Lutz. Bloomington, 1955.
Hantsch, Hugo. *Leopold Graf Berchtold: Grandseigneur und Staatsmann*, Graz, 1963, Volume II.
Haselmayr, Friedrich. *Diplomatische Geschichte des Zweiten Reichs von 1871-1918. Der Weg in die Katastrophe*. Volume II: 1914-1918. Munich, 1964.
Haussmann, Conrad. *Schlaglichter: Reichstagsbriefe und Aufzeichnungen*, ed. U. Zeller, Frankfurt am Main, 1924.
Hazlehurst, Cameron. *Politicians at War: July 1914 to May 1915. A Prologue to the Triumph of Lloyd George*, New York, 1971.
Helfferich, Karl. *Der Weltkrieg*, Berlin, 1919, Volumes I-II.
Herre, Paul. *Kronprinz Wilhelm: Seine Rolle in der Politik*, Munich, 1954.
Herwig, Holger H. "Admirals versus Generals: The War Aims of the Imperial German Navy, 1914-1918," CEH, September, 1972, pp. 208-33.
Herzfeld, Hans. *Die moderne Welt, 1789-1945*, Braunschweig, 1961.
———. "Zur deutschen Politik im ersten Weltkriege: Kontinuität oder permanente Kriese?" HZ, 191, pp. 67-82.
———. "Die deutsche Kriegspolitik im ersten Weltkrieg," VfZ, July, 1963, pp. 224-45.
Higgins, Trumbull. *Winston Churchill and the Dardanelles: A Dialogue in Ends and Means*, New York, 1963.
Hildebrand, O. *Bethmann Hollweg: Der Kanzler ohne Eigenschaften? Urteile der Geschichtsschreibung. Eine kritische Bibliographie*, Düsseldorf, 1970.
Hindenburg, Paul. *Aus meinem Leben*, Leipzig, 1920.
Hoffmann, Max. *Die Aufzeichnungen des Generalmajors Max Hoffmann*, ed. K.F. Nowak, Berlin, 1929, Volume I.
Hohn, Reinhard. *Sozialismus und Heer. Der Kampf des Heeres gegen die Sozialdemokratie*. Bad Harzburg, 1970, Volume III.
Holborn, Hajo. "Moltke and Schlieffen: The Prussian-German School," in *Makers of Modern Strategy: Military Thought from Machiavelli to Hitler*, ed. E.M. Earle, G.A. Craig and F. Gilbert, New York, 1970.

Hölzle, Erwin. *Der Osten im ersten Weltkrieg*, Leipzig, 1944.

——. "Das Experiment des Friedens im ersten Weltkrieg, 1914-1917," GWU, September, 1962, pp. 465-522.

Hopwood, Robert F. "Interalliance Diplomacy: Count Czernin and Germany, 1916-1918," Stanford University PhD dissertation, 1965.

Horne, Alistair. *The Price of Glory: Verdun 1916*, New York, 1962.

House, Edward. *The Intimate Papers of Colonel House*, ed. C. Seymour, London, 1926, Volume I.

Howard, Michael. "Lest We Forget," *Encounter*, January, 1964, pp. 61-7.

Hubatsch, Walther. *Der Weltkrieg, 1914-1918*, Constance, 1955.

Huldermann, Bernhard. *Albert Ballin*, Oldenburg/Berlin, 1922.

Janssen, Karl Heinz. *Macht und Verblendung: Kriegszielpolitik der deutschen Bundesstaaten 1914-1918*, Göttingen, 1963.

——. "Der Wechsel in der Obersten Heeresleitung im Jahre 1916," VfZ, October, 1959, pp. 337-71.

——. *Der Kanzler und der General: Die Führungskrise um Bethmann Hollwegs und Falkenhayn, 1914-1916*, Göttingen, 1967.

Jarausch, Konrad H. *The Enigmatic Chancellor: Bethmann Hollweg and the Hubris of Imperial Germany*, New Haven, 1972.

Jaszi, Oscar. *The Dissolution of the Habsburg Monarchy*, Chicago, 1929.

Joffre, Joseph J.C. *Memoirs*, New York, 1932, Volume I.

Joll, James. *Britain and Europe: Pitt to Churchill, 1793-1950*, London, 1950.

——. "The 1914 Debate Continues," PP, July, 1966, pp. 100-13.

Jordan, W.M. *Great Britain, France and the German Problem, 1918-1939*, London, 1943.

Jusserand, J.J. *Le Sentiment américain pendant la guerre*, Paris, 1931.

Kautsky, Karl. *Sozialisten und Krieg*, Prague, 1937.

Kerner, Robert J. "Russia, the Straits and Constantinople, 1914-15," JMH, I, 1929, pp. 400-15.

Kielmansegg, Peter Graf. *Deutschland und der Erste Weltkrieg*, Frankfurt, 1968.

King, Jere. *Generals and Politicians: Conflict between France's High Command, Parliament and Government, 1914-1918*, Berkeley, 1951.

——. *The First World War*, New York, 1971.

Klein, A. "Der Einfluss des Grafen Witte auf die deutsch-russischen Beziehungen," University of Münster PhD dissertation, 1933.

Klein, Fritz. *Deutschland von 1897/98 bis 1917*, Berlin, 1961.

——, ed. *Politik im Krieg 1914-1918: Studien zur Politik der deutschen herrschenden Klassen im Ersten Weltkrieg*, Berlin, 1964.

——, ed. *Deutschland im Ersten Weltkrieg*, Volume I, *Vorbereitung, Entfesselung und Verlauf des Krieges bis Ende 1914*, Berlin, 1970.

Koehl, Robert L. "A Prelude to Hitler's Greater Germany," AHR, October, 1953, pp. 43-65.

Koschnitzke, R. "Die Innenpolitik des Reichskanzlers Bethmann Hollweg im Weltkrieg," University of Kiel PhD dissertation, 1951.

Koszyk, Kurt. *Deutsche Pressepolitik im Ersten Weltkrieg*, Düsseldorf, 1968.

Kotowski, Georg. *Friedrich Ebert: Ein politische Biographie,* Wiesbaden, 1963, Volume I.

Kraft, H. "Das Problem Falkenhayn. Eine Würdigung der Kriegsführung des Generalstabschefs," WG, 1962, pp. 49-78.

Kuczynski, Jürgen. *Der Ausbruch des ersten Weltkrieges und die Sozialdemokratie,* Berlin, 1957.

Kühlmann, Richard. *Erinnerungen,* Heidelberg, 1948.

Küsten, Heinz. "Die Kriegsziele des deutschen Imperialismus zu Beginn des ersten Weltkrieges (1914-1916)," University of Berlin PhD dissertation, 1961.

Lancken-Wakenitz, O. *Meine 30 Dienstjahre 1888-1918, Potsdam, Paris, Brüssel,* 1931.

Lansing, Robert. *War Memoirs,* New York, 1935.

Lasswell, Harold D. *Propaganda Technique in the World War,* New York, 1927.

Lehmann, Hartmut. "Österreich-Ungarns Belgienpolitik im ersten Weltkrieg. Ein Beitrag zum deutsch-österreichischen Bündnis," HZ, 192, pp. 60-93.

Lemke, Heinz. "Georg Cleinow und die deutsche Polenpolitik 1914-1916," in *Politik im Krieg,* Berlin, 1964, pp. 134-66.

——. "Konferenz über den ersten Weltkrieg," ZfG, 1964, pp. 1428-32.

Lewerenz, Lilli. "Die deutsche Politik im Baltikum," University of Hamburg PhD dissertation, 1958.

Liddell Hart, B.H. *The Real War 1914-1918,* Boston/Toronto, 1930.

——. *The Strategy of Indirect Approach,* London, 1941.

Liebig, Hans. *Die Politik von Bethmann Hollwegs: Eine Studie,* Munich, 1919.

Linde, G. *Die deutsche Politik in Litauen im Ersten Weltkrieg,* Wiesbaden, 1965.

Link, Arthur S. *Wilson,* Oxford/Princeton, 1960, Volume III.

Lloyd George, David. *War Memoirs,* London, 1938, Volume I.

Lowe, C.J. "The Failure of British Diplomacy in the Balkans 1914-1916." CJH, March, 1969, pp. 73-100.

——, and Dockrill, M.L. *The Mirage of Power. British Foreign Policy, 1914-1922,* Volume II, London, 1972.

Ludendorff, Erich. *Meine Kriegserinnerungen, 1914-1918,* Berlin, 1919.

——. *Kriegführung und Politik,* Berlin, 1922.

Lynar, Ernst W. Graf, ed. *Deutsche Kriegsziele, 1914-1918,* Frankfurt/Berlin, 1964.

Magnus, Philip. *Kitchener,* New York, 1959.

Mann, B. *Die baltischen Länder in der deutschen Kriegszielpublizistik 1914-1918,* Tübingen, 1965.

Mann, Golo. "Der Griff nach der Weltmacht," NZZ 28 April 1962.

——. "1914-1939: Der zweite Weltkrieg war die Wiederholung des ersten," *Die Zeit,* 21 August 1964.

——. *Geschichte und Geschichten,* Frankfurt, 1961.

Marder, Arthur J. *From the Dreadnought to Scapa Flow: The Royal Navy in the Fisher Era, 1904-1919.* Volume II: *1914-1916, The War Years: To the Eve of Jutland,* London/New York, 1963.

Margutti, Albert. *La Tragédie des Habsbourg,* Vienna, 1919.

Martin, Lawrence W. *Peace Without Victory: Woodrow Wilson and the British Liberals,* New Haven, 1958.

Marwick, Arthur. "The Impact of the First World War on British Society," JCH, January, 1968, pp. 51-64.

Matthias, Erich. *Die deutsche Sozialdemokratie und der Osten 1914-45,* Tübingen, 1954.

May, Arthur J. *The Hapsburg Monarchy, 1867-1914,* New York, 1968.

———. *The Passing of the Hapsburg Monarchy, 1914-1918,* Philadelphia, 1966, Volume I.

May, Ernest R. *The World War and American Isolation, 1914-1917,* Cambridge, 1959.

Mayer, Arno J. *Political Origins of the New Diplomacy, 1917-1918,* New Haven, 1959.

Meenzen, Johann. "Aussenpolitik und Weltfriedensordnung der deutschen Sozialdemokratie 1914-19," University of Hamburg PhD dissertation, 1951.

Meinecke, Friedrich, *Strassburg, Freiburg, Berlin, 1901-1919: Erinnerungen,* Stuttgart, 1949.

———. *Politische Schriften und Reden,* Darmstadt, 1958.

Meyer, Henry Cord. *Mitteleuropa in German Thought and Action, 1815-1945,* Hague, 1955.

Michon, Georges. *The Franco-Russian Alliance, 1891-1917,* London, 1929.

Moltke, Helmut. *Erinnerungen, Briefe, Dokumente, 1877-1916,* ed. E. Moltke. Stuttgart, 1922.

Mommsen, Wolfgang J. *Das Zeitalter des Imperialismus,* Frankfurt, 1969.

———. "The Debate on German War Aims," JCH, July, 1966, pp. 47-72.

———. "Die italienische Frage in der Politik des Reichskanzlers von Bethmann Hollweg, 1914-1915," QFAB, 1968, pp. 282-308.

———. "Die Regierung Bethmann Hollweg und die öffentliche Meinung, 1914-1917," VfZ, 1969, pp. 117-59.

Morley, James W. *The Japanese Thrust into Siberia, 1918,* New York, 1957.

Moses, John A. *The War Aims of Imperial Germany: Professor Fritz Fischer and His Critics,* St. Lucia (Queensland, Australia), 1968.

Mowat, R.B. *A History of European Diplomacy, 1914-1925,* London, 1927.

Mühlmann, Carl. *Deutschland und die Türkei, 1913-1914,* Berlin, 1929.

———. *Das deutsch-türkische Waffenbündnis im Weltkriege,* Leipzig, 1940.

———. *Oberste Heeresleitung und Balkan im Weltkrieg 1914-1918,* Berlin, 1942.

Müller, Georg Alexander. *Regierte der Kaiser? Kriegstagebücher, Aufzeichnungen und Briefe des Chefs des Marine-Kabinetts Admiral G.A. von Müller 1914-1918,* ed. Walther Görlitz, Göttingen, 1959.

Musilin, Alexander. *Das Haus am Ballplatz,* Munich, 1924.

Naumann, Victor. *Profile,* Munich, 1925.

———. *Dokumente und Argumente,* Berlin, 1928.

Neck, Rudolf. "Kriegszielpolitik im ersten Weltkrieg," MOS, XV, pp. 565-76.

Nicolai, Walter. *Nachrichtendienst, Presse und Volksstimmung im Weltkrieg,* Berlin, 1920.

Nicolson, Harold George. *Sir Arthur Nicolson, Bart., First Lord of Carnock—A Study in the Old Diplomacy*, London, 1930.

Ostfeld, Hermann. *Die Haltung der Reichstagsfraktion der Fortschrittliche Volkspartei zu den Annexions—und Friedensfrage in den Jahren 1914-1918*, Kallmünz, 1934.

Page, Walter H. *The Life and Letters of Walter H. Page*, ed. B.J. Hendricks. New York, 1925, Volumes I and III.

Paleologue, Maurice. *Journal intime de Nicolas II*, Paris, 1934.

———. *La Russie des tsars pendant la grande guerre*, Paris, 1921, Volume I.

Pares, B. *The Fall of the Russian Monarchy*, London, 1939.

Patemann, R. *Der Kampf um die preussische Wahlreform im Ersten Weltkrieg*, Düsseldorf, 1964.

Patin, W. *Beiträge zur Geschichte der deutsch-vatikanischen Beziehungen in den letzten Jahrzehnten*, Berlin, 1942.

Paulus, Günther, "Der Bankrott der Militärdiktatur 1918," in *Politik im Krieg*, pp. 230-52.

Payer, Friedrich. *Von Bethmann Hollweg bis Ebert. Erinnerungen und Bilder*, Frankfurt am Main, 1923.

Petzold, Joachim. "Zu den Kriegszielen der deutschen Monopolkapitalisten im ersten Weltkriege," ZfG, 1960, pp. 1396-1415.

Pingaud, Albert. *Histoire diplomatique de la France pendant la grande guerre*, Paris, 1940, Volume I.

Pitt, Barrie. *1918: The Last Act*, New York, 1963.

Pogge-von Strandmann, H., ed. *Walther Rathenau, Tagebuch, 1907-22*, Düsseldorf, 1967.

Pohl, Hugo. *Aus Aufzeichnungen und Briefen während der Kriegszeit*, Berlin, 1920.

Poincaré, Raymond. *Au Service de la France: Neuf années de souvenirs*, Paris, 1928, Volumes IV and V.

Pokrowski, M.N. *Der imperialistische Krieg*, Moskau, 1928.

Poll, Bernhard. *Deutsches Schicksal*, Berlin, 1937.

Potiemkine, Vladimir. *Histoire de la diplomatie*, Paris, 1947, Volume III.

Pretsch, Gerhard. "Dietrich Schäfer—der Alldeutsche," WZKMU, 1959/60, pp. 729-35.

Pribram, A.F. *Austrian Foreign Policy, 1908-1918*, London, 1923.

Rachfahl, F. *Deutschland und die Weltpolitik*, Stuttgart, 1923.

Radoslavov, Vasil. *Bulgarien und der Weltkrise*, Berlin, 1923.

Rathenau, Walther. *Briefe*, Dresden, 1926, Volume I.

Rathmann, Lothar. *Stossrichtung Nahost 1914-1918*, Berlin, 1963.

Recouly, Raymond. *Les Heures tragiques d'avant-guerre*, Paris, 1922.

Redlich, Fritz. "German Economic Planning for War and Peace," RP, July, 1944, pp. 319-26.

Redlich, Joseph. *Das politische Tagebuch Joseph Redlichs: Schicksalsjahre Österreichs 1908-1919*, ed. Fritz Fellner, Graz/Cologne, Volumes I-II.

Reiners, Ludwig. *In Europa gehen die Lichter aus. Der Untergang des wilhelminischen Reiches,* Munich, 1955.

Renouvin, Pierre. *La Crise européenne et la première guerre mondiale,* Paris, 1962.

———. *Histoire des relations internationales,* Paris, 1955, Volumes VI-VII.

Renzi, William A. "Italy's Neutrality and Entrance into the Great War: A Re-examination," AHR, June, 1968, pp. 1414-33.

Richter, Werner. *Gewerkschaften, Monopolkapitalisten und Staat im ersten Weltkrieg und in der Novemberrevolution, 1914-1919,* Berlin, 1959.

Riddell, Lord. *Lord Riddell's War Diary, 1914-1918,* London, 1933.

Ritter, Gerhard. *The Corrupting Influence of Power,* Hadleigh, Essex, 1952.

———. *Der Schlieffenplan: Kritik eines Mythos,* Munich, 1956.

———. *Staatskunst und Kriegshandwerk. Das Problem des "Militarismus" in Deutschland,* Munich, 1960, Volume II, 1964, Volume III.

———. "Die Zusammenarbeit der Generalstäbe Deutschlands und Österreich-Ungarns vor dem ersten Weltkrieg," in *Festschrift für Hans Herzfeld, Zur Geschichte und Problematik der Demokratie,* Berlin, 1958, pp. 523-49.

———. "Bethmann Hollweg im Schlaglicht des deutschen Geschichts-Revisionismus," SMH, May, 1962, pp. 799-808.

———. "Bethmann Hollweg und die Machtträume deutscher Patrioten im ersten Jahr des Weltkrieges," *Festschrift für Percy Schramm,* Wiesbaden, 1964.

———. "Eine neue Kriegsschuldthese? Zu Fritz Fischers Buch 'Griff nach der Weltmacht,' "HZ, 191, pp. 646-668.

———. "Die politische Rolle Bethmann Hollwegs während des ersten Welt-krieges," in *Comité International des Sciences Historiques,* XII Congrès International des Sciences Historiques, Vienna, 29 août-5 septembre 1965, Vienna, 1965, IV, Rapports, pp. 271-78.

———. *Der erste Weltkrieg. Studien zum deutschen Geschichtsbild,* Schriftenreihe der Bundeszentrale für Politische Bildung, Bonn, 1964, Heft 65.

Rohlfes, Joachim. "Französische und deutsche Historiker über die Kriegsziele," GWU, 1966, pp. 168-88.

Rohrbough, Philip E. "Brockdorff-Rantzau and the Politics of World War I," University of Washington MA dissertation, 1969.

Rosenberg, Arthur. *The Birth of the German Republic, 1871-1918,* New York, 1931.

Rothwell, V.H. *British War Aims and Peace Diplomacy 1914-1918,* Oxford, 1971.

Rupprecht, Crown Prince of Bavaria. *Mein Kriegstagebuch,* Berlin, 1928, Volume I.

Salandra, Antonio. *Italy and the Great War: From Neutrality to Intervention,* London, 1932.

Sazonov, Serge. *The Fateful Years, 1909-1916,* London, 1928.

Schädlich, Karl-Heinz. "Der 'Unabhängige Ausschuss für einen Deutschen Friedens' als ein Zentrum der Annexionspropaganda des deutschen Imperialis-mus im ersten Weltkrieg," in *Politik im Krieg,* Berlin, 1964, pp. 50-65.

Schäfer, Theobald. "Das militärische Zusammenwirken der Mittelmächte in Herbst 1914," WW, 1926, pp. 213-34.

Scheidemann, Philipp. *Memoiren eines Sozialdemokraten*, Dresden, 1928, Volume I.

Schellenberg, Johanna. "Die Herausbildung der Militärdiktatur in den ersten Jahren des Krieges," in *Politik im Krieg*, Berlin, 1964, pp. 22-49.

Schieder, Wolfgang. *Erster Weltkrieg. Ursachen, Entstehung und Kriegsziele*, Cologne/Berlin, 1969.

Schorske, Carl E. *German Social Democracy, 1905-1917. The Development of the Great Schism*, Cambridge, 1955.

Schröter, Alfred. *Krieg-Staat-Monopol 1914 bis 1918*, Berlin, 1965.

Schwabe, Klaus. "Zur politischen Haltung der deutschen Professoren im ersten Weltkrieg," HZ, 193, pp. 601-34.

———. "Ursprung und Verbreitung des alldeutschen Annexionismus in der deutschen Professorenschaft im ersten Weltkrieg. Zur Entstehung der Intellektuelleneingaben vom Sommer 1915," VfZ, April, 1966, pp. 105-38.

———. *Wissenschaft und Kriegsmoral: Die deutschen Hochschullehrer und die politischen Grundfragen des Ersten Weltkrieges*, Göttingen, 1969.

Seeckt, H. *Aus meinem Leben, 1866 bis 1917*, ed. Fr. von Rabenau, Leipzig, 1938.

Seymour, Charles. *American Diplomacy during the World War*, Baltimore, 1942.

Sheehan, James J. "Germany, 1890-1918: A Survey of Recent Research," CEH, December, 1968, pp. 345-72.

Shukman, Harold. *Lenin and the Russian Revolution*, New York, 1967.

Silberstein, Gerard E. "The Central Powers and the Second Turkish Alliance, 1915," SR, March, 1965, pp. 77-89.

———. "The Serbian Campaign of 1915: Its Diplomatic Background," AHR, October, 1967, pp. 51-69.

———. *The Troubled Alliance: German-Austrian Relations, 1914-1917*, Lexington, Ky., 1970.

Siney, Marion C. *The Allied Blockade of Germany, 1914-1916*, Ann Arbor, 1957.

Smith, C. Jay. *The Russian Struggle for Power, 1914-1917: A Study of Russian Foreign Policy during the First World War*, New York, 1956.

———. "Great Britain and the 1914-1915 Straits Agreement with Russia. The British Promise of November, 1914," AHR, July, 1965, pp. 1015-34.

Snell, John L. "Socialist Unions and Socialist Patriotism in Germany, 1914-1918," AHR, October, 1953, pp. 66-76.

Spender, J.A., and Asquith, Cyril. *Life of Herbert Henry Asquith, Lord Oxford and Asquith*, London, 1932, Volumes I-II.

Spindler, Arno. *Der Handelskrieg mit U-Booten*, Berlin, 1932, Volume I.

Spring-Rice, C. *Letters and Friendships of Sir Cecil Spring-Rice*, London, 1929, Volume II.

Stadelmann, Rudolf. "Friedensversuche in den ersten Jahren des Weltkrieges," HZ, 156, pp. 485-545.

Steglich, Wolfgang. *Die Friedenspolitik der Mittelmächte 1917/18*, Wiesbaden, 1964, Volume I.

Stegmann, Dirk. *Sammlungspolitik 1897-1918. Parteien und Verbände in der Spätphase des Wilhelminischen Deutschland*, Cologne, 1970.

Stenkewitz, Kurt. *Gegen Bajonett und Dividende*, Berlin, 1960.

Stern, Fritz. "Bethmann Hollweg and the War. The Limits of Responsibility," in *The Responsibility of Power,* Historical Essays in Honor of Hajo Holborn, ed. L. Krieger and F. Stern, New York, 1967.

Straus, Oscar. *Under Four Administrations,* Boston, 1922.

Stürgkh, J. *Im deutschen Grossen Hauptquartier,* Leipzig, 1921.

Suchomlinov, W.A. *Erinnerungen,* Berlin, 1924.

Swartz, Marvin. *The Union of Democratic Control in British Politics during the First World War,* Oxford, 1971.

Sweet, Paul R. "Leaders and Policies: Germany in the Winter of 1914-1915," JCEA, October, 1956, pp. 229-53.

Tabouis, Geneviève R. *The Life of Jules Cambon,* London, 1938.

Tardieu, André. *Avec Foch,* Paris, 1939.

Taylor, A.J.P. *A History of the First World War,* New York, 1966.

——. *The Struggle for Mastery in Europe, 1848-1918,* Oxford, 1957.

——. *The Habsburg Monarchy, 1809-1918. A History of the Austrian Empire and Austria-Hungary,* New York, 1965.

——. "What Else Indeed?" NYRB, 5 August 1965, pp. 9-10.

——. *English History, 1914-1945,* Oxford, 1965.

——. *The Course of German History,* New York, 1962.

——. "The War Aims of the Allies in the First World War," in *Essays Presented to Sir Lewis Namier,* ed. A.J.P. Taylor and Richard Pares, London/New York, 1956, pp. 475-505.

Taylor, Edmond. *The Fall of the Dynasties: The Collapse of the Old Order, 1905-1922,* Garden City, 1963.

Terraine, John. *Impacts of War 1914-1918,* London, 1970.

Thieme, H. *National Liberalismus in der Krise: Die nationalliberale Fraktion des preussischen Abgeordnetenhauses, 1914-1918,* Schriften des Bundesarchives, Hamburg, 1963, Volume XI.

Thimme, Friedrich, ed. *Front wider Bülow,* Munich, 1931.

Thoumin, Richard, ed. *The First World War,* New York, 1964.

Tirpitz, Alfred. *Erinnerungen,* Leipzig, 1919.

Tisza, Stephan. *Briefe, 1914-1918,* Berlin, 1928.

Torrey, Glenn E. "German Policy toward Bulgaria, 1914-1915," Unpublished MA thesis, University of Oregon, 1957.

——. "Rumania and the Belligerents, 1914-1916," JCH, 1966, III, pp. 171-91.

Trevelyan, G.M. *Grey of Fallodon,* London, 1940.

Trumpener, Ulrich. *Germany and the Ottoman Empire, 1914-1918,* Princeton, 1968.

——. "Turkey's Entry into World War I: An Assessment of Responsibilities," JMH, December, 1962, pp. 369-80.

——. "German Military Aid to Turkey in 1914: An Historical Re-evaluation," JMH, June, 1960, pp. 145-9.

Tuchman, Barbara. *The Guns of August,* New York, 1962.

Turner, L.C.F. "The Mobilization of the Russian Army in 1914," JCH, January, 1968, pp. 65-88.

Vagts, Alfred. "M.M. Warburg & Co.: Ein Bankhaus in der deutschen Weltpolitik, 1905-1933," VfSWG, September, 1958, pp. 289-388.

Valentin, Viet. *Deutschlands Aussenpolitik von Bismarcks Abgang bis zum Ende des Weltkrieges,* Berlin, 1921.

Valentini, R. *Kaiser und Kabinettschef. Nach eigenen Aufzeichnungen und dem Briefwechsel des Wirklichen Geheimen Rats R. von Valentini,* ed. B. Schwertfeger, Oldenburg, 1931.

Valiani, Leo. "Italian-Austro-Hungarian Negotiations 1914/15," JCH, 1966, 3, pp. 113-36.

Vietsch, Eberhard. *Wilhelm Solf: Botschafter zwischen den Zeiten,* Tübingen, 1961.

———. *Arnold Rechberg und das Problem der politischen West-Orientierung Deutschlands nach dem 1. Weltkrieg,* Coblenz, 1958.

———. *Bethmann Hollweg. Staatsmann zwischen Macht und Ethos,* Boppard, 1969.

Vigezzi, Brunello. "Die Politik der 'Pfänder,'" in Wolfgang Schieder (ed.), *Erster Weltkrieg.* Cologne/Berlin, 1969, pp. 373-407.

Volkmann, Erich O. *Der grosse Krieg, 1914-1918,* Berlin, 1938.

———. *Der Marxismus und das deutsche Heer im Weltkriege,* Berlin, 1925.

Wacker, Frida. *Die Haltung der deutschen Zentrumspartei zur Frage der Kriegsziele im Weltkriege, 1914-1918,* Lohr am Main, 1937.

Wahnschaffe, Arnold. "Der Reichskanzler von Bethmann Hollweg und die preussische Wahlreform," DR, June, 1922, pp. 193-203.

Weber, Frank G. *Eagles on the Crescent: Germany, Austria and the Diplomacy of the Turkish Alliance, 1914-1918,* Ithaca, 1970.

Weber, Max. *Gesammelte politische Schriften,* Munich, 1921.

Werner, Lothar. *Der Alldeutsche Verband, 1890-1918: Ein Beitrag zur Geschichte der öffentlichen Meinung in Deutschland,* Berlin, 1935.

Westarp, Kuno. *Konservative Politik im letzten Jahrzehnt des Kaiserreiches,* Berlin, 1936, Volume II.

Whitlock, Brand. *Belgium,* New York, 1920, Volume I.

William, Crown Prince. *My War Experiences,* London, 1922.

Wohlgemuth, Heinz. *Burgkrieg, nicht Burgfrieden. Der Kampf K. Liebknechts, R. Luxemburgs und ihrer Anhänger um die Rettung der deutschen Nation in den Jahren 1914-1916,* Berlin, 1963.

Wolff, Theodor. *Der Marsch durch zwei Jahrzehnte,* Amsterdam, 1936.

Woodward, E.L. *Great Britain and the War of 1914-1918,* London/New York, 1967.

Zechlin, Egmont. "Friedensbestrebungen und Revolutionierungsversuche: Deutsche Bemühungen zur Ausschaltung Russlands im ersten Weltkrieg," Beilagen zu *Das Parlament, Aus Politik und Zeitgeschichte,* 17 May 1961, 14 June 1961, 21 June 1961, 15 May 1963.

———. "Das 'schlesische Angebot' und die italienische Kriegsgefahr 1915," GWU, September, 1963, pp. 533-56.

——. "Deutschland zwischen Kabinettskrieg und Wirtschaftskrieg," HZ, 199, pp. 347-458.

——. "Bethmann Hollweg, Kriegsrisiko und SPD 1914," *Monat,* January, 1966, pp. 17-32.

——. "Motive und Taktik der Reichsleitung 1914: ein Nachtrag," *Monat,* February, 1966, pp. 91-5.

——. "Probleme des Kriegskalküls und der Kriegsbeendigung im Ersten Weltkrieg," GWU, February, 1965, pp. 69-88.

——. "Die Illusion vom begrenzten Krieg: Berlins Fehlkalkulation im Sommer 1914," *Die Zeit,* 17 September 1965.

——. *Die deutsche Politik und die Juden im Ersten Weltkrieg,* Göttingen, 1970.

Zeman, Z.A.B. *The Breakup of the Habsburg Empire 1914-1918: A Study in National and Social Revolution,* Oxford, 1961.

——. *A Diplomatic History of the First World War,* London, 1971.

——, and Scharlau, W.B. *The Merchant of Revolution: The Life of Alexander I. Helphand (Parvus),* Oxford, 1965.

Zwehl, Hans. *Erich von Falkenhayn, General der Infanterie: eine biographische Studie,* Berlin, 1926.

INDEX